Dedication

Thank you to all my family and friends who have supported me both through the writing of this book and the running of my business.

With special thanks to Alex and James, my supportive husband and son.

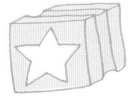

CRAFT A CREATIVE BUSINESS

FIONA PULLEN

CONTENTS

First published in 2015

Search Press Limited,
Wellwood, North Farm Road,
Tunbridge Wells, Kent TN2 3DR

Reprinted 2015

Text copyright © Fiona Pullen 2015

Design copyright © Search Press Ltd 2015

Photographs used with permission. All photographs by Fiona Pullen except for page 22, by
Lyra Loves; page 23 top, by Holly Booth Photography; page 23 bottom, by Welbeck Tiles Ltd; page
78, by Roddy Paine Photographic Studios; page 83, by Peppermint Fizz; page 85, by Kangan Arora;
and page 88, by Charlotte's Web.

Logos remain property of their owners

ISBN: 978-1-78221-052-8
ebook ISBN: 978-1-78126-295-5

The Publishers and author can accept no responsibility for any consequences arising from the
information, advice or instructions given in this publication

Printed in China

FOREWORD

BY PERRI LEWIS

It is good to daydream. When you are tied to a desk in a job you don't love, there is no better escape than thinking about what you could be doing instead – designing gorgeous wedding invitations instead of putting together presentations; crafting pieces of metal into beautiful silver pendants instead of making spreadsheets; having free reign to pursue your own ideas instead of following your boss' agenda... Come Sunday night, it is even easier to find yourself daydreaming. After a weekend flexing your creativity by poring over Pinterest, exploring craft fairs or whipping up a few homemade gifts, it is no wonder so many of us begrudge the nine-to-five that awaits.

There is something a whole lot better than daydreaming about a more creative life. It is not trying to pack it all into two little days at the end of the week; it is making that life happen for you, all the time. It is leaving behind the career you never cared for and starting out on your own, creating a business from scratch that gives you the freedom to do it your way. This might sound like the stuff of clichéd postcards and inspirational Pinterest boards, but there is plenty of proof that it can be done.

As Fiona explains in her introduction overleaf, the statistics prove that there has never been a better time to make the jump: the creative business is big business. This is not simply because people like you have stopped daydreaming and starting doing, it is because the world is changing: there is now a bigger audience for your creative talents than ever before.

Shoppers are fed up with paying for mass-produced, identikit tat, made by faceless companies who hide the true cost of their products. Instead, they want to buy from people like you, who can tell them about provenance and prove

Perri Lewis *is a craft journalist, author of* **Material World: The Modern Craft Bible,** *and the Creative Director of the online craft tuition platform* **Mastered.** *You can also find her blogging at:* **perrilewis.wordpress.com**

that the goods are made without exploiting anyone. They are looking for stories too – why that dress was made like that or what the inspiration was behind that bag – and you can give them these stories, no matter what your small creative business. You can speak to them directly at fairs, you can blog about your process, you can showcase your personality, individuality and craftsmanship and give them the personal attention they want. These are just some of reasons why people are willing to pay you to do what you love.

Your sketchpad and craft box can be turned into a thriving new company if you underpin your creativity with a strong business grounding. Talent, skills and ideas will only pay the rent if you learn how to use them wisely, but you likely need only encouragement and a little bit of business nous; Fiona's book is here to give you a big fat dose of both.

It can be done, really. Across the world there are thousands of creatives living a more fulfilling life because they made that move. Hopefully this book is your first step towards making those daydreams a reality.

INTRODUCTION

The creative industries are booming. In the UK, the government announced the craft industry outperformed all other industries, with a growth of ten per cent in 2012. Craft generates over eight million pounds an hour and employs over one-and-a-half million people in the UK. The Craft & Hobby Association (CHA) conducted its own research on the craft industry in 2013 and found that seventy-one per cent of women in the UK – more than eighteen million – had crafted at some time during that year, and more than half of those said they have an active creative hobby. What better time to start a craft business?

Your business and this book

Although many creative people can easily identify what products to make or what services to offer, they find the technical sides of running a business harder to manage. It can be difficult to find the time to make your products while learning about accounts, legislation, social media, search engine optimisation, marketing and all the other aspects of the business. I intend this book to be a guiding hand to help you through those sides of the business as quickly and easily as possible, allowing you more time to enjoy the creative parts.

Being lucky enough to be both creative and business-minded, I have spent the past few years avidly learning as much as possible while starting up and running my own business, **The Sewing Directory.** I have been sharing this information through the business guides on my website, in magazines, in training sessions and at seminars in my role as affiliate business expert for the CHA UK.

I decided it was time to lay out all I had learned so people can access it all in one place, and that leads us to this book.

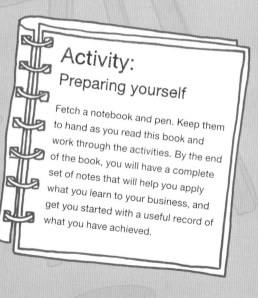

Activity:
Preparing yourself

Fetch a notebook and pen. Keep them to hand as you read this book and work through the activities. By the end of the book, you will have a complete set of notes that will help you apply what you learn to your business, and get you started with a useful record of what you have achieved.

You can, of course, read this book from cover to cover, but it is designed to be dipped into so that you can go straight to the aspect you want to learn about at any given time. Each chapter has a different coloured background so you can see at a glance if you are in the right part of the book.

If you have ever read any of my business guides you will know that I like to provide detailed information, tips on how to apply the information to your own business, and useful links for you to learn more, should you wish to do so. I have continued this format with this book: you will find activities like the one on the opposite page, with exercises to get you putting the information into practise; information boxes (see below left) that provide illustrative examples, important notes, and insights from other professional craft businesses.

There are also tips (see below right) with notes and advice drawn from my own experiences.

There are also spaces where you can fill in your own notes in the book. Furthermore given how there are new websites and useful articles popping up daily there is space for you to add your own links or notes at the end of each section. If you come across something you think other creative business owners would benefit from reading please do tweet me the link (@craftabiz) so that I can share it.

I hope you find this book useful and wish you every success with your creative enterprise.

KEEPING IN TOUCH

Things change rapidly in the world of business, so I have set up a website to accompany this book: **craftacreativebusiness.co.uk.** This site will be updated with changes that may affect your business, and explores some of the subjects covered in this book in more detail.

The site also contains downloadable material to help you with your business planning. Where relevant, this is noted in the text along with a link.

You can also follow me on Twitter **@craftabiz** for lots more useful links, tips and news.

My experience

My background is not in the creative industries; I took a degree in law then worked in the legal team of a firm of loss adjusters. While on maternity leave in 2009, I wanted something which would better fit around my son.

Having built the website for my mum's dressmaking business I could not find anywhere to promote it online, and so formed the idea of The Sewing Directory as a service for small businesses who wanted an affordable way to promote themselves online.

I avidly studied everything I could find about running my own business and still do to this day. The world of business constantly changes, so it pays to keep on top of these changes to use them in a way that benefits your business.

WHERE D

SELF-EMPLOYMENT AND YOU

The first thing you need to consider before getting into the nitty-gritty of setting up your own business is whether self-employment is for you. There are many benefits to self-employment, but there can be a lot of downsides too. I am not going to sugarcoat it and make self-employment sound like the easy option, but equally I can tell you that having set up my own business, I cannot imagine working for anyone else ever again!

I love running my own business and most of the entrepreneurs I have spoken to say the same. This section of the book will help you to make sure you are prepared for what self-employment involves.

A NOTE ON WEBSITES AND LINKS

For clarity, any prefixes to web addresses (URLs), such as 'http' or 'www' have been removed. Most browsers will automatically account for this, so you can type the addresses in just as they appear.

I have included a list of useful links to websites referenced repeatedly, or intended for further reading, at the end of each section. Where space and readability allows, I have included a link within the text.

THE REALITIES OF SELF-EMPLOYMENT

Being self-employed means that you can ensure that you spend most of your day doing things you love. You are in control. If it is a sunny day and you want an afternoon at the beach, you do not have to ask anyone's approval. If you are just having one of those days where you do not feel like doing anything, then you can take some time off.

You do not have to wear a set work wardrobe dictated by anyone else. If you are working from home, then you also have no commute with which to contend either. Another great advantage is that your earning potential is unlimited. Unlike most jobs where you have a fixed monthly wage, you have the potential to work more and earn more; and ideally, as your business grows, so will your income.

The downside of having an unfixed wage is that you could earn less than expected so you need to have a contingency fund ready to cover any quieter periods. You will also probably find that you work many more hours than you ever did in regular employment. Several years into running my business I find I often still work sixty hour weeks. It can also be hard to take holidays or sick days because you normally will not get paid for them, and you know you have to make up the work when you get back.

If you are not afraid of hard work, are passionate about your idea, and love the thought of being your own boss, then read on.

> ## Making it work for me
> Using my business as an example, I can fit my hours around my young son and his school holidays; and because I run an online business I can work from almost anywhere: I can sit on the sofa watching television while I work!

Is self-employment for you?

To set up and run your own business, there are certain character traits which will help to ensure that it becomes a success. You need to be:

Self-motivating You will be your own boss, so there is no one else to tell you what to do and when to do it. You have to be able to stick to the deadlines you have promised your customers or the other businesses with which you are working. You will need to make sure that you spend the day being productive rather than procrastinating. We all have days like that sometimes, but you alone will be responsible for making sure it is not most of your days!

Organised Any business has a lot to co-ordinate. From buying in supplies to setting up a website; and from doing the administration to managing your accounts, there are many tasks to be done. When self-employed, you need to be able to structure your working week to make sure you keep on top of all of these routine aspects of running a business, as well as spending time doing the things you love or find more stimulating.

Willing There are likely to be many things in which you have no experience that you nevertheless have to confront when you are self-employed. Some things like accounts, sales, marketing or administration can be delegated to other members of staff – if you have them – or you can hire freelancers to help you with specific tasks. However, doing so will reduce your profit when you are paying someone else to do them. A willingness to approach and complete tasks with which you are unfamiliar or inexperienced is particularly important if it you are working alone, as you cannot delegate the daunting tasks to other people.

Positive Quite often people are investing not just in your product, but in you as a person. If you are positive and friendly, people are more likely to want to work with you or buy from you. Furthermore, there will be days where things do not go your way. You have to be able to pick yourself up and carry on, rather than become demotivated and give up.

Adaptable If you can respond quickly and are willing to adapt your business plan to suit demand, you can keep on top of current trends, customer demands and other changes in your industry. This responsiveness is a crucial advantage that small businesses naturally have over more bureaucratic larger businesses. Their corporate structure means that it takes time for changes to be implemented, whereas a responsive business can do it straight away and reap the rewards.

Honest Trust has to be earned over time and, if you are true to your word, your reputation for being trustworthy will spread. Equally a bad reputation spreads quickly in this highly-connected age, and it can be very hard to win back lost good will.

Driven It is your energy and drive that will help determine the success of your business. Particularly when you are starting out, you need to be prepared to work seven days a week, to work past midnight to fulfil an urgent order or forgo a day out to catch up on work. Your drive and willingness to make these short-term sacrifices will help in making your business a success in the long term.

Passionate Most of all, you should love what you do. Then you will not mind the nights, paperwork, and lack of free time because it will be as much fun as it is a job. Passion will come across to your customers and make them more interested in being involved with you. It is quite easy to tell when someone is not passionate about what they are doing and it can be a big turn-off to potential customers.

Some of these traits can be learnt. There are books and courses that can teach you how to improve your organisation, how to cultivate a positive attitude or to learn how to stay motivated. Other traits, like honesty, passion and willingness to put in the work necessary to make your business succeed need to be there from the start. Take a good, honest look at yourself and your personality traits to see if you have what it takes to run your own business.

Before you begin

Before you invest money into your business idea, take the time to research your market and make sure there is a demand for the product or service you plan to offer. It could be an amazing concept but if the market is already saturated, or you are trying to pitch it to the wrong people, you will struggle to succeed.

Correctly identifying your market from the outset will save you a lot of time, money and heartache in the long run. Many people are so excited by their business concept, and so keen to get it up and running that they are tempted to skip the research and planning stage. Avoiding this temptation can make the difference between eventual success or failure for your business.

Identifying your target market

Are you aiming your product or service at people with children? People with large incomes? People who are buying for special occasions? People decorating their home?

Try to narrow your target market down as much as possible. It is no good saying that every woman between the ages of twenty and sixty would buy your product, because the truth is they will not. You need to pinpoint, as precisely as possible, what need you are satisfying for your customers. Why would they want or need to buy your product? It is much more cost effective if you are pitching to a narrow, well-targeted audience than trying to appeal to everyone. It is also a lot more likely to help you grow a successful business.

Once you have thought about your ideal customer and how they spend their time, you need to establish if there is a demand for your product. This can be done in a variety of ways, which are summarised on the opposite page.

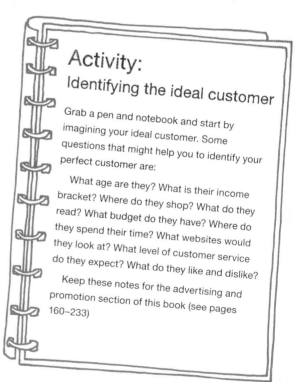

Activity:
Identifying the ideal customer

Grab a pen and notebook and start by imagining your ideal customer. Some questions that might help you to identify your perfect customer are:

What age are they? What is their income bracket? Where do they shop? What do they read? What budget do they have? Where do they spend their time? What websites would they look at? What level of customer service do they expect? What do they like and dislike?

Keep these notes for the advertising and promotion section of this book (see pages 160–233)

Ask your customers You could poll some of your target customers by doing a market research questionnaire, either in person or online. Ideally, go to the places where you identified your target customers like to spend their time – both offline and online – and ask them to take part in your survey. You will likely get a higher response rate if there is some kind of incentive to complete the survey, such as being entered into a prize draw.

Do not just ask friends and family; they are more likely to say what you want to hear. Well-intentioned though this may be, honesty is what you need.

Competitor research Research which businesses already exist that offer a similar kind of product or service to what you are planning to offer. Do they seem to be busy? Do they seem to have a lot of customers or are they struggling?

If the latter, is there space for your business in the market too or is the demand not as great as you anticipated? Identify whether they are struggling because they are doing something wrong that you could avoid. Look at where they advertise and how they attract customers. Consider their strengths and weaknesses. What could you learn from them and what could you do better or differently?

Speak to the experts Try speaking to experts in the area you want to go into. Contact relevant magazines and any businesses within your niche, and gauge whether they think your idea is viable. While this approach risks someone else copying your idea, you can get invaluable feedback, so you have to decide if it is worth the risk. Speaking to the experts can be a gamble, but the people already in the industry will have the best idea about what works and what does not. You can get a lot of useful input from speaking with them.

Trials Rather than going through the cost of buying or renting premises, or producing large quantities of products to stock a website or online shop, you could speak to a local shop or an online retailer and see whether they would stock a few of your products on a trial basis.

Such trials can help you to see if there is a demand for your product and if you have priced it correctly. The shop owner may also be able to give you feedback about how it sold compared with other related products.

If you are planning to start teaching your craft, approach an established workshop provider and enquire about becoming a guest tutor. This will allow you to trial your lesson plans without too much cost or hassle.

Focus groups A focus group can be a great way to get honest feedback about your business idea as well as suggestions on how to improve it. You may need to offer some kind of enticement to get people to take part and you will need a place to hold it. Again, try to avoid using your friends and family as your focus group as you are less likely to get honest, unbiased feedback.

Research potential markets

The research you do while investigating whether there is demand for your product will help form the rest of the plan for your business. Finding out where your customers spend their time, what they read, what sites they visit, and their other habits and preferences will help you to decide where you should advertise your business.

Finding out what budget your customers have, and what their income level is, will help you when it comes to pricing your product; while analysing your competitors will help you decide on your business' USP (see pages 22–24).

Market research surveys

One of the easiest methods of research is to conduct a market research survey; but how do you decide what to include, and how do you encourage people to get involved?

Before the days of the internet, entrepreneurs would stop people in the street asking them to take part in a survey. Nowadays we can do it all from the comfort of home, by harnessing the power of social media and using programs like Survey Monkey (a free online questionnaire tool). While the online world can offer useful tools, it is up to you to use them appropriately. If you are planning to run a local business, it may be more useful to get out on the streets and talk to local residents about your idea. These people are your potential audience – and customers – so you need to be connecting with them, rather than people you have contacted online who live hundreds of miles away.

Whether you are running your surveys online or offline, there are a few basic things to consider when planning your questionnaire.

Length Most people are unlikely to complete a survey that will take them more than two or three minutes, so keep your survey short and tightly focused to get a higher participation rate.

The objective Have very clear objectives in mind while you are planning the survey. What do you want to find out?

Clarity Aim to be as specific as possible with your questions, in order to ensure you get the information you want in the shortest survey possible.

Language Leading people into a response you want to hear will not help you. You want their honest opinion, not to spoonfeed them answers. Keep the language as neutral as possible.

EXAMPLE SURVEY QUESTION

How much would you be prepared to pay for a unique and hand-painted wooden sign for your child's bedroom?

A) Less than £10.00

B) Between £10.00 and £15.00

C) Between £15.00 and £20.00

D) More than £20.00

Using closed questions Closed questions are those where the participant has to choose an answer from set responses, as in the example survey question on the opposite page. Closed questions will make it much easier to collate your results into usable data.

Using open questions Bearing the above in mind, it may be worth including one open question at the end of the survey. An open question allows people to give as much detail as they like, and not have to choose from set answers. This will let them to expand on anything they wanted to say in response to the earlier questions. You will often see a 'further information' or 'is there anything you would like to add?' option at the end of a survey.

Location Consider where you will ask people to answer your survey. If you try to stop a mother with children in the street she is likely to refuse you, but if you asked her while she was sitting down at a park or play place, watching her children play, she may be more able to give you a couple minutes of her time. Equally, commuters rushing to work in the morning are less likely to have time to stop than people sitting in a coffee shop or on a train.

Use of the internet You will reach more people if you post a link to your survey on your actively updated social media pages and ask your friends to share it than if you post it on your old neglected blog. If you approach a few complementary businesses and ask them to share it with their followers, that can also lead to a greater response.

Rewards People often respond well to a little enticement. Many surveys use the lure of a prize to get people to participate. Consider offering a cash prize, high street vouchers or a few of your products to tempt participants to reply. Do not forget that you need the participants to give you a way of contacting them if they have won!

Respect for privacy Adding a line to reassure people that you will not be using the data to market to them or passing it on to other companies is always a good idea and will encourage a greater response rate.

Anonymity Some people do not want to leave their details. Making contact details a non-compulsory part of your survey will probably result in more people taking part. It may also encourage people to be more honest because they know you cannot track their response back to them.

Timings and lifestyle

If you are sending your survey by e-mail, consider the lifestyle of your target participants to get the best response. Sending a survey to an office worker's personal e-mail will get a better response if sent during the evening or weekend, when they have leisure time to read and fill it in.
Similarly, if the recipient is likely to be out partying on a Saturday night, that is not the best time to send it to them!

19

Making use of the survey results

Once you have conducted your survey, do not forget to analyse the data generated by your survey. Pay attention to what people are saying – if most people responded they would only pay an amount for your product that is less than it would cost you to make, then you really need to re-think your business concept. If the majority say they read magazine X, then do not advertise in magazine Y simply because you can get a cheaper deal.

It may be tempting to ignore any negative feedback but this can often be the most valuable feedback of all. Although you do not have to take every single comment on board – you cannot please everyone, after all – but you should be aiming to satisfy the majority of your potential customers. We often get too attached to our ideas, which makes it hard for us to see them objectively, so make the most of having objective viewpoints of your concept.

If you have asked the right questions during your market research, you will have a wealth of information which will tell you what people want from your business, where and how to market it, and what price people are prepared to pay for it. Make sure you analyse the data you have gathered to help you make key decisions about your business. It is also worth storing it for future reference.

Finally, remember that there is nothing to stop you conducting more market research at a later date. In fact, this will allow you to continue to refine your business, and make sure you are continuing to offer what your customers want.

Activity: Giving your customers what they want

Having imagined your ideal customer (see the activity on page 16) now it is time to apply the results of your market research to what your customers will expect from you. From the information you have gathered answer the questions below:

- What does that customer want from your product or service? What look? What function? What results when using it?

- What is the best way to reach that customer with your marketing?

- What is the customer likely to pay and what do they expect in return?

- What problem are you resolving for the customer with your product, or how will it enhance their life?

- What criteria does your customer use when choosing your product or service? Price? Style? Customer service? Ease of purchase? A combination?

MARKET RESEARCH TIPS
FROM BEFAB'S ZOE & SOLLI

BeFab (befabbecreative.co.uk) is a printer of creative fabrics. The owners, Zoe and Solli, spent over six months planning and researching their business concept, including running several market research surveys.

- Use the resources around you that can help with research and reviewing business plans. An example is Business Gateway (bgateway.com), which offers professional resources and support, such as workshops and advice, to businesses.

- Regional libraries have staff that can assist research too; whether to back up your own findings or discover new information.

- Companies House holds the registration details of all limited companies in the UK. They will have details of your competitors, when they started, some financial information and their business classification.

- When researching your competitors, make sure you identify things that they do which you can or want to do better, in order to better serve your customers.

- Use online tools – survey tools, mailing tools and social media – to promote and collect information, as well as build your customer base in advance.

- Framing your survey questions is really important. Make questions short – people often want to help but are busy, so make things easy for them – but also give the space to give additional information if they want to.

- Trusted friends may not have the knowledge of the business idea but if they have the skills to review documents for grammar and spelling, give pointers in helping you research the chosen subject, or to otherwise assist, get them involved.

- Accept that no matter how much research you do you will not know everything. You have to take a leap of faith; but you will likely be surprised at how much you know.

Your USP

USP stands for 'unique selling point'. When planning your business you need to think about why people will choose to buy from you and not someone else. What makes you different from the other businesses already out there?

Your new business will be up against established businesses who already have a customer base, and if you are simply offering the exact same thing as other businesses, you need to give customers a reason to buy from you rather than one of your competitors. Having something unique about your business will help to make it stand out from the others, and help to convince people to try your business out.

An obvious way to ensure your business has a USP is to sell a product or service that does not yet exist. However, businesses can become very successful by taking something that has been done before, and doing it in a different way. You may have an innovative website in mind that will give the buyer a superior buying experience; or you could plan to sell in a totally different way. You may be combining products that are not usually sold together or you may intend to deliver customer service to a level that is way above your competitors.

If you can establish a niche for your business to occupy, it will be a lot easier for you to both market and sell your product, plus you will have less competition. The examples on these pages highlight a few companies that have excellent USPs that have helped them to become successful.

Image credit: Lyra Loves.

LYRA LOVES

USP: Individualised products

This company makes dolls for children which are made to look like the intended recipient, or a superhero version of them. Many people make dolls and toys for children; but not many make ones that are mini versions of the children themselves!

lyraloves.com

JUDITH BROWN JEWELLERY

USP: Unusual supplies

Judith combines vintage haberdashery supplies and lace-making techniques into her jewellery making, producing beautiful unique designs. For instance, she makes necklaces from old hook and eyes and push studs, and earrings from zip pulls or lace.

judithbrownjewellery.co.uk

Image credit: Holly Booth Photography.

WELBECK TILES

USP: Unusual products

Welbeck Tiles produces 'patchwork tiles' – ceramic tiles with prints of beautiful patchwork fabrics on them which when put together look like a patchwork quilt on your wall.

Welbeck Tiles' USP is their prints, they have ditzy floral designs which look just like real fabric.

welbeck.com

Image credit: Welbeck Tiles Ltd.

Market research is a great way to help you find a USP. Ask people what they want, what do they not currently get elsewhere or what they do not like about existing businesses that offer the same products as you. Find out how you can fill a gap in the market and what you can do or offer to stand out. Even once you are up and running you can continue this research by asking customers why they chose you rather than a competitor. They may help to identify a USP that had not occurred to you.

This kind of research does not have to be done through the use of a survey. If you have identified where your target market hangs out, go and join in – whether through online forums, blogs, or at industry events, local cafés or hobby groups. Make friends, join conversations and find out what they really want. If people have come to know you before you start marketing your business to them you are likely to get a much better response. Plus if they have helped you plan the business they then develop an emotional connection to your products too.

Once you have identified a potential USP, double check to make sure none of your competitors are doing the same thing. If you promise to be the only company offering a product or service and your customers find that other businesses do the same, you will have lost their trust.

UNIQUE MARKETING

Your USP does not have to be restricted to your product or service. It could be a clever way of marketing or showcasing your work or products. A great example of marketing your products in a unique way is the 'Fat Quarter Gang'. Like many businesses, Art Gallery Fabrics wanted to get bloggers to demonstrate what could be made with their products. They put a fun – and unique – twist on it by establishing a street gang style for the blog. Bloggers with tongue-in-cheek street names like Stash Slasher, Queen Quilta and MC Hemmer posed for photographs wielding their sewing scissors and rotary cutters.

This unique marketing idea ensured people were talking about their fabrics and sharing links to the projects written by the contributors. It also helped establish their brand as being fun, modern and different.

artgalleryfabrics.typepad.com/weblog/fat-quarter-gang

Activity: Creating your company's USP

Grab your notebook and start writing down what makes your business different from the others.

- Is it your products?
- Is it the way you deliver your product or service?
- Will it be your website?
- Will it be the way you market your concept?

Finally, make sure you tell everyone about it! People will not know how you differ from other similar businesses unless you tell them. If you use Fairtrade or organic materials, make sure this is prominently displayed on the front of your site/shop and highlighted in your product descriptions and your marketing materials. If you promise next-day delivery, remind people of this frequently. If you give a percentage of your profits to charity then make sure this is clearly communicated. The more people know about your USP, the more chance you have to convince them that they should buy from you and not someone else.

CRAIG DE SOUZA'S TIPS ON STARTING A CREATIVE BUSINESS

Craig works for the Craft & Hobby Association (cha-uk.co.uk), a not-for-profit trade body whose goal is to increase growth in the craft industry and support businesses within the sector.

- *Passion* It goes without saying that if you do not have passion for the industry then it is a non-starter. Loving what you do will make running your business more rewarding.

- *Point of difference* The craft industry is renowned as being one that goes through 'boom periods' where the market becomes flooded with people who have jumped on a bandwagon. Make sure you are not a 'me too' company and have some innovation in product, or a real USP if you are providing a service. Look at what your potential competitors are doing, identify your differentiation and stay true to it.

- *Cash is king* As with any business, you need to prepare a detailed business plan, which includes not only profit and loss and a balance sheet, but also a cash flow forecast to ensure you have adequate funding to get you through at least the first year. This is normally the reason most new start-ups fail so plan ahead to make sure you always have cash in the bank.

- **Support of friends and family** It may seem exciting, but as with any business you will go through some tough times so having the love and support of those around you will go a long way in helping your business survive and thrive.

- **Keep it real** Do not have your head in the clouds – walk before you can run, do not over stretch yourself and recognise your limitations. Otherwise, there is the worry you could either implode or run out of financing, in which case it does not matter how great your ideas are.

Study your competitors

Looking closely at the opposition is an essential part of any business plan. Not only do you want to know what other businesses are out there but you want to know what they do well and what they do not. Why do people keep coming back to them, and what do their customers not like about them?

Identify the areas where your competitors excel, and try to think how your business could deliver those things to at least an equivalent standard, if not a better one. Try to pinpoint exactly what it is that makes those parts of their business good. For example, is their website great because it is bright and colourful, because the photography on it is clear, or because it is easy to navigate? This will help to give you a list of the things you want to achieve with your business.

Aim not to simply copy other businesses, but instead be inspired by their strengths and work out how you can apply the lesson to your own business. If you can see that a good website helps to sell a product the same as yours then you know you need to work hard on your web design. It does not mean you should try to copy their website design.

Imagine that you are considering setting up a fabric shop in your local town. There is already a local fabric shop near you that is always busy and stocks a good selection of dressmaking fabrics. However, the owner has a reputation for being incredibly rude to his customers. Local people say that if there were other places where they could get the same fabrics nearby they would not go to the shop. This information would let you know that what people are seeking is a good range of dressmaking fabrics with nice, polite customer service. With this information, you would know that being friendly and welcoming is as important as having a good selection of dressmaking fabrics in making people come to you instead of the other shop.

That is the kind of information you may not pick up in a survey, or even through looking online, as people are often reluctant to badmouth local businesses publicly. However, spending time at places where you can hear honest word of mouth reviews – local sewing groups and classes, in the case of the example given here – will pay dividends as you will meet your potential customers and hear what they have to say about your competitors.

Looking at the things your competitors do not do well will help you spot gaps that need filling. Perhaps there are things that you can offer that they do not. Do they stock complementary products? If not, perhaps you could. Perhaps you have identified that your customers like to be able to get everything they want in one place and in one transaction: look into whether your competitors can achieve this or not. If your competitors can not deliver an important service, or supply a vital item, work out why and aim to become the business that can. If your competition is slow at posting orders, find a way to send things out more quickly. This will give a higher level of customer satisfaction. By analysing the mistakes of your competitor's businesses, you can learn without having to make the same mistakes yourself.

Check out the competition online

Take a look through your competition's social media accounts and see what people are saying about/to them. This will give you an idea of what people like or do not like about their business.

Try searching for online reviews too. Many forums have places where people can recommend businesses or warn people about businesses to avoid; it is worth taking a read through the relevant comments in those as well.

Activity: Reviewing the competition

Draw up a three-column table as shown below. In the first column name at least five of your main competitors. In the second column make a note of what they do well; perhaps 'nice website', 'good prices', 'good online reviews', 'it is easy to find things in their shop' or similar. In the third column make a note of the things they do not do well: 'Items not priced properly in the shop', 'misleading advertising' or 'overpriced', for example.

Competitor name	Strengths	Weaknesses

Forward planning pays off

When I set up The Sewing Directory it was a unique concept and I knew I had to make a big impression before anyone else copied the idea — indeed, several competitors have appeared in the years since my company made its debut.

I prepared an extensive marketing plan which involved me exhibiting at several large shows where key people and businesses in the industry would find out about my site. I also ensured I had a big presence in magazines, key websites, blogs and on social media. So many became aware of my site that when competitors tried to copy my idea, people would notify me.

Quality really counts. If your products are of a superior quality, people will want to buy your products and not an inferior copy.

A good service will attract positive reviews and a strong reputation which will keep people coming back to you.

Customer satisfaction is very important as well. If your customers are happy with the product or service you are offering, they will not be looking around for someone else doing the same thing. They will feel loyal to you even if approached by other businesses.

Getting started

Once you have decided that running your own business is for you and have identified that there is a market for your product or service, it is time to plan the finer details. What you are going to charge, calculating what profit you can expect and setting your business goals. For the purposes of the pricing exercises in this section, I will use a jeweller making necklaces as an example.

Creating a business plan

Even if you do not want to work to a set business plan, it pays to keep all your notes together in one place. Keep a dedicated business notebook or folder so you can refer back to it in the future. You can download business plans online which have space for you to note the details of your market research and the results, your USPs and your analysis of competitors. Several banks have business plans available for free on the business sections of their websites.

Bplans has over five hundred business plan templates available on its site, many of them free, along with advice on completing a business plan. Some computer software, such as Microsoft Office 2003 or later, includes business plan templates in the free templates that come with the software. I set my own business up through The Prince's Trust using the free business plan template available on their website under the Enterprise Programme section. Links to all of these services are on page 45.

Pricing

Pricing is a very difficult subject when you are first setting up your business. Once you start selling your products at a certain price it can be hard to change it in the future, so it is really important to aim to get the pricing right from the outset. However, until you actually start selling it can be hard to know if you will be able to sell your products at the price you want to achieve. Unfortunately it is all too common in the handmade market to see people selling at cost or even at a loss. Often people only think about the materials cost and not the time or overheads when calculating their price. There are several different formulas for calculating price which we will cover in this section.

Cost pricing

There are three factors which are critical to pricing calculations. We will cover each of these in turn to make sure you are arriving at figures which are as accurate as possible when calculating your price.

• **Costs** What you spend to make your product or provide the service you offer.

• **Time** How long it takes you to make your product or provide your service.

• **Profit** How much profit you want to make on top of costs and time expense.

Costs

Your costs are all the expenses involved in making your product. If you offer a service you will normally still have costs too – website hosting, business cards and stationery, electric, travel costs and so forth. When selling a product your costs could include:

- **Materials** If you are paying postage costs for your materials or tools to be sent to you, do not forget to factor those in too.

- **Tools**

- **Rent**

- **Services** These include electricity, gas, telephone rental and other similar bills.

- **Travel**

- **Products used in giveaways**

- **Website** This includes one-off fees like setup and domain purchase, as well as ongoing maintenance and hosting.

- **Stationery** This includes printer cartridges, business cards, compliment slips and other similar items.

- **Packaging/labels**

- **Selling fees**

- **Waste** This includes supplies used and items produced that are not suitable for sale.

- **Labour** If you are employing anyone else in your business.

Some of the costs listed will be easily calculated per item; like the example to the right, for a glass bead necklace. The other costs listed will need to be split over all your products and taken into account. These are your overheads. The easiest way to do this is to calculate your overhead cost per month (the total amount you pay in rent, services, travel etc.) and then split the result across the average number of products you expect to sell per month.

Assuming the overhead cost of the necklace example is thirty pence, we have a total production cost of £8.80 for our bead necklace.

Note that I have not included postage of the item to your customer, because most people add the postage on separately to the item price when selling online or by mail order. Postage varies depending on how many items are being purchased and what delivery option people choose. However, if you offer free postage, then you will need to factor this into your costs.

Do remember that prices of your supplies or overheads change over time. Periodically check and adjust your figures.

COSTING GLASS BEAD NECKLACES

Assume the following prices for your materials.

- Beading wire: £3.00 per 3m (3¼yd)

- Czech glass beads: £3.50 per 50g (1¾oz)

- Magnetic clasp: £2.00 each

If each necklace you are making requires 1m (1yd) of wire and 75g (2½oz) of beads, your material costs can be calculated as follows:

- £1.00 for the wire

- £5.25 for the beads

- £2.00 for the clasp

This gives you a total materials cost for each necklace of £8.25. If your packaging/labelling costs 25p then you add that on top to get a cost of £8.50.

Activity: Recording your costs

Write down all the costs involved in making your products and cost them out per product. Each time you add a new product to your range do this calculation again and write it here or in your notebook so you have all the costs together in one place.

Product	Cost	Time	Profit	Minimum sale or wholesale price

Time

The £8.80 figure for the glass bead necklace example on the previous page excludes the time element of production, an important consideration. To cost out your time you need to know two things: how long it takes you to make each product or to provide the service you sell, and how much you expect to be paid per hour.

Products The simplest way to calculate the time involved to make a product is to time yourself. We all have days when we are more productive than others, so do this two or three times on different days and then take the average time. Make sure you also factor in the time it takes you to set up, pack away, and the time it takes you to package your product.

Services If you provide a service, the majority of your price will come from the time you take, so make sure you count every minute. You may think the odd few minutes here and there will not matter, but over the year it could make a huge difference to your income. Furthermore do not forget to factor in travel time and preparation time.

For example, if you teach craft workshops you may spend half an hour setting up and the same tidying away after. If you forget to count that time in your price calculations you are working unpaid for an hour each time you run a workshop.

When it comes to working out your hourly wage rate, you need to balance up the price for which you can realistically sell your products or charge for your services against what you want to earn per hour.

Minimum wage

If you are a resident in the UK, visit gov.uk/national-minimum-wage-rates to see what the current minimum wage is and work up from there as a starting point.

US state governments and EU countries have similar webpages for checking minimum wages.

We would all love to pay ourselves a very generous wage, but the chances are that most of us would never sell our products if we factored a huge hourly rate into our price. That said, do not sell yourself short. You are doing a skilled job and should be paid accordingly. As you gain more experience or qualifications, remember to put your hourly rate up – you have earned it!

Profit

As with the hourly wage calculation, there is no set figure to which to work. Deciding upon your profit is again a balance between what you want to achieve and what you can realistically charge. A lot of crafters appear to add around fifteen to thirty per cent profit, but this will varying depending on your market.

You need to bear in mind if you are planning to sell wholesale that retailers will expect to buy at half the retail price. So you need to be able to cover your production costs and make a profit on around half the retail price.

You can use the calculated starting price (£15.00 in the example) as your retail price – the amount you charge customers if you are selling your product directly. However, if you intend to sell wholesale, then your retail price should be double the starting price you calculated. This is to ensure that you are not undercutting the retailers who stock your products – as mentioned above, they will expect to buy your products at half the price they sell them; so if you want to keep your profit, you must take this into account when selling to wholesalers. In the glass bead necklace example, if you are selling the necklaces wholesale you would sell it to the retailer for £15.00, and the retailer would then charge the customer £30.00. This gives a basic formula to help you calculate a price for your products:

• Production costs + time + profit = retail price; if you are only selling the product directly to the customer.

If you are selling wholesale the formula becomes:

• Production costs + time + profit x 2 = retail price. Half of this is the price you want to sell the product at wholesale.

PRICING THE GLASS BEAD NECKLACES

Returning to the necklace example, if one necklace takes you twenty minutes to make, and you want to earn £12.00 an hour, that gives a time cost of £4.00. The other production costs were £8.80 (see 'Costing glass bead necklaces' on page 29).

This gives you a total production cost of £12.80, to which we add a profit margin of around twenty-five per cent of the production cost – an appropriate amount in the market in which it will be sold – would be £2.20.

This gives a basic total of £15.00, which is your starting price.

Changing prices

If your raw materials vary in price, or are subject to frequent price increases you may want to add an extra ten per cent or so to your profit to account for the fluctuations in price, rather than having to keep increasing your prices or cutting your profit.

Competition pricing

This pricing method involves looking at a group of your competitors and then taking an average of their prices to calculate your own. This method of working out your pricing is quick and simple, and you know customers will buy at this price. In addition, looking at what your competition charge may reveal a 'going rate' for your product or service.

The downside of this method is it takes no account of the costs and time involved in making your product and could lead to your not making a profit. Other people may be able to produce the item more cheaply than you and make a profit on it when you cannot. There are also many 'hobby sellers' who craft because they love it and simply want to earn enough to buy more materials to make something else.

The combination method

I suggest combining the two methods and calculating your prices based upon your costs, then looking at the competition and see how your price compares to theirs. If yours is a lot cheaper then perhaps you could increase your profit.

Remember that cheaper is not always better. Customers will wonder why your product costs less than your competitors and may assume that it is made with cheaper materials, or by someone less skilled. If other people are able to sell the same product at a higher price there is no reason why you should not be able to.

If your price is too high for the market

If your product is going to be a lot more expensive than all your competitors you have a few options:

Pitch to a more expensive market Promote your product as being high end and aim it at those with a larger budget. Popular examples of this are Cath Kidston, Jan Constantine and Poppy Treffry, who are able to sell their homeware at high prices. Like you, even these big, well-established names had to start from nothing and build up their brand. This point also relates to the market research discussed earlier and pinpointing your ideal customer.

Change your product to add value People are prepared to pay a little extra for something unique. If your product is different from all the others, you can get away with charging a little extra. Alternatively could you use more luxurious supplies to justify a higher price. Use wool felt instead of polyester felt, for example, or precious stone beads instead of glass beads. Adding personalisation is another way to justify raising your prices.

> ### Remember online fees
>
> If you are selling through a site like Etsy, Folksy, Misi or similar, make sure you include any fees involved in selling your product such as payment processing fees and listing fees in your price. You should also account for the time you spend in listing your products online.

Source cheaper supplies It is tempting to stick with the supplier(s) you know but you need to make money or your business will not survive. Shop around to find a better deal. I highly recommend attending industry trade shows to find new suppliers. There you will find hundreds of wholesalers, with many products on display and show discounts. Take a look at my website (see page 45) for a list of wholesalers.

Invest or innovate to speed up production Could you invest in a tool or piece of machinery to speed up your work? A different technique or process that could make things quicker, like batching, could help, too. For example, cut out ten bags at once, sew the bags in a batch and then photograph and list them at the same time, rather than making one from start to end before going onto the next one.

Experimenting with your prices

Your pricing is not set in stone, and you do not have to follow a formula to the letter. Such suggestions are good starting points but a lot of handmade products are unique and require a unique price.

Once people get used to paying a set price for something they are generally unhappy if prices increase. As a result, it is better to start at a higher price and lower your prices than to raise your prices. If in doubt when starting out, go higher. If you do need to increase the price it is often better received if you are able to give a justification. People are more understanding if they know you had to increase your price because the price of cotton has increased, or the rent of your shop has risen.

You can trial special offers such as free postage, or money-off sales to see how this affects your income. Running a short-term offer like this gives you a chance to gauge the response and measure the financial effect before you commit to it permanently.

Remember that your prices will need to be regularly reviewed. As your experience and skills grow you can charge more; as your brand grows and becomes more established you can also increase your price. If your materials become more expensive or you move to more expensive premises you may need to increase your costs.

> ### Experimenting with my start-up
>
> When starting up my company, The Sewing Directory, I began with high prices. After a few months I ran a summer sale at a forty percent discount to see if it would make a difference to my sign-up rate.
>
> The sale price proved such a hit that I made it my permanent price and ended up with hundreds of businesses signing up. If I had gone the opposite way and put my prices up I could easily have lost several customers instead.

Setting your goals

A really important part of running a business is to plan ahead, to set goals and then check your progress towards those goals. All too often people write up a business plan before they launch then never return to it once the business is up and running. It is easy to get bogged down in the day-to-day work and never look at the longer term. It may be that you love the creative side of things but not the business side so you tend to ignore it. The reality is that unless you focus on the business side you will not be able to continue doing the creative side. If you do not have clear business objectives in mind, or a good idea of how your business is performing, how do you know if you are going where you want to go?

Activity: Defining your goals

I want you to think about what success means to you. Does it mean being able to work from home, or working around your children's timetable? Does it mean being able to do something you love all day? Does it mean making as much as you used to in your old job? Does it mean earning some extra money for holidays and treats? Is it funding your hobby? Is it having your work admired? Making it into a big gallery or exhibition? Is success to you measured in money? In time? In a frame of mind? A set of circumstances? Is it a combination of factors?

For me success is being able to work from home, doing something I enjoy, while working around my son and earning more than a part-time wage. Now it is your turn. Once you have thought this through, write out and complete the following sentence:

Success to me is ...

Read through your definition of success and pick out the key elements. Jot them down in your notepad. Leave space to add more at a later date.

For example the key elements of success for me are:

- Being able to work from home.

- Enjoying my work.

- Being able to fit my job around my son.

- Earning more than a part-time wage.

The elements you have written above are your goals. They are what you want from your business. Now that you know what your goals for your business are, you need to start thinking about how you are going to achieve them.

When planning how to achieve your goals it is a good idea to make sure each goal is specific as possible so you know precisely what you are aiming for. Take each goal and break it down. For example, one of the key elements of success I identified was earning more than what I consider a part-time wage. I quantified this goal by working out my monthly salary if I returned to work part-time in my previous office job. With this figure in mind, I can quantify that goal and work out precisely how much I am aiming to earn.

Some goals are harder to define than others. How do you set a target for enjoyment, for example? You need to think about what that means to you. To me, enjoying my work is looking forward to doing it as opposed to dreading it, and being willing to work extra because I enjoy what I am doing.

I am happy to say I have achieved that goal. However, I did not achieve it from the outset. When launching my business I had to do a lot of sales, and I hate sales! I am not a natural sales person and I feel very uncomfortable trying to sell myself and my products to people, especially cold calling. So I worked very hard to get to a point where I no longer have to actively sell to people. As a result, my brand and reputation grew, and people began to approach me instead of me having to approach them.

Once you have defined your goals you will know exactly what you want from your business. You will have something to measure against to see whether you have achieved your goals at the end of each year, or month, depending how often you want to review. Now concentrate on how you are going to get there. I think the best way to tackle this is to get the negatives out of the way first.

Activity: Breaking down your goals

Take the list of goals from the previous activity and break down each one as far as you can. Define what you have to achieve to reach that goal, and be as precise as possible.

Put a figure on the income you would need to earn: the number of sales you want to achieve each week, the exact number of magazines you want to be featured in, or the percentage of customers you want to return.

Outsourcing

If there is a particular task that is preventing you achieving your goals, consider outsourcing it. If you spend months dreading doing the accounts, hire an accountant.

Sometimes it is worth spending money on these things for your own peace of mind and to allow you to concentrate on the things you love.

Identify what is getting in the way of achieving your goals. Is there too little space to work from home? Can you not sell many products because you do not have the necessary supplies? Are your prices so low that you are not making much profit? Are customers not completing their purchase because your website is awkward? Is your website not getting much traffic? Are people struggling to find you because you do not promote yourself well enough? We all have hurdles we need to overcome. Rather than ignoring them – tempting as that may be – tackle them head on!

As with your goals you need to identify and define any obstacles to your success, and then think about what you can do to overcome them. Make them part of your business plan. Do not panic and think you need to overcome them all at once. Write them down, then gradually work through each one, trying to think of some ideas for overcoming them. You could pick one per month to concentrate on, or set some time aside to address them all at once.

If you cannot think of solutions to them, ask around. See if anyone else has had the same problem and find out how they overcame it. Consult online forums, or read magazines for interviews with entrepreneurs or crafters to see how they tackle things. Look at business advice sites, forums, books or magazines for tips on pricing, time management, contracts, dealing with suppliers, promoting yourself and so on. There are plenty of helpful resources available; some of my favourites are listed on page 45.

Activity: Removing obstacles

Use your notebook to write down the things that are stopping you from achieving your goals, then note down ways that you can try to overcome them. As with your goals, try to go into as much detail as possible, as this will help when you are looking back over this in months to come.

You may also find long-term solutions start to come to you as you work out short-term solutions. You may not be able to tackle the whole problem at once but you could well resolve part of it immediately. For example:

Problem

- Lack of space. My work papers are piled up all over the house because I do not have a dedicated work area. I am working from a laptop on the sofa and getting backache. My business cards are strewn all over the house because the boxes are within the reach of my child who thinks they are fun to play with.

Short-term solutions

- Invest in a small table that goes over the sofa or just in front of the sofa for the laptop. Alternatively, clear the kitchen table to use for working on.

- Move furniture around until I can make space for a filing cabinet. File all papers into the filing cabinet. If I cannot make that space, get some filing boxes and store them under the bed so all documents are together in one place.

- Move the business cards into a high cupboard or shelf away from the child's reach.

Long-term solution

- Save up enough money to convert the garage into an office or look at hiring an office space locally.

Breaking goals and obstacles down into smaller parts makes them a lot more achievable and helps to keep you motivated – you no longer have seemingly insurmountable problems, you have a to-do list of achievable tasks. Now if you find yourself with an hour to spare pick one of the solutions you have written above and make it happen. Before you know it those pesky problems getting in the way of your goals will be gone.

Once you have looked at ways of dealing with potential obstacles to success, begin planning how you are going to reach your goals. Consider each of your goals in turn and establish what steps you need to take to achieve each one.

If your goals are financial, figure out how much you need to sell to reach your goal, and then how you plan to do that. If you want to turn over one thousand pounds a month and your products cost twenty pounds each, write down that you need to sell fifty products a month.

Be realistic

Keep your goals realistic. Do not set yourself up for failure by setting impossibly high targets.

That is the easy bit done; now on to the how. Do you sell at craft fairs? If so, what do you normally sell at one of those? Do you sell through platforms like Folksy and Etsy (see pages 165)? If so, make notes of your average sales per month on those platforms. If you sell through your own website make a note of that too. If you add those up and you normally sell forty units per month, start thinking about how you can increase that to fifty. Some ideas that may help you achieve your goals are below and on the following pages.

GOAL: MORE SALES

- Attend extra craft fairs or shows.
- Find a new online platform to sell through.
- Start selling wholesale.
- Send out press releases to relevant magazines and websites.
- Run a sale/give out a discount code.
- Improve your SEO (search engine optimisation) to bring more traffic to your site.
- Find more or better stockists.
- Place some adverts.

GOAL: MORE TIME OFF

- Start using a program like Hootsuite or Tweetdeck to schedule your social media updates.
- Work later on a couple of evenings to have an extra day a week off.
- Review your processes to see if there is anything you can stop doing or do more efficiently.
- Raise your prices so you earn more for fewer hours of work.
- Assess whether you can afford to hire help.
- If you have staff, delegate more tasks to them.

GOAL: BUILD BRAND AWARENESS

- If you can afford it, increase your advertising or try advertising in new places to reach different people.
- Write for blogs, sites and magazines. It means people will be seeing your brand name/logo in several different places.
- Create a viral blogging campaign. Blog coverage is very good exposure for a brand.
- Interact with people more frequently on social media, and post content that is likely to be shared.
- Make sure your branding is consistent across all platforms.
- Attend shows, local craft fairs, and networking events to get your name out there.
- Put yourself forward for awards and competitions. If you win, the resultant publicity will help promote your brand.

GOAL: REDUCE COSTS AND INCREASE PROFIT

- Make things in batches to increase productivity. This also works for doing things like social media updates or writing blog posts. It is quicker to preschedule, write or plan several at a time.
- Research suppliers and make sure you are getting your materials at the best price. Attend trade shows to compare several suppliers at once, and see if you can benefit from show discounts.
- Buy in bulk if you can afford to, as you often get bigger discounts that way. If you cannot afford to, see if there are any local crafters who would share a big order with you.
- Review your pricing – are you charging as much as you could be?
- Review your product lines. If certain items are not selling well, reduce their price, clear the stock and fill their place with better-selling products.

GOAL: INCREASE TRAFFIC TO YOUR WEBSITE

- Do a search engine optimisation (SEO) review and make sure your site is well-optimised.
- Guest post on blogs and websites to drive traffic to your site, or write for magazines that will include a link to your site on the page.
- Try advertising online – on blogs, websites, Facebook, Google ads or similar.
- Keep adding fresh interesting content to your site to attract visitors and help your SEO.
- Build your social media following and post occasional links back to your site.

Reviewing your goals

There is no point setting goals for your business and then forgetting about them. You need to regularly revisit your goals and review how your business is performing towards those goals. You need to see if you are on target to meet your goals and, if not, what you can do to help reach them. You also need to see whether your goals need revising. Our priorities change over time, so your goals may need updating. What was important to you last year may not be important to you this year. If your business is doing a lot better than predicted, why not set higher goals?

One common thing with entrepreneurs of all types is over-working which results in getting run down, exhausted, or even ill. (I have certainly been there and done that!) If this happens then you may decide that your focus is no longer increasing your profits but perhaps taking more time off.

How frequently you review your goals is up to you, you may want to set aside some time each month to do it or if you think that you are not likely to stick to that make it once a quarter. It is also worth doing a big annual review to look back over the whole year.

Activity:
Planning your goals

Go back to your notepad to make notes on how you plan to reach your goals. If you write them in the form of a check list you can easily cross them off as you go.

Remember your goals are not set in stone. As your business or personal circumstances change, amend your goals accordingly. You may also need to adapt them to fit customer demand.

Write down events such as the launch of a new website, a big sale, a new product range launch, closing the shop while you went on holiday, or exhibiting at a big show – anything that happened during the year which may have affected your statistics, and what dates those things occurred. This will allow you to account for peaks and troughs in the figures in a few years' time when you look back.

You may want to add some extra statistics to your annual review form depending upon the nature of your business, and what your focus is. It can also help to break down the sales of individual items over the year so you can see what is selling well and what is not. This will help you plan your stock for the next year.

It is worth keeping an eye on your conversion rate (the percentage of visitors to your shop or website that end up buying something) so that you can see if any changes you make, such as to the layout of your shop or website, have any impact on the number of conversions.

If you complete the business review form each year you will be able to see the growth of your company from year to year. You can also identify any areas that are not improving, or growing at a slower rate than others, so you can focus on improving them. Once you have more than one year's worth of figures, compare the current year with previous years.

My reviewing habits

Personally, I review my figures every month to check that I am on track for my financial target, and keep an eye on my site statistics daily so that if I spot a drop one day I can add something the following day to boost interest.

I also do a big review at the end of the calendar year. This may seem odd because my business year runs from April–April (the UK financial year). However, I find I have more time to review at the end of December as my business has a natural lull between Christmas and New Year. This has the added benefit of giving me three months to address any shortfall I identify so that I still hit my goals by April, the end of my accounting year.

Activity:
Reviewing your business

Complete the business review form opposite so that you have a starting point for future reviews. This will give you a snapshot of your business as it stands on this date. If you trade through premises or on a craft stall then pick a week to count your average number of customers and visitors to your shop/stall. Try to use the same week each year so you can accurately measure any growth. Write down which week you have used so you know for the next year. The easiest way to log these figures is to keep a notebook by your till and track the number of customers/browsers.

Photocopy the form before you begin if you want to use it more than once or download copies from my site (see page 45) if you do not want to write in your book.

40

BUSINESS REVIEW FORM

Financial

- Annual turnover
- Annual outgoings
- Annual profit
- Average monthly profit
- Number of sales in the last year
- Average monthly number of sales

Online statistics

- Hits in the last year
- Number of Facebook/Twitter/other social media site fans
- Number of blog followers
- Number of online sales in the last year
- Conversion rate (percentage of website/shop visitors that end up buying something) in the last year

If you sell both online and offline complete the following:

- Annual turnover from online sales
- Annual profit from online sales
- Average monthly profit from online sales

Offline statistics

- Total people that visited your stall/shop in a week
- Total number that purchased from you that week
- Total number of browsers in that week (visiting/looking but not buying)
- Conversion rate in that week
- Income that week from offline sales
- Income in the whole year from offline sales
- Average monthly income from offline sales

Taking it further

If you have worked through the exercises, you will have ended this section with a written list of business goals, a to-do list of things which will help you achieve your goals, and the up-to-date statistics of your business. The important thing is to make business planning and reviewing part of your routine. Schedule in regular reviews at intervals which best suit you. Aim for mini reviews every month or two and a big annual or bi-annual review.

Learn to use the tools that will help you with your reviews. Keep your accounts up to date so you can review your financial standing regularly (see pages 54–56 for more on accounts). Learn to use analytical tools like Google Analytics to keep an eye on your web stats (see pages 181 and 190 for more information on search engine optimisation and analytics).

Follow-on activities

Because goal setting and reviewing are so important to your business I have added a few extra activities below to help you continue to monitor your business on an ongoing basis.

Activity: Creating your ideal day

When you are doing something day in and day out you sometimes need to take a step back to assess. Your goals can often change over time as your business evolves or your personal circumstances changes. That is why it is worth taking a day out and starting from scratch with your goals rather than just using the same list as before.

Schedule in a day every six or twelve months where you are away from your business, with a clear mind and no interruptions. Grab your notepad and a pen, visualise your ideal working day and answer the questions below.

- Where are you on that ideal day?
- How does your day start?
- What tasks do you do during that day and what results do you achieve?
- What frame of mind are you in?
- What hours do you work?
- How does your day end?

With that ideal day in mind, and thinking about what success means to you (see page 34), draw up a list of goals that work directly towards achieving that ideal working day. How can you change your business to get you doing more of what you want and less of what you do not want to do? Have your goals changed since the last time you did them? If you identify new goals, remember to break them down into the smaller tasks you need to do to help you achieve them (see page 35).

Sometimes your business can be dragged in directions you have never really planned. Opportunities present themselves and we take them without checking whether they fit with our goals. Regular reviews will help you think such opportunities through so that you can decide whether these things are worth pursuing or if they are just distracting you from your main goals.

Activity: Twenty-four goals in twelve months

Referring to your to-do list (see page 36), and your list of goals (see pages 34), use the table below to allocate one thing from each list to each month of the year. Do not make this one of the big goals or problems, but one of the smaller steps you will need to take to help achieve your goal or overcome your problem. You can download this form from the website (craftacreativebusiness.co.uk) if you do not want to write in the book.

For example, I might add 're-vamp my blog' to the first box for January, and 'sort all my filing into a filing cabinet' into the second box. I might add 'create a press pack' for my February task and 'find a good mailing list program' from my problem list, and so forth.

Month	Task from your to-do list	Item from your list of goals
January		
February		
March		
April		
May		
June		
July		
August		
September		
October		
November		
December		

Start from whichever calendar month it is at the moment and aim to complete the two tasks for this month in the next few weeks. You do not have to do them both at once – start with one now and the other later in the month. When you have completed the task, cross it off or colour the box in so that you know it is done. Think of the sense of achievement you will have when you look at that table in a year's time and see how much you have managed to do.

Do not panic if you cannot do the tasks for one month. Leave them in the table and go back to it later in the year. You will find that some tasks are a lot quicker than others, so one month you may manage three or four tasks and other months only one. The main thing is to aim to have all twenty-four tasks done at the end of twelve months.

Activity: Make an in-depth business plan

A business plan will help you focus on your goals, and also to plan the long-term future of your business, budget your outgoings, forecast your incomings, research your market and much more. If you never wrote a business plan when you started your business, now is a good time for you to do it. If you did create a business plan, now is the time to update it.

There are several different sites offering business plan templates as well as advice on how to complete them. Several banks have free templates on their sites (some are listed in the 'Useful links' box opposite). Find your bank's website, go to its business page and look for links to its business plan templates, start-up guides and other useful information.

Writing a thorough business plan is a time-consuming job, but it will give you a much better idea of what you want to achieve when you have finished.

Activity: Studying trends

Using a spreadsheet program (such as Microsoft Excel or Google spreadsheets) or some graph paper, make a graph showing your profit each month for the last year (or two or three years, if you have the records). If you run an online business, do the same thing for your monthly hits as well.

These graphs will likely show you that some months you earn more than others, or get more site traffic, and other months a lot less. If you do it with a few years' worth of data you will be able to see if it is the same months each year.

Note down why you think particular months are better or worse than the others. Do you get a sudden rush of traffic and sales in the pre-Christmas period because people are buying presents? Is the summer quieter because people tend to be away on holiday? Do you have a big peak in January and February because you sell lots of products suitable for St. Valentine's Day?

Concentrating on the months where you have a dip in your income or site traffic, brainstorm how you can improve those figures in those months.

Is it worth running a sale? Doing extra advertising? Launching a new product that ties in with a seasonal event that month? Putting some fresh content on your site? Changing your social media strategy?

Bear in mind that some things cannot be overcome. Rather than wasting your time and energy fighting, consider how to usefully use the time. Over December, many people spend less time browsing websites or interacting on blogs or social media: they are busy preparing for Christmas, spending time with their family or simply having time off work. After a couple years of trying to think of ideas to boost my site traffic over that period, I decided to accept it and take some time off myself then too.

Studying these trends can help you plan your business strategy. There is no point putting lots of great content on your site at a time of year when hardly anyone is looking at it. Equally, if you find that certain shows or events on particular months are always quiet and do not make you money, avoid those next year.

USEFUL LINKS

Here are some useful online links to help you with the topics we have discussed in this section.

My website

craftacreativebusiness.co.uk

Start-up advice

bgateway.com

business.wales.gov.uk/starting-business

enterprisenation.com

europa.eu

gov.uk/browse/business/setting-up

hmrc.gov.uk/startingup

shell-livewire.org

uk.moo.com/startup-business-toolkit

Business plan templates

barclays.co.uk

bplans.co.uk

business.gov.au

lloydstsb.com

santander.co.uk

sba.gov

Advice on planning your business and setting goals

enterprisenation.com

entrepreneur.com

schoolforstartups.co.uk

thedesigntrust.co.uk

Pricing

createandthrive.com

etsy.com/blog

ohmyhandmade.com

thedesigntrust.co.uk

ukhandmade.co.uk

Market research

help.surveymonkey.com

marketingdonut.co.uk/marketing/market-research

smarta.com

YOUR LINKS AND NOTES

You can use this space to keep a list of links to websites and services you find helpful.

LEGAL

MATTERS

YOUR BUSINESS AND THE LAW

It is sometimes tempting to 'switch off' when looking at the legal and financial aspects of running a business. However, if you want to make a success of your business it is important to do it correctly. You do not want to end up being fined, closed down or even imprisoned because you did not do what you should have done. This chapter gives a simple introduction to the things you should be thinking about and where you can get more information.

We begin with a brief summary of the laws which can apply to creative businesses. Depending upon the exact nature of your business, not all of those listed will apply to you, but do take a read through and think about which ones relate to you. There is an extensive links section at the end of this chapter, so do use these to get more information on all the legislation mentioned here. If you are unsure about any of these requirements, either use the contact numbers on the websites in the links list to get more information or seek professional legal advice.

Disclaimer

I am not a legal or financial expert. This chapter is intended simply to give you an idea of where to start when considering the legal requirements of setting up your business. You should always double check the current rules and laws by either using your government website, trading standards, the tax office or seeking professional legal advice.

Learning the law

Familiarising yourself with local legislation and regulation is essential for any start-up business owner. These laws may cover anything from what you sell to how you sell it, and extends to the people you employ.

Employment laws

Once your business grows to the point where you start employing other people there are more laws that will become applicable to you, including minimum wage laws, pension laws, tax laws and working time regulations. The government website or tax office website for your country of residence is the best place to start obtaining this information.

Health and safety

Depending on where you work and whether you employ people, there may be health and safety regulations that apply to you. These can dictate how you train staff, how you manage risks and how you deal with first aid and accidents. If you check the useful links section at the end of the chapter you will find details of where to get more information on this subject.

EMPLOYMENT TIPS FROM KAY HEALD

These tips on employment regulations are from Kay Heald, who runs the human resources consultancy, Heald HR (kayhealdhr.co.uk).

Much business advice suggests that start-ups outsource services and engage freelancers instead of employing staff in order to keep costs down. However, while outsourcing services is usually beneficial, there can be drawbacks to engaging freelancers for regular patterns of work over long periods. An alternative option might be to initially employ part-time staff on short-term contracts, then review them after a twelve month period, once the business is more established.

Whatever you do, budget for a good HR advisor who can:

- Help you explore the best option(s) for your business.
- Draw up written agreements/contracts clarifying duties, expectations, who owns copyright and rates of pay.
- Put statutory policies in place, e.g. Disciplinary, Grievance, etc.
- Clarify the working arrangements with regard to HMRC and employment law, to avoid any tax or employment liabilities

Do this up front as clear documentation can help avoid costly litigation in the event of misunderstandings or breakdowns in any relationships.

Selling and distance selling around the world

In the majority of countries there are legal requirements about the selling of products both online and in person. In the UK, the rules include making sure that your product matches its description, that the description is not misleading, that the product is of satisfactory quality, and that is fit for purpose (Sale of Goods Act 1979). When selling online you need to ensure you provide the customer with your identity, your full address, details of the delivery and payment options and details of their cancellation rights amongst other things. The Office of Fair Trading website has in-depth information on all the regulations you need to consider. Online sellers also have to look into cookie regulations, marketing rules and data protection.

TOY SAFETY REGULATIONS

In most countries there are strict regulations for selling products that will be used by children. When selling toys within the UK or the European Economic Area, your products are required to be CE marked to confirm that they meet safety standards. If you fail to comply with this regulation you can be fined or even sent to prison. If you are unsure of whether your product needs CE marking it is best to contact Trading Standards to find out. There are also regulations about chemicals and materials used in children's toys as well as rules governing choking risks.

There is a UK-based company called Conformance (conformance.co.uk) that gives advice, training and self-certification packs for product safety and CE marking. Conformance also has a 'knowledgebase' section on its website which gives answers to many commonly asked questions.

For the requirements of the US government, there is a very useful site called the Handmade Toy Alliance (handmadetoyalliance.org) which is a great resource on this subject. The legislation you need to be aware of when making toys in the USA is the Consumer Product Safety Improvement Act (CPSIA). The full details can be found online at cpsc.gov.

Australia has various Australian Standards which govern toy safety. The Australian Toy Association website (austoy.com.au) is a good place to start when seeking advice on toy safety.

Another useful resource when it comes to toy safety is the International Council of Toy Industries website (toy-icti.org/info/toysafetystandards.html) which has advice on toy safety standards around the world.

In the USA the Federal Trade Commission is the main agency that regulates e-commerce rules. There is a lot of information on its website about advertising, marketing and selling regulations as well as advice on other financial and legal aspects of running a business. For Australia, the Australian Competition & Consumer Commission is a good place to start your research.

Wherever you live, when selling online you must look into the rules regarding online marketing in your country (such as the Can-Spam in the US), the rules regarding domain registration (try Nominet for UK domains) and labelling laws.

CLOTHING REGULATIONS

As with toys, certain legal requirements must be met when you are producing clothing. Some countries also have labelling requirements. For example, textile products in the UK should contain a label, either on the product itself or on the packing, which indicates the fibre contents of the product. Certain products are exempt, so do double check the up-to-date list of exemptions online.

The Product Safety Australia website has details of the mandatory requirements for labels for clothing, household textiles and furnishings for those either manufacturing or importing into Australia.

In America the Federal Trade Commission (FTC) and the US Customs and Border Protection agency dictate labelling requirements. The main Act you need to be looking at is the Textile Fiber Products Identification Act which can be found on the FTC website.

A lot of regulations apply to children's products in general; whether clothing or toys. For children's clothing there are particular rules about the flammability of the fabrics used, and about hood cords, for example. Many of the useful links given in the box on toy safety regulations (see the box opposite) will also give advice relevant for making and selling children's clothing.

The form of your company

There are different forms that your business can take. Each one carries its own set of legal restrictions and requirements, but also benefits too. Sole traders, for example, have full legal liability for their business which can make it easier to get credit accounts, but does leave you personally responsible for the business debts. It also affords you privacy because your accounts are not publicly published. Other options include limited liability companies or partnerships, which protect the owner from the potential liability of the business (in most circumstances) but often have more stringent accounting requirements.

Your company name

There are many factors, both legal and non-legal, to consider when choosing a name for your business. The name should represent your brand, appeal to the target market, and be unique. If you intend to incorporate you need to check if the name you are thinking of has already been registered. You may also want to check the trademark database too (see page 67 for relevant website links).

There are also restrictions on words that you are allowed to use in your business name. Company names are not allowed to be misleading or suggest illegal activity; nor are they allowed to be too similar to companies that already have established goodwill. Again the websites in the links section will give you advice about what is and is not allowed when it comes to naming your business. Your business name may also be required to reflect the legal status of your business, for instance with the addition of 'Ltd' after the name in the UK, or 'LLC' in the US.

Checking whether the domain names and social media names for your proposed business name are available is not a legal requirement, but well worth doing. You do not want to have to use social media names which are too different from your brand or hard to remember. Normally when someone is searching for a brand on social media they will simply type the name. If that leads them to another company, it can get very confusing. You do not want your customers or prospective customers to be following someone else on social media thinking they are following you.

Activity:
The right form for your business

Investigate what company forms are available in your country and decide which one best suits your requirements.

Dormant social media

Depending on the platform, if there is an inactive social media account with your business name you may be able to request that the name be transferred to you.

Trademarks and patents

If you have unique branding or a unique product idea that you want to protect, it may be worth investigating trademarking your logo or patenting your product. The best place to find out whether your idea has already been registered, or how to go about registering it and the costs involved is to visit the intellectual property office website for your country. You can also find out more about protecting your ideas and designs on pages 58–61.

Working with children

If you are planning to hold events that will involve children or teaching children, there are certain legal requirements you have to satisfy beforehand. There are background checks that need to be performed on you and your staff, and there is sometimes a set ratio of adults to children that needs to be observed.

The adult–child ratio can differ based upon the intended activities, any special needs the children have, and the ages of the children. The NSPCC website (nspcc.org.uk) gives you suggested guidelines for the ratio in the UK.

Renting commercial premises

Renting property from which to trade is not the same as renting a domestic property. The lease will be very different, so make sure you read through every clause, and consider getting a solicitor to look over it. The lease will normally transfer several responsibilities over to you during the term of your tenancy, so you need to understand which responsibilities you are taking on, and which will remain with the landlord. You may become responsible for fire safety, gas safety, maintaining electrical equipment, as well as certain repairs and maintenance to the property.

RENTAL TIPS FROM DOMINI LUCAS

Domini Lucas runs Space to Sew (spacetosew.co.uk), a popular sewing school.

Renting commercial premises is different from renting residential premises. You have to sign a commercial lease tying you in for a number of years. If your landlord is unscrupulous you could also find yourself pushed into expensive repairs or upkeep unnecessarily.

Leasing

- Engage a good solicitor to represent your interests: do not sign a lease presented to you by an estate agent, or drafted by the owner's solicitor alone.
- Have the solicitor negotiate a break clause in case your business runs into difficulties.

Planning

- Check the property has the right planning use for your business or you could be tied in without permission to trade.
- It may be possible to apply for 'change of use'. Ask a planning consultant, who can also help with submitting the application.

Taxes and accounts

Taxation and accounts are areas that can seem very daunting when you first start up your business. They sound very complex and change rapidly. This often leads to new business owners simply paying an accountant to deal with it! However, tax and accounts do not have to be as complex as you think. So long as you keep a proper log of what money is going in and out of your business, you have the information you need to do your own tax returns.

Keeping track of your cashflow

When it comes to keeping track of what is coming in and out of your business there are a few things that you need to do:

Set up a separate bank account for your business.

You can run your business through your personal account, but it will make doing your accounts more complicated. Disentangling business transactions from among personal ones, several months after the money was spent, can be very difficult.

Business bank accounts do not need to cost a fortune. As well as making your accounts easier it makes you look more professional to be able to make or receive payments in your business name. For the same reasons, if you are processing online payments, consider setting up a business account with whichever online payment provider you choose to use. See pages 177–179 for more information on selling online and online payments.

Keep all your receipts

The tax office may ask to see your receipts, so you need to keep them safe. In addition, if you ever have a problem balancing your accounts, it helps to be able to go through the receipts and double check each payment amount.

It is easiest if you keep all of your receipts in one place so that you do not have to waste time searching for them if you need them. Keep a big box file with all your receipts in for the current tax year, and at the end of each year put them all in a large envelope and write the tax year on the front of the envelope. You can print out online receipts and store them with the others, or simply save them all in one e-mail or computer folder. If you choose the latter option, make sure to back up the folder regularly.

Log your transactions

This is so much easier if you do it as the money comes in and out, rather than trying to do it all at the end of the month or year. You can do this with dedicated accounts software like Sage or Quick Books, or, if you are more of a pen and paper person, by keeping an accounts book and writing down the transactions as you go. You can buy accounts books with all the columns ready marked in from most stationers.

My business bank account

I pay nothing for my business bank account. My bank allows me to process online payments and cheques for free, which is all I need for my business. Shop around and compare what the different banks offer to see which is best for you.

Keeping track of my accounts

I download monthly statements from the various accounts I hold as pdf documents and save them in two different places as back-up.

You can also find free accounts templates online. The Microsoft website holds accounts templates for Excel, and there are a couple of useful ones on the Arts Council website.

Try to establish a habit of updating your accounts around the same time each day, make it part of your daily routine. Use whichever method you are most confident with, and the one you are more likely to stick to. If, like me, your business involves being online quite a lot then a computerised method is probably best. If you are working in a studio or shop away from the computer you may find it easiest to have a paper book and write things down as you go. The main thing is that you need to be logging yours transactions as close as possible to when they happen. Then once a week or once a month have a look over your accounts and make sure the figures add up and that you have not missed any transactions in error, or made any mistakes.

BACK UP FREQUENTLY

Given that a lot of business is now done online, the chances are that many of your receipts and account statements will be online too. Make sure you back up frequently so that you do not risk losing these. Either print them up and keep paper copies, use a service like Dropbox to back them up online, or use a USB stick or external hard drive.

I am a big fan of Dropbox, not only is it free but it automatically synchronises with your computer so you do not need to remember to back up – it is all done for you automatically. In addition, because the service provides online storage, you can access your accounts and receipts from any computer or device.

Recording my transactions

I use a spreadsheet that I update at least once a day to track The Sewing Directory's cashflow.

I have a sheet for incomings, a sheet for outgoings, a sheet for monthly profit and a front sheet which tells me the current solvency of my business, drawing data from the other sheets so that it updates every time I spend or receive any money.

You do not need to be a spreadsheet wizard to make a spreadsheet like this, it just uses a couple of basic formulas to check the figures balance.

Activity:
Pick a logging method

Think about what accounts logging method will work best for your business. Use the useful links at the end of this section of the book to compare some of the different options and see which appeals most to you.

Know your tax limits

Rather than waiting until the end of the year to see what you owe, look up the current tax limits for your country, how much you can earn before you have to pay tax, and what the tax rate is once you cross that threshold. You can normally find those figures on your government website or tax office website. Check them each year as they tend to change annually.

Take care to read through the notes on the tax office websites for your country because there can be extra costs you need to account for. For instance in the UK, once your tax bill passes a certain limit, you have to pay money in advance towards next year's tax bill (payment on account). You do not want to wait until you submit your tax return before finding out things like that!

Activity: Tax limits

Look up what the tax limits are in your country, and what rate you have to pay once you cross that threshold. Write those figures below, and copy them into your notebook/logbook.

Tax limit	Rate

I recommend totalling up your figures at the end of every month and checking them against the tax limit. Once you cross the tax threshold, calculate how much you owe at the end of each month and make sure you put that money aside. If you do this throughout the year you do not need to worry about finding money to pay your tax bill.

You might also consider setting up a second business account in which to keep your tax money to make sure you do not spend it. If possible, choose a high-interest account so that you can earn interest on your set-aside funds while you wait to pay your tax bill.

Avoid last-minute panic

Bureaucracy can slow things down — in the UK the HMRC can take up to three weeks to send out the necessary information to access and fill out a tax return online, for example, and I am sure there will be similar delays elsewhere. Do not leave things too late!

Depending on where you live, there may be other contributions or taxes to pay during the year, so make sure you account for them and set the money aside. For example, in the UK you may have to pay class 2 National Insurance contributions during the year. Register on the HM Revenues and Customs (HMRC) website to let them know you are self-employed and they will send you a bill for the National Insurance contributions.

Accountant or not?

If after reading the above, you still do not think you can handle your own accounts, consider looking into outside help such as local accountants or online firms. Equally, you might decide to learn more about accounts yourself. Most areas have business support including accounts or tax training. There are also accountancy books available and online training courses. Tax offices and government websites are very useful sources of information as well.

If you cannot handle your accounts yourself, it is best to get professional help rather than risk submitting late or incorrect accounts which could result in fines. Try not to leave it too close to the end of the tax year before looking for someone as most accountants will be very busy then and may not be in a position to take on new businesses.

Teaching yourself accountancy

I attended free courses at my local tax office just before I launched my business, and then did one of its free online webinars a couple years later for a refresher. Both experiences gave me a chance to ask questions as well as find out the current regulations.

You can also ring the tax office with any queries you have; I have done so several times and they are very helpful. In my experience they would much rather you did that than guess what you should be doing and submit incorrect accounts.

Expenses of working from home

In the UK, you can now claim a fixed rate to cover the expenses of working from home. Search the HMRC site for simplified expenses to find out more.

SETTING MONEY ASIDE

Whether you decide to set up a separate business account for tax funds or not, it always helps to keep an extra float in your business to cover any unexpected costs like new machinery you need, extra supplies for a large order or an unexpected trip you need to take.

Set an amount that you want to keep in your account at all times, that would cover any possible expense you could foresee. For instance if your business involves you using a sewing machine, keep enough aside to replace or repair it in case it breaks.

Copyright

Copyright is a legal concept which gives the person who created the original work rights over how that work is used or distributed. Not everything can be copyrighted. Ideas cannot be protected and nor can names, but written works such as books, poems and plays can be; as can photographs, drawings, paintings, computer software, sound recordings and more. These, along with trademarks, registered designs and patents, are collectively known as intellectual property or IP.

IP TIPS FROM DIDS MACDONALD

Dids MacDonald is the Chief Executive of ACID (acid.uk.com), an organisation that raises awareness and encourages respect for intellectual property.

- Create an IP strategy and ensure that it is communicated within and outside your company. IP communication sends a clear message that 'original design and design integrity equals value' for both the purchaser and the originator!

- Be active when dealing with IP issues. Become 'IP savvy' and create an informed understanding within your team.

- Create an IP portfolio of your design and trademark registrations. Include any patents you may have and guard your trade secrets carefully.

- Clarity of IP ownership is essential, so agreements should underpin most commercial relationships. It's good to know you have the small print to rely on if things go wrong. Never underestimate the risks of sharing a good idea unless you know there are safeguards.

- Choose your battles carefully. Never sue on principle; only if there is a quantifiable loss and a clear IP case to pursue. Consider dispute resolution/mediation as an alternative to litigation. It's good to talk!

Trademarks, registered designs and patents

Unlike copyright these protections do not occur automatically but are paid-for registration of the visual appearance of your design (registered design), the processes or features that make your design work (patents) or your logo (trademarks). These need to be registered via the Intellectual Property Office website if you are based in the UK or the Patent and Trademark Office if you are in the USA. These sites gives you full details of what exactly can be registered and how to do so.

INDEPENDENT DESIGNERS AND THE HIGH STREET

There have been several high-profile cases of high street stores breaching independent designers' copyright. Kate Davies, owner of Kate Davies Designs, found an owl jumper of her design being sold through the high street store Debenhams. After hundreds of her followers made complaints, Debenhams agreed to donate £5,000 to a charity of Kate's choice.

Another recent case is that of illustrator HiddenEloise and Paperchase. Paperchase allegedly stole and traced one of her illustrations to put on its notebooks, totebags and albums. Her blog post about this went viral, and resulted in Paperchase saying it they would investigate and the items being withdrawn from sale.

A lot of the recent cases have been fought through social media; perhaps as a result of the cost and difficulty that faces a small business pursuing this kind of case through the courts. In a similar case to Kate Davies', Claire's Accessories released a range of necklaces almost exactly like those designed by Tatty Devine at a fraction of the price. Tatty Devine put a post on its blog comparing both sets of necklaces. This very quickly went viral on social media and led to Claire's Accessories trending on Twitter. An undisclosed settlement was reached between the two companies soon afterwards.

Learning to protect your copyright

Copyright is an important issue for any business. The advent of the internet has made it easier for people's designs to be copied. People can now see your products on your website, social media and any online marketplaces you sell through, which makes it easy for them to copy your designs.

Fortunately, the internet also makes it easier for you to find out when this has happened. Companies are commonly notified of breaches to their copyright by their social media followers. You can also use tools like Google image search to see if anyone is trying to pass your designs off as their own.

So how can you protect your copyright? Copyright is established automatically as soon as the item, design or brand is created: there is no need to notify an official register where you can log your designs, but you can join an organisation like Anti Copying In Design (ACID).

ACID is a not-for-profit organisation which provides help and support in protecting designers' intellectual property. They charge a membership fee in exchange for access to their design databank, initial free legal advice and access to their intellectual property resources. They have IP affiliates in many countries and operate an IP tracker which tracks the sending of any intellectual property or confidential information. They also have the ACID Marketplace, an online safer trading conduit. Designers have the safety of knowing their designs are on the ACID database and are protected by a buyers' charter.

The University of Arts London also has a good copyright site called Own It. This site has a series of useful articles about copyright and intellectual property as well as a legal advice service which is free for some people and available at a nominal fee for others. It also suggests several other places where you can get intellectual property legal advice too. The UK Intellectual Property Office website is a great resource for information on protecting your IP.

In Australia, the Australian Copyright Council provides free legal advice services, and seminars around the country, plus a bookshop of useful books. It also has free downloadable advice documents on its website as well.

In the USA, you can register your copyright with The US Copyright Office. Copyright will still exist even if you do not register it with the Copyright Office, but if may help to protect you if you do register.

How can I prevent copying?

Unfortunately the short answer is that in many instances you cannot prevent others copying your work. However, there are steps you can take to minimise the risk.

Notices Include a copyright notice on your site and on products with the year, your name or business name and the copyright symbol © or the word 'copyright'.

Watermarks When putting product photographs online, watermark them. There are several sites and software programs that allow you to do this including PicMonkey, Pixlr and TSR Watermark Image. Pixlr is also available as a free phone app so you can watermark and upload images directly from your phone.

Check the internet Use programs like Copyscape or Google image checker to see if anyone is using your content elsewhere on the internet.

Use the law Legally protect your designs where possible using patents, trademarks and registered designs.

Record your work Keep a record of what you create and when. If your copyright is breached you need to be able to prove that you created it first. Records will help prove your case. Digital methods such as uploading to your blog, or saving digital copies with a file creation date are less useful than hard copies (see box, right) as the dates are easier to manipulate.

Branding Create and use a recognisable logo or other branding so people can check it is your original product and not an inferior copy.

Registration If it is a product or brand name you want to protect, register all the relevant domains to prevent other businesses from being able to use them. These domains can all be linked to feed through to your main website.

Insurance If you think your designs are at a big risk of being copied you may want to get intellectual property insurance. It will cover your legal costs and any judgment costs up to the policy limits.

Impact Aim to make a big impact and to be the best. Things like your business concept are hard (if not impossible) to protect. By making sure you are the most well-known and the best, you will still be known as the person to go to even if people copy your idea and set up competition. Creating and maintaining a high-profile presence means that most people will have heard of you before anyone has a chance to copy your ideas.

The copyright symbol

To get the © symbol when using a Windows PC hold the ALT key and type 0169. If you are using a Mac hold the OPTION key and press G. The copyright symbol can be expressed by a C in brackets too (C).

Poor man's copyright

In the UK you can take steps to protect your idea by depositing a hard copy with a bank or solicitor, or sending it to yourself by special delivery (which gets the envelope date marked) and then not opening the envelope. This is known as 'poor man's copyright'. Note that this does not provide concrete protection.

Licensing

If your designs are proving very popular you may want to look at licensing them to other businesses so that you get paid for them being used. You still retain the intellectual property rights to that design but you give them permission to use it in a certain way. Because the design remains yours you can still use those designs in other ways, subject to the contract you sign. There are three common ways to get paid for your licensed designs:

One-off payment The benefit of a one-off payment for use of your IP is that you know exactly how much you will get paid for the job and when. The downside is that if it becomes a huge hit and sells in very large quantities you do not get any extra money.

Royalties This means you get a percentage of each product sold. Essentially, you share the risk with the company to which you license your designs. If it is a hit you could stand to make a lot more money than with a one-off payment, but if it does not sell well you could earn very little from it. With a royalty deal you will benefit from continuing to promote the products to help ensure high royalties. Make sure this is something you are willing – and able – to do.

Royalties with an advance This minimises the risks slightly for you because you get an agreed sum up front and then royalties if the item sells well enough. Normally you get a lower rate of royalties than if you went for royalties only, and the advance will be deducted from the royalties you earn. Therefore you need to earn more royalties than you had in advance if you want to receive any more payments after your advance.

LICENSING TIPS FROM NEL WHATMORE

The artist Nel Whatmore has licensed her designs to be used on fabric, homewares and stationery (nelwhatmore.com and nelpatterns.com).

- Keep a good digital file of all your paintings that you feel will sell the best. I could say get a good digital file done of every painting, but that would be rather unnecessary and very expensive.

- Never sell the copyright to your work: only the license to use it for a period of time.

CREATING A LICENSING AGREEMENT

A licensing agreement between you and the person or company licensing your designs helps to ensure clarity regarding:

- What exactly is being licensed.
- What it can be used for and where those products can be sold (geographically).
- How much you will get paid, and when.
- How the royalties will be calculated, if applicable.
- How long the agreement will last.
- What will happen if either party wants to terminate the agreement early.
- Whether you can still use that design on your own products or license to another party to use for different products.
- A quality clause to make sure your brand is not associated with substandard products.

The Intellectual Property Office and the Own It website have more information on licensing.

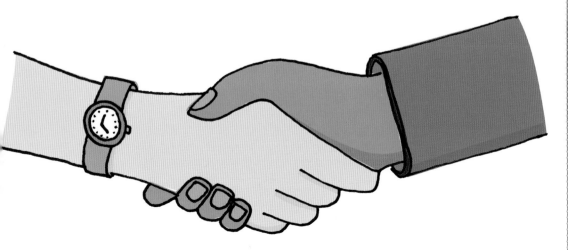

Insuring your craft business

There are many reasons why you could need insurance for your craft business, from insuring the tools of your trade against theft of damage to making sure you have protection in place if one of your products causes injury or illness.

Insurance

It may seem tempting to keep costs down by not being insured, especially when you are only making a very small profit on your business. However, if someone is injured by one of your products or tripped on part of your craft stall at a show or event, you could be looking at thousands in damages. Insurance can provide peace of mind that you will not have to be having to pay out a fortune some time in the future, and it is often surprisingly affordable.

When it comes to finding the right insurance you could approach a local insurance broker who would be able to provide you with quotes from several insurance companies. You can also search online for the type of insurance you want and the country you are based in. Alternatively I have put some useful links for you in the links section.

There are five main types of insurance that people running a craft-related business need to consider:

Product liability If you supply products then you are responsible for any injury to a person, or damage to their property, which may occur as a result of the use of your product (provided they were using it properly). Product liability insurance can meet the cost of any claims that arise. Depending on the level of harm caused and the amount of people affected, this kind of claim can run into the tens or even hundreds of thousands, so this sort of insurance helps gives you peace of mind.

Public liability Public liability covers any injury or property damage that occurs to a member of the public in connection to your business. If you teach sewing and someone in your class sustains an injury, or trips over some goods you laid out at a craft market, this is the insurance you need. It can be used to defend any claim made against you as well as for compensating any injured party.

Tradesman insurance If you do not have traditional retail premises, you may find that tradesman's insurance may be a better fit for your business. This can provide cover for your tools and premises, and also any liability that may arise as a result of you running your business.

SPECIAL CASES

Exhibiting

Many craft fairs will not let you have a stall unless you can show them your public liability insurance certificate.

Working from home

If you run your business from your house, you need to notify your home insurers because it may invalidate or alter the terms of your existing home insurance policy.

Professional indemnity If you give advice as part of your business – if you are a business consultant or a craft teacher, for example – this insurance will help to protect you from claims of professional negligence. If you offer a service such as social media management you also need professional indemnity.

Employer's liability If you employ anyone to help you with your business, then you need employer's liability insurance. This protects you from claims from employees injured or which became ill as a result of their work while in your employment. This type of insurance is compulsory in the UK and you must have a minimum coverage of five million pounds.

Other insurance you may also want to consider is accident and sickness insurance (to help you pay the mortgage or other bills if you are unable to work), vehicle insurance if you use a business vehicle, intellectual property insurance, and cancellation insurance for shows and events, so that you do not end up out of pocket if they do not go ahead for any reason.

INSURING A FAMILY BUSINESS

If your business is not a limited company, you may be exempt from the requirement for employer's liability insurance.

For more information please look at the Employers' Liability (Compulsory Insurance) Act 1969. This can be viewed online at legislation.gov.uk.

EXCLUSIONS AND EXCESSES

Exclusions

It is important to note that all insurance policies have exclusions, so make sure you have a good look through your policy to understand what is and is not covered. For instance most policies will not cover claims that arise as a result of your negligence, or if you fail to comply with health and safety or product safety laws. Some policies may only cover selling at events and shows and not online; or only cover trading from commercial premises, not from home. Always double check the small print.

Excesses

Most insurance policies will require you paying an excess/deductible if you claim. This means you are responsible for the first part of any claims payment. If you accept a larger excess, it will often give you cheaper insurance premiums. However you must make sure it is an amount you would be able to pay if you did have to make a claim.

USEFUL LINKS

Toy safety

CE marking information: gov.uk/ce-marking

UK trading standards: tradingstandards.gov.uk

Product safety advice (UK): conformance.co.uk

UK product safety regulations:
gov.uk/product-safety-for-manufacturers

British Standards Institution: bsigroup.com

Australian Standards: standards.org.au

Australian toy association: austoy.com.au

Product Safety Australia: productsafety.gov.au

Toy safety advice (USA): handmadetoyalliance.org

US toy safety legislation: cpsc.gov

International toy standards:
toy-icti.org/info/toysafetystandards.html

Clothing and labelling regulations

Clothing and footwear regulations (UK):
gov.uk/clothing-footwear-and-fashion

Product safety including clothing (UK):
gov.uk/product-safety-for-manufacturers

**Trading Standards Institute advice on labelling
(UK):** tradingstandards.gov.uk/advice/advice-
business-ftbussum20.cfm

**Regulations, including 1007/2011 on textile
labelling (EU):** eur-lex.europa.eu

Relevant UK legislation: legislation.gov.uk

Labelling requirements (Aus):
productsafety.gov.au

Federal Trade Commission (USA): ftc.gov

Customs and Border Protection (US): cbp.gov

Further reading on toys and clothing:
etsy.com/teams/6861/keeping-up-with-cpsia/
discuss/8567574

Selling regulations

Office of Fair Trading (UK): oft.gov.uk

Domain registration (UK): nominet.org.uk

Federal Trade Commission (US): business.ftc.gov

Small Business Administration (US):
sba.gov/content/online-business-law

Australia Competition & Consumer Commission:
accc.gov.au

Australian Government Business:
business.gov.au

Health and safety

Health and Safety Executive (UK): hse.gov.uk

**Occupational Safety and Health Administration
(US):** osha.gov

Safe Work Australia: safeworkaustralia.gov.au

Business structure

UK Companies House: companieshouse.gov.uk

Australia: asic.gov.au

USA: sba.gov

Business names, trademarks and patents

Companies House (UK): companieshouse.gov.uk

Intellectual Property Office (UK): ipo.gov.uk

Small Business Administration (US):
sba.gov/content/how-name-business

US Patent and Trademark office: uspto.gov

**Australian Securities and Investments
Commission:** asic.gov.au

Trademark and patent database (Aus): ipaustralia.
gov.au

Renting commercial premises

Advice for commercial tenants (UK): gov.uk/
renting-business-property-tenant-responsibilities

Ten tips for negotiating a commercial lease:
bit.ly/196Zmr9

A sample commercial lease agreement: lawdepot.
com/contracts/commercial-lease-agreement/

**Information for commercial tenancies and retail
shops (Aus):** commerce.wa.gov.au

Accounts

Accounting software:
sage.co.uk; intuit.co.uk/quickbooks/accounting-software.jsp; accountz.com/

Accounts templates:
artscouncil.org.uk/funding/information-funded-organisations/tools-templates/management-accounts-templates; office.microsoft.com/en-us/templates/results.aspx?qu=Budgets&av=zxl

Tax office (UK): hmrc.gov.uk

Australian Tax Office: ato.gov.au

Dropbox: dropbox.com

Copyright and licensing

Crafts & Copyrights: craftsandcopyrights.com

Copyright advice (UK): ipo.gov.uk

Anti Copying In Design: acid.uk.com

Own It: own-it.org

Copyright Council (Aus): copyright.org.au

Copyright Office (US): copyright.gov

Tatty Devine blog post: tattydevine.com/blog/2012/02/can-you-spot-the-difference

Katie Davies blog post: katedaviesdesigns.com/2012/07/12/thankyou-knitters

Watermarking images

TSR Watermark Image: watermark-image.com/

Pixlr: pixlr.com

PicMonkey: picmonkey.com

Copyscape: copyscape.com

Insurance

Links to craft insurance providers (UK):
craftacreativebusiness.co.uk/craft-insurance

Useful guide to insurance on The Crafts Report website: craftsreport.com/beginning-business/177-craft-business-insurance.html

List of insurers for artists and crafters (US):
studioprotector.org/OnlineGuide/Safeguarding/GettingtheRightInsuranceCoverage/InsuranceResources/BusinessInsurancePlans.aspx

Arts and craft business insurer (Aus):
ruralandgeneral.com.au

Market and trade exhibitors insurers (Aus):
aami.com.au

YOUR LINKS AND NOTES

You can use this space to keep a list of links to websites and services you find helpful.

PRESEN

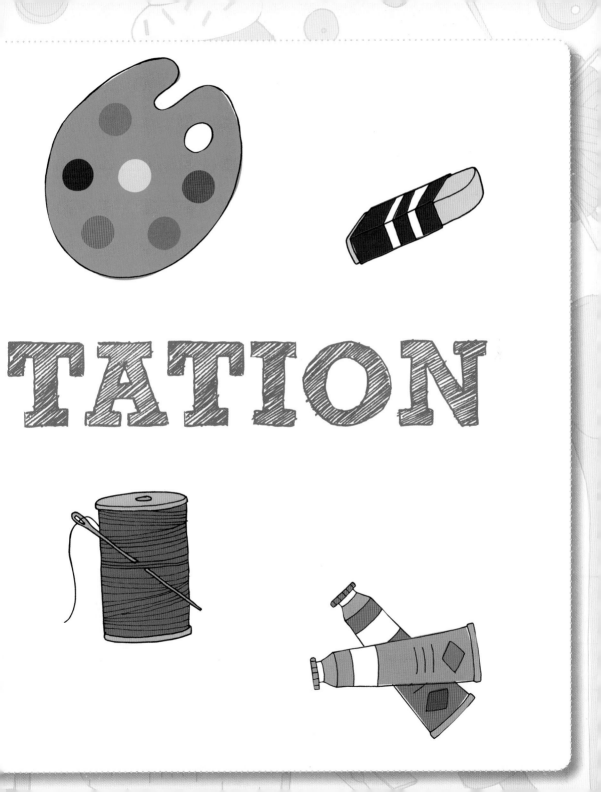

TATION

PRESENTING YOUR BUSINESS

This section focuses on the visual side of your business, including branding, product photography and visual marketing. The visual impact your business makes on your potential customers is incredibly important, and ensuring your brand and products are presented well can be a critical factor of success.

Visual presentation ties in to many aspects of your business, from advertising to social media and web design. As the saying goes, 'a picture is worth a thousand words'.

Branding

When you are launching your business, think about the impression you want to make with your branding. Identify who you need to appeal to, then reflect on what message you want to send to that target audience.

Consider the core values of your business and how you can communicate those through your branding. Do you want to be seen as fun and quirky? Sensible and trustworthy? Innovative and creative? Cool and trendy? Your aims are to make your business recognisable through your branding, and to appeal to your target audience at the same time.

Be distinctive

Take a good look at your competitor's branding before deciding on yours in order to avoid any potential confusion. In addition, bear in mind that most large brands have trademarked their logos: make sure yours is not too similar.

Colour

Different colours can trigger different responses in your audience. For instance, red suggests energy, yellow happiness, green nature, while blue symbolises trust and loyalty. The colours of a brand are often what will stick into people's memories. The blue and yellow of Ikea is instantly recognisable to most people, just like the red and yellow of McDonald's. Colour makes an instant impact, so make sure you think through your choice properly.

Vibrant clashing colours can put off people who want something more subtle and sophisticated, whereas muted browns and greys will probably not appeal to people looking for a vibrant brand.

Getting the colour wrong can instantly rule out a large number of potential customers. The gender and age of your potential audience can influence your colour choice. Many women prefer subtle soft colours such as pastel shades whereas men are often more attracted by bright bold colours. However, bright pink may put off as many men as it attracts. Similarly, striking black and white can be too boring for a younger audience. Focus on your intended audience to make sure the branding you choose will appeal rather than deter them.

There are also the practicalities to consider. You want colours you can easily recreate on different platforms, whether printed on paper or viewed online. Cost can be an issue too: if you are planning to print a lot of flyers, for instance, it is often cheaper to print in black and white than in colour.

IDENTIFYING COLOUR ONLINE

Colours used online are represented by what is known as a hex colour code. This code consists of a six-digit string of letters and numbers, and it specifies the precise colour. The digits represent the red value, green value and blue value of the colour. For example the hex number for blue is #0000FF; as the shade of blue varies the code will change, so navy blue is #000080.

Knowing the hex colour code of your branding makes it much easier to ensure consistency across your brand.

If you see a colour online that you like but do not know the hex number you can use a colour picking tool like ColorZilla to find out. This installs a tool on your browser bar that allows you to pick colours from any site whenever you want. There are web addresses for a few colour pickers in the links section on page 102.

Blue – #0000FF

Navy – #000080

Picking colours

Start by choosing a main colour for your scheme, then establish complementary colours that work well together with your choice. The easiest way to do this to look at a free online colour wheel tool like Colour Scheme Designer. This allows to you experiment with various colour combinations until you find the one that suits your brand.

Another useful site for choosing your brand colours is Design Seeds. This site extracts colours out from an image to create a colour palette. There are numerous images and corresponding colour palettes on the site for you to browse for inspiration. Many of them are combinations you probably would not have come up with by yourself. If you look on the sidebar of the site there is the option to pick palettes based upon their dominant colour. This can be useful if you have a rough idea what colours you want to go for but need help deciding on the specific combination.

USING A COLOUR WHEEL

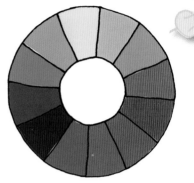

There are three ways you can use a colour wheel (see right) to choose your colour scheme.

- Analogous colours These are the adjacent colours on either side of your main colour. Blue and pink are analogous to purple, for example.

- Complementary colours A complementary colour is the hue directly opposite your chosen colour on the wheel. Purple is the complementary colour to yellow, for example.

- Triads Draw an equilateral triangle in the middle of the colour wheel, with your first colour on one of the points. The other two corners of the triangles with give you your other two colours to use. Using purple as your starting colour would result in orange and green being on the other points of the triangle, for example.

Activity: Choosing colours

Make a list of the key words you want associated with your brand and then think about which colours would best epitomise those words. Then using a free online colour tool like Colour Scheme Designer or Design Seeds, experiment until you find the exact hues that you want to represent your brand.

Make a note of the hex numbers of those colours so you can re-create the exact same hues across all your branding.

Colour name	Hex colour code

Lettering

Consider the typeface or font you will use. This covers those fonts you will use in your main logo (see opposite), but also on your website and in promotional materials. These do not all need to be the same font but aim to create a cohesive style across all of your branding – too many different typefaces risks diluting this effect.

As with colours, you want your typeface to represent the spirit of your brand. There are fonts in a variety of styles – modern, vintage, quirky and traditional. When choosing a font, make sure that is it easy to read. Ideally you want something with well-defined lettering, and good spacing between the letters to make sure people do not struggle to read it. As great as some of the novelty fonts look when reading just a word or two, they can be very hard going when trying to read an entire page of them.

SERIF VS SANS SERIF

You may have noticed that fonts are classed into two categories, serif and sans serif. Serif fonts have small finishing strokes on the end of the character and sans serif do not. See the examples below:

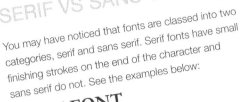

SERIF FONT

SANS SERIF FONT

It is generally thought that serif fonts are easier to read in print, and sans serif on screen.

Activity: Choosing your fonts

Experiment with a few typefaces to see how they look in different sizes, and across different media – online and in print. Do remember to see how the numbers look too.

Once you have decided which fonts you want to use make a note of them below, or in your notebook.

Logo

Once you have decided upon the colours and typeface you will use, you need to think about how you will combine them to create your logo. Will your logo be just lettering, just an image, or a combination of the two? Will it have a design unique to you? It helps to consider where you will be using your logo when considering the design. If it is going to be on small labels, your logo should not be too detailed or involve a lot of text. If it will be the centrepiece of your advertising and promotional materials and your website design, ensure it is eye-catching. An ideal logo can be easily recreated in a variety of sizes – large for posters or a shop sign, but also on a smaller scale for letterheads and business cards.

If you are unsure which colours, fonts and logos will resonate best with your target audience, then ask them. You could create a few different versions of branding for your business and conduct some market research to see which they like best, or show them a selection of colours, fonts and business keywords to see which appeal most to them.

Complexity

A logo does not need to be complicated. Simpler, iconic designs are often more effective. Think of the Nike swoosh, the Apple logo, or the Twitter bird: all are instantly recognisable and easy to use in different situations.

LOGO DESIGN

In addition to professional programs like Photoshop or Adobe Creative Suite, there are plenty of free design programs, such as Pixlr or PicMonkey, that you can use to create your logo. There are also several logo creator websites that will help you. Search for 'logo maker' and you will get a selection of sites from which to choose.

However, if graphic design is not your forte, then outsource it. A poor logo can make even a very good creative business look unprofessional. It is critical to get your logo right, so leave it to the professionals if you are not sure what to do. Many graphic design and illustration services have surprisingly affordable rates: there are graphic designers on services like Fiverr.com who will design a logo for as little as $5. Check the reviews to see what other people think of those services you are considering approaching.

Activity:
Creating your logo

Using your research into colours and lettering, work on ideas for your logo. If you do not want to do it yourself ask around for recommendations of graphic designers and illustrators. You can always do a rough sketch on paper and then send it to someone to digitise and tidy it up for you.

As an alternative to having a single logo, consider making two; one a shorter or smaller version of the other. The Facebook logo below is a good example:

Message

Branding is not all about appearance: the principles behind your brand are just as important. Some of these principles can be conveyed in your visual branding, but they are also portrayed in the way you do business and the way you interact with your customers.

Creating a strong set of brand principles will not only help you stand out from your competitors but will also help to make your customers feel loyal to you. If your brand message resonates with them they are much more likely to return to you again in the future.

Write a list of words that you want people to associate with your business, and plan how to demonstrate those key words through the way you run your business. Think about how can you communicate these principles through your branding, through your interactions with your customers and through your products or service. For example, if you want to be perceived as being helpful, go that extra mile to make sure you assist your customers wherever possible. If you want to build a reputation for being reliable, put systems in place to ensure deliveries are sent quickly with a low error rate.

Think about what you can do to make sure you deliver what you promise. Customers will learn what your brand principles are and come to expect them from you, so make sure you do not set standards that are impossible to keep up. It is much better to over-deliver than under-deliver.

Strapline

A slogan or strapline for your business that can be used in your promotion can help to communicate your message. It should summarise what your business stands for, what it provides, and how it will help fulfil the customer's needs.

If you are struggling to come up with a strapline, ask friends, family or customers how they would describe your business or business concept to another person. They might help you come up with something really creative and original. However, do not try to make it too obscure or unusual. A subtle play on words might make a clever or amusing slogan, but if some of your potential customers do not understand it, it will not benefit your business. Equally, your slogan should not be too vague or too 'off the wall'. Remember that it needs to tell people what your business is about – or at least give them a hint and make them want to learn more. A good strapline will help you connect with existing and potential customers, and encourage them to look further into what it is you do. If people can instantly tell from your strapline that you offer what they want, then you are onto a winner!

My strapline

The strapline for The Sewing Directory is: 'Making it easier to find great sewing resources.' That short sentence encapsulates the core principles of my site. Can you summarise what your business does in just a few words?

Applying your branding

Once you have finalised the message you want to convey with your branding, and how you are going to do it, think about how to apply your branding to your business. Places you can apply your branding include:

- Your website

- Business cards

- Flyers

- Adverts

- Banners or posters for shows or your shop

- Packaging and labelling

- Headed paper

- Your social media accounts

The fronts of my current business cards for The Sewing Directory.

PROMOTIONAL MATERIALS

Free trials

There are many companies, such as Avery, Moo and Vistaprint, that allow you to create your own promotional materials by simply uploading your logo and choosing a colour scheme that matches your branding.

Most of these companies offer new customer deals with free trials, discounted products, or sample packs. Make the most of these offers to experiment with your branding and determine what works best for you.

Business cards

Get good quality business cards where possible, even if you pay a little more. As the first thing you give to potential customers or contacts, they need to make a good impression.

Brand consistency

When you have settled on your brand identity you need to ensure you keep it consistent so that people learn to recognise it as your business. People may see information about your business in several different places but if your branding is the same throughout, they will come to realise it is the same business they are seeing.

Often your business will evolve over time and you may want to come back and review your strapline, and branding every year or so to make sure it is still relevant to your current business. As an example, I changed my strapline after I had been trading for a couple of years.

Finding a balance between developing your business and keeping true to your core principles is a rewarding challenge.

Moo business cards

It is tempting to go for bulk over quality; I did that when I first started. However, I have since found it is worth having business cards that 'wow' people. Personally I like Moo best for this. It lets you use a range of images so that you can tailor the card to the people you are giving them to, plus it has some very high quality finishes. You can also create product labels or stickers through its site as well.

Take a look at the inspiration section of the Moo website for some great branding ideas and useful tips.

HOW I CHOSE MY BRANDING

The process for developing the Craft a Creative Business brand is a good example of the approach you should take. For the website, I wanted to combine business with creativity. I decided I would portray several different crafts in the branding; and without becoming too corporate, I wanted to include some elements of business too.

I knew what I wanted in terms of design, but graphic design is not one of my talents, so I employed a graphic designer whose style I have long admired, Lucy Farfort (lucyshappyplace.com), to turn my ideas into reality. Following my brief, she created a good quality design that could be used in different aspects of my branding, from banners on my site to web adverts and logos. The results are pictured here.

The brand name is a play on words that clearly communicates the goal of both the book and site: namely, to help you craft a creative business.

Photography

I cannot emphasise enough the importance of your product photography, particularly when you are selling your products online. Unlike in a shop, where people can see and handle your products to examine the quality, online they are fully dependent on the photographs that you give them. Photographs really are the key to selling your products. No matter how amazing your products might be, if you are displaying them in poor quality photographs you will struggle to get a sale.

In the art and craft industries this seems to be where many people fall down. So many stunning products are let down by poor photography, which unfortunately puts off many potential customers. With so much competition online, good photography can really help make your products stand out from the competition's.

Even if you do not sell products, you will still need to have some good photographs to help promote your business – images of yourself, your work space and your team to send to people who want to write a feature on your business; or stock photographs you can use on your site and social media. The advice in this section will be just as useful for those photographs as for product photography.

The good news is that you do not have to be an expert photographer to produce good quality images. This chapter includes lots of useful guidance and tips which will help you to improve your photographs. Digital cameras are most common nowadays, so most of the information in this section has been written assuming you are using one.

Image credit: Roddy Paine Photographic Studios.

Further reading

If you would like to learn more about improving your photography I recommend reading *The Crafter's Guide to Taking Great Photos* by Heidi Adnum. This book is an in-depth guide to both producing and editing art and craft photography.

COMMON PHOTOGRAPHIC TERMINOLOGY

Diffusion Scattering light in several directions. You can diffuse a camera flash by putting fabric or paper over it. You can diffuse light from a lamp or natural light by using a reflector.

DSLR Digital single lens reflex. Unlike a digital compact camera, where the viewfinder only estimates what the sensor is seeing, DSLR cameras have a mirror that reflects the light going into the camera's sensor to the viewfinder, so the user sees exactly the same image as the sensor.

Resolution This refers to the amount of detail recorded by an image. The higher the resolution the more detailed and clearer the image. Digital cameras measure their resolution in megapixels (MP): the higher the MP, the more detail the camera can record. High MP cameras can take larger images without the picture quality deteriorating or becoming blurry.

DPI Dots per inch. The DPI measures the density of dots per inch of a digital image when printed. Printed images are made up by a series of very small printed dots; the more dots per inch, the clearer and more detailed the image.

Exposure The amount of light collected by the camera in a single photograph. Most cameras let you adjust the amount of light collected by the camera by adjusting the ISO speed. When working in low light you can increase the ISO on the camera to get sharper photographs.

Pixel size The size of a digital image is often referred to in pixel size, or 'px'. When booking an online advert the person hosting the advert will tell you what size image is needed to fill the space – 180 x 150px, for example. An advert made to those dimensions ensures there will be no loss of image quality from resizing, and no need to crop the image to make it fit the space.

JPEG/GIF/PNG File formats for digital image files. There are hundreds of different image file types but those three are the most commonly used on the web, and will be suitable for most uses.

Camera

You do not need to rush out and spend hundreds or thousands of pounds on a high-end camera to take good photographs. You can produce good images with the majority of cameras and even with your phone. Most mobile phones include a digital camera that can produce images that are suitable for viewing on webpages. Some have very high quality cameras on them which produce images as good as most digital compacts. However, the camera on your phone will probably not produce high enough quality images for press photographs (see page 224). If your mobile phone images are not high enough quality you may want to look at getting or borrowing a camera too.

One of my site contributors takes and edits all her photographs on her iPhone and they look great and are perfect for web use. However, do check the size and image quality of pictures from your phone if you intend to also use them in print. If you are going to be printing a lot of large detailed images you will want a high-resolution camera. High-resolution cameras used to be very expensive but as technology improves the price comes down.

You can pick up a decent digital compact camera fairly affordably. Most of these have pre-set modes and you can essentially 'point and shoot' as soon as you take it out of the box. It is worth reading through the manual, visiting the manufacturer's website or searching for instructional videos to learn about the full capabilities of the camera. These are great if you are a beginner or do not want to get too involved in the technical side of photography.

If you have a little more budget you could go for a DSLR camera. These are more expensive cameras that give you a lot more control over the settings, and work better in low or varying light conditions. If you are keen to learn more about photography these cameras will give you a lot more chance to experiment and will usually result in higher quality images. You can also change lenses on a DSLR, giving you more creative options.

If you are unsure of what camera to go for, ask around to get feedback from other people on the cameras they use. If there is anyone whose photography you admire, contact them to find out what camera they prefer to use. You can also ask on forums or social media for recommendations, or take a look at review websites.

My camera

I use a 16.1 mega pixel camera, a Panasonic Lumix, which cost under £90. It is worth looking out for sales and special offers to get a discount, or free accessories like a case or memory card.

Other useful equipment

Tripod A tripod keeps your camera still so avoids any blurring and giving you a sharper image. You can buy these cheaply, or you can improvise by resting your camera on surfaces. The heavier your camera, the stronger and sturdier your tripod will need to be.

Backdrops The background to your image can make a big difference. It can just be your wall, or you can buy or make fabric or paper backdrops to use especially for your photography. Just remember that you do not want your backdrop to distract people from your product.

Light tent These are great for creating a brightly lit image with a plain background. Light shines in from the top and then bounces off the sides onto your product in the centre, giving a more even exposure and resulting in less shadow. If you use a plain background, it means all the focus of the photograph is on your product.

You can buy pop-up light tents with interchangeable backgrounds online for very little. There are also numerous tutorials online about how to make your own using a cardboard box. There is a link to one in the useful links section.

81

Image size and quality

Is important to remember how you plan to use your photographs as this will dictate the quality you require. To check the image size, file size and quality of an image on your computer, right click on the file and select 'properties'.

Images for your website

Image size and quality can be a lot lower for web images than images which will be used in print – in fact, small web images are a benefit: they take up less server space, load more quickly when people view the web page, and you can upload them to your site or shop a lot faster too. You normally need a file size of around 100kb with a width of around 1000 pixels to cover the full width of a page. Most cameras will produce images a lot larger than this. You can put your camera on its lowest settings to reduce the image size. Alternatively, you can reduce images shot at a higher quality by altering the size or compressing the file on your computer. There are many free image compressor sites online which will do this for you, such as compressnow.com, or you can use image editing software on your computer to do it yourself.

Images for print

In my role as a freelance journalist for *Sewing World* magazine, a common problem I face when featuring people's products is that their images have been taken with their websites in mind and are neither large enough, nor good enough quality to use in print. Magazines usually require images with a minimum resolution of 300 dpi and a file size over 1MB. Journalists often have tight deadlines and cannot wait for you to re-shoot images. If you do not have a good enough image when they call, you could lose out on valuable coverage!

When taking images for your website, adjust your camera to its highest quality settings, take some print-quality pictures, and store them all in a folder called 'Press'. This ensures you have the images ready if a journalist wants to feature your business or products in print. Once they know you supply high quality images, they are more likely to come back to you for future features.

By storing all of the high resolution images you take in a separate dedicated folder, you are less likely to accidentally compress the image or to try and upload the large image to your website. It will keep them separate from your lower quality, smaller web images.

Managing your press images

Be careful which images you delete from this folder – you never know when they will come in useful. There are a few I deleted which would have been ideal for a recent article a magazine wrote about me. I was kicking myself for not having kept them!

If you are short of space on your computer then put them on a USB stick or CD ROM and keep them somewhere safe for when the press come knocking!

Activity: Organising images

Create a press folder on your computer and go through your current photographs, checking the size/quality and moving any suitable for magazine use to your press folder. If you do not have any suitable images, take some.

PHOTOGRAPHY TIPS FROM HILARY PULLEN

Hilary Pullen is a social media manager and photographer. She also runs the popular UK Craft Blog website (ukcraftblog.com).

If your photography stands out from the crowd, your products are far more likely to be noticed by customers and shared by influential bloggers and magazine editors!

Clear and detailed photographs give a buyer confidence in your product. The photographs should replicate the real-life shopping experience of picking up the item.

My top tips for immediately boosting sales

- Never post a blurry, dull image on your blog, social media or in your shop. It looks unprofessional and it will not sell your beautiful handmade product. Take the time to ensure all of your images are bright and in focus. Invest in a tripod to enable you to take photographs with a slower shutter speed. This will allow more light in without any camera shake.

- Composition and framing are important. Use interesting angles, as images laid flat and taken square-on look dull. Your images do not need to be identically composed for every product but they should look like a 'family' in order to create that branded feel.

- Get in close and show your customers the details – beautifully clear images of stitching and seams will give the buyer extra confidence.

Light

Light is one of the essential components of good photography. One of the most common problems with craft photography is dark images, where it is impossible to properly see the colour or the detail in the products. Here are some suggestions for how to get good lighting for your photographs.

Daylight Daylight produces a broader and more even light source than artificial light. Natural light is ideal for product photography, but avoid strong direct sunlight as it casts harsh shadows. Try photographing your products next to a large window; using a net curtain to diffuse the light if it is too strong. Even on a cloudy day you will likely get more light outside than you will inside. In fact, an overcast day is better for your photography than a bright sunny day as it will produce less stark shadows.

Lamps/spotlights Artificial lighting produces a more intense and narrower light than daylight, and now that most of us have energy-saving bulbs in our houses, it is much harder to get a good photograph using a regular light. Try a daylight lamp, which is bright but less harsh than most other artificial lights.
   It is best to buy a desk lamp which allows you to move the head, or use a spotlight – either one designed for studio shoots, or a portable one if you often photograph in different locations – so that you can angle towards the area you are shooting. Use directional light to highlight certain aspects of your products and create interesting shadows on other parts. Try lighting your products from different angles to see the different effects you can produce.

Light tent As mentioned on page 81, you can buy or create your own light tent for your photographs. The sides of the light tent diffuse the light giving a more even spread of light and softer shadows than direct lighting. You can also use a neutral backdrop ensuring that the focus is on your product and not on anything around it.

Flash The camera flash can often be very bright and can overpower the shot making it look very white. However you can soften that light by diffusing it. This can be done by placing something like tissue paper, white fabric, paper or thin white plastic over the flash. This spreads out and softens the light so it is less harsh on the item you are trying to photograph.

Reflectors You can make your own reflectors by wrapping foil around cardboard to increase the light when taking photographs. Try using crumpled foil so it will bounce the light all around, or if you do not have foil you can use white card. You then need to point your light source at the reflector, and angle the reflector to shine on the item you are photographing.

My lamp

If it is a bit gloomy when I am taking photographs, I often use a Swan desk lamp with a daylight bulb to shoot my photographs.
   The head of this lamp can be moved to find the best position to light what I am photographing.
If a daylight lamp is out of your budget, try a daylight bulb in a regular lamp.

Shadows, reflections and a true image

When photographing artwork, make sure the light is not casting any unwanted shadows or reflections on your work. Ideally, you want bright soft lighting, such as natural light. Hang or prop your artwork up and try to set the camera up opposite at about the same height.

Aim to ensure the colours in your image are as close as possible to the colours in your photograph. Look at the screen on your camera and adjust the colour and exposure settings on your camera if the colours do not look the same.

PICTURES OF YOU

It is worth taking a few good pictures of yourself, your work area and any behind-the-scenes type pictures for the 'about us' section on your site, and for anyone who wants to interview you.

To the right is a good example of a generic picture which can come in useful for different purposes. It is a photo of Lisa Comfort who runs a sewing café called Sew Over It (sewoverit.co.uk) in London.

This image is friendly and welcoming and the background shows what Lisa does. This picture would work well on the 'about' page of her website, accompanying a press feature about Lisa and her business or on her social media accounts.

If you have a few of this kind of image you will find they can be multipurpose.

Image credit: Sew Over It.

Background

There are three main choices for backgrounds for your photographs.

Plain Using a plain background makes it easier to use the image for different purposes. You can add text around the product for promotional images or you can cut around the image and combine a few product images together to make one new image. This is not so easy to do with textured backgrounds or if all the images have different backgrounds.

You may want to experiment with different coloured backgrounds to see which makes your products look the best. Generally a muted white works better than a bright white one, it is not so harsh on the eye. The same applies for black, a dark grey can often work better than a bold black. If your product has a lot of detail it is best to go for a plain background so that the focus remains on the product. Once you have found the background you like, stick with it to ensure consistency.

Textured Using a textured background such as fabric, wood or bricks can make an image more interesting than a plain background; but be careful that it does not detract attention from your product. Some textured backgrounds can really complement the product, haberdashery items photographed on fabric, for example; or country chic style products photographed on distressed wood.

If you do not have the background you want, you can buy textured backgrounds specifically for photography. Alternatively you could try buying a roll of wallpaper or a length of fabric with an interesting texture and hanging them behind where you are photographing your products.

Lifestyle This is a staged background intended to show your products in use. This helps the potential buyers imagine how they could use your product. For instance you could photograph your cushions on a chair, one of your paintings hanging on a wall above a fireplace, or your Christmas decorations on a Christmas tree. For jewellery, clothing, bags or shoes it is useful to see what the product looks like being worn as well as against a plain background. Similarly for home decor products, it is good for potential purchasers to see them where they would be in a house. Not only does it help the buyer think about what the product would look like on them, or in their home, but it also gives a good indicator of scale. You can even take this a step further and create a background around the theme of your products even if that is not where your product will be used (see the lifestyle example in the box, opposite).

Lifestyle photographs help your products to tell a story. However, be careful that the background does not detract from your product. If you are going to have other items in the photograph, try to ensure they are yours where possible. That way if anyone likes one of the other items it will still lead to a sale for you. For instance, if you photograph a ring you have made in a jewellery box surround by other jewellery items, make sure those other items are yours too. Tell people in the product description that they can find the other items elsewhere on your site.

A sense of scale

It can be hard to tell the scale of an item when there are no other items in the shot. Clearly indicate product size in your description or include something else in the shot which indicates scale. I have noticed a lot of fabric photographers include a spool of cotton, or a coin to show the scale of the print.

PEPPERMINT FIZZ – EXAMPLES

Peppermint Fizz (etsy.com/uk/shop/peppermintfizz) make unique handcrafted textiles, cards and gifts. Their shop on Etsy is filled with examples of fantastic photographs.

Plain

The plain white background used here makes the bright colours of the cushion stand out.

Textured

These background bricks give an interesting texture and show the scale of the cushion, but do not distract you from the product itself.

Lifestyle

A beach-themed cushion in the pebbles propped up against a sign that says 'to the beach'; this is obviously not where the product will be used, but it fits the theme of the cushion and makes this photograph stand out from competitors' photographs of cushions on a sofa.

The rule of thirds

If you want to make something in your photograph stand out, it is best not to place it in the centre of your image. Instead imagine the image was divided into thirds both horizontally and vertically by lines. When people look at an image they naturally tend to look at these points rather than at the middle of the image, so placing the focal point at one of the points that the lines intersect makes for a more pleasing photograph.

The focal point of this photograph – my son's face– sits where the grid lines intersect.

Multiple photographs

When selling your products online, you ideally want to use a combination of different photograph types. This will show off your products to best effect.

- At least one shot of the item on a plain background, with the full focus is on the product.

- If your product is available in different variations or colours, include a group shot showing the different options that are available.

- A lifestyle shot of the item in use.

- Close-up shots of any details. These photographs should show your product from as many different angles as possible – even inside. This lets people see your product in its entirety as they would if they were physically handling it in a shop.

GROUPS OF PHOTOGRAPHS

These shots, of a Rajput turquoise spinning ring by Charlotte's Web (notonthehighstreet.com/charlottesweb). show a good example: a large central lifestyle shot to show as much of the product as possible, surrounded by close-up details on plain background so the customer can clearly see the object from all sides.

Image credit: Charlotte's Web.

Editing your photographs

Once you have taken your photographs you may want to do a little touching up to make them look even better. It may seem like a lot to worry about, but once you get used to the editing programs and what works best for your photographs it will take less than a minute to really enhance your images. There is an abundance of free editing software available that will allow you to make most of the common edits I recommend below, such as PicMonkey or Pixlr (both available online), or even Microsoft Paint, which comes pre-installed on most Windows computers.

If you are doing extensive photo editing, you might like to invest in a professional program like Photoshop, but this can be an expensive option. One great advantage of using such programs is that there is an abundance of useful tutorial videos available online, mostly for free. The Photoshop website and YouTube are the best places to find these videos.

As with all of your branding try to stick to a consistent style with your images to help make your brand more recognisable. Once you have created and edited your images make sure you give them relevant names so that you remember precisely what they are. Most importantly do not forget to back them up! You do not want all that hard work to be lost.

The following pages explain some of the common edits you might want to apply to your photographs, along with pictures of examples where appropriate, all based on the image below.

Free software

Because most paid-for software has abundant support online, and because I use free photo editing software myself, this section will concentrate about what you can do with free programs. There is a list of free editing software and associated links in the useful links section of this chapter (see page 102).

This image, of Kona cotton fabrics from Plush Addict (plushaddict.co.uk), provides the basis for the edited images on the following pages.

Main image:
Re-sized (enlarged). Note the
pixellation and loss of quality.
Inset: Re-sized (reduced).

Re-sizing (1) This edit will change the size of your image, which is useful to ensure that you do not put unnecessarily large images onto your website. You can usually type in the exact number of pixels you want your image to be and whatever software you are using will re-size it for you. Sometimes you have to reduce by percentage instead so there can be some mathematics (or a little guesswork!) involved. Do note that increasing the image size will reduce the quality resulting in the image looking blurry and low quality.

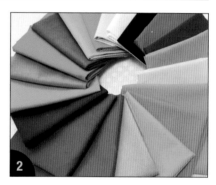

Cropping (2) If there is a bit too much space around your product, or you want to cut out some unnecessary distractions from around the edge of the image, cropping allows you to cut out the part you want and get rid of the rest.

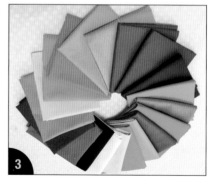

Rotation (3) If your photograph came out horizontal when it should be vertical (or vice versa) you can do a 90-degree or 180-degree rotation to correct the orientation. You can also do a freehand drag rotation to correct a distracting tilt or intentionally pull your image around to a more quirky angle.

Do bear in mind that directional lighting can look a little odd when the image is rotated. If the light is even throughout the picture you can minimise this problem.

This image has been rotated by 180°.

This image has a banner and text overlay, plus a logo overlay in the top left-hand corner.

Text (4) This very useful tool allows you to add your product name, a description, tag line, message, price or enticement to buy to your image. There is a huge selection of fonts to choose from. Remember to use one of your chosen fonts to ensure brand consistency.

Watermark (5) Adding a digital watermark helps to protect your images. This can be done by either uploading your logo, or adding your business name or website as text to an image. Once you have it in the right position you can then fade it a little so it enables people to see the image beneath the watermark. You do not want the watermark to obstruct people's view of your products.

Overlays (6) An overlay is something added over the top of your image. When you put text straight onto an image it can be a little difficult to read unless you have an area of plain background to put it on. Overlay a white box, then fade it out a little so you can still see the image behind it, and then add your text on top. It makes the text stand out a lot more, and is easier to read.

You can also get themed overlays to add things like hearts, banners, buttons, or seasonal designs. For example, if you have a photograph of your jewellery that you want to promote for St. Valentine's Day, instead of re-shooting the image with heart props nearby, you can simply add a heart overlay to the image. You can also add your own overlays so you can upload your logo and add that to the image.

Brand your images

I always add my web link to my images as part of my branding. That way, if people share the images on social media, people can see the original image came from my site, and already have the address.

Borders (7) Adding a border can be a nice way to frame your image. Experiment with the different borders available to see which best fit with your style. Do not forget you can alter the size and colour of the borders too. Once you have found one you like, try to stick with that one to ensure brand consistency.

Exposure (8) Altering the exposure settings will allow you brighten a dull image, or tone down an over-exposed photograph. It also allows you to increase the shadows or bring out the lighter parts of an image.

You can also adjust the contrast. Increasing it makes the colours darker and bolder. Lightening an image can wash it out a little, but you can increase the contrast to make the colours more vibrant again.

Colour (9) You can change the colour saturation of an image, increasing it to bring out the colours more or decreasing it to tone down the colours. You can adjust the colour temperature too, making it warmer (more yellow), to make an image more summery or to give it a romantic, candlelit feel; or colder (more blue), for bright blue skies or wintry images.

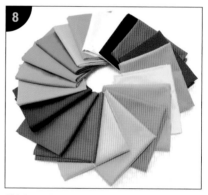

This image has been lightened. To avoid a washed-out look to the edited picture, I subsequently increased the contrast.

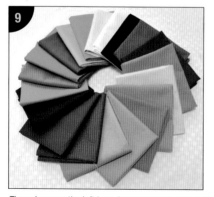

The colours on the left have been warmed, and cooled on the right. I have exaggerated the effect in these images so you can see the difference. You would not normally adjust the colour to such an extreme!

Blur or sharpen (10) Adding a subtle blur effect across an image can make it seem a little dreamy or abstract; while sharpening can help if you have accidentally blurred your image. You can also use these tools selectively so you can apply them to certain parts of your image: sharpening your product and blurring the items in the background ensures the focus is on your product.

The right-hand side of this image has been selectively blurred to draw attention to the left-hand part, which remains in focus.

Effects (11) Various different effects can be applied either to the whole image or to just part of it. One common and effective change is to desaturate (remove the colour) most of the image in order to draw attention to the one part you leave in colour. On PicMonkey this effect is called Focal B & W. You could use this to make a certain part of your product stand out, or your product stand out from everything else.

There is also a focal blur effect which has a similar effect of highlighting one specific part of an image, making one part of the image clear and the rest blurry.

There are other effects you can apply to the whole image such as sepia to give it a vintage look, frosting the edges of the image, softening or boosting the image, or giving it a variety of colour washes to change the tint of the image.

Main picture: focal black and white effect applied to the top right corner. Inset: sepia effect and frosted edges.

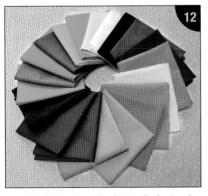

Textures (12) If you wanted a textured background for your picture but did not have one, you could add your own after you have taken the photograph. You can either upload your own texture or use one of the selection they have available including metal, water, paint and fabric.

The dotted background has been edited out and replaced with a fabric texture.

FABRIC SALES SHARABLE

This image is a good example of a edited 'sharable' – an image designed to catch the eye and bring traffic to a website.

It was created to go on a page on my website that has details of the latest fabric sales. Beginning with one of my own fabric stock images for the background, I added a frosted effect around the outside so the edges of the image were not so harsh. I then used two overlays – a rectangle at the top left and a ribbon at the bottom – to make the text stand out from the background. I also added my weblink (URL) so that if people share the image without crediting me or linking back, people can still find my site from the image.

I share this image regularly on social media to encourage people to visit this page and find the latest fabric sales and offers.

Fabric Sales

Discounted sewing supplies

www.thesewingdirectory.co.uk

Activity: Choosing your editing software

Decide which editing software you want to experiment with and upload an image. Try out as many of the different editing tools as possible to experiment with different effects and combinations. Once you know what they all do, write down your favourites to come back to in the future.

Auto correct/ wizard

Some software has an 'auto fix' option which is a combination of a few different effects to bring out the best in your image. I have to say personally I have not found these to be as good as doing it yourself but if you are in a rush it could be worth a try.

What else you can use your images for?

As well as using product photographs on your site or online shops there are many other ways you can use your photography to promote your brand.

Social media Social media platforms are perfect for promoting your brand with good quality images. Certain platforms like Pinterest, Facebook and Instagram really work well for visual marketing. Remember to include your business name or web address on the images so that if they get shared all the viewers also see your brand name.

Stock images It is useful to use your own images as stock images when writing blog posts, content for your site newsletters or guest posts for other sites. It saves you having to pay for stock images (see pages 97–99) and gets your products out in front of more people.

Business cards What better way to promote your products than to have images of them on the back of your business cards? It is much more attractive than just a logo. Some companies, like Moo, allow you to use different images on each of your business cards at no extra cost.

Catalogues As you build your range you may one day want to produce a catalogue so people can see your full product range at a glance.

To generate press coverage Magazine editors and website owners/bloggers, are often on the lookout for visually attractive content to share with their readers. If you send them a press release, there is more chance they will use it if it is accompanied by really professional looking eye-catching images.

On leaflets Instead of just using text, make your leaflets really visual by using some of your best images with a small amount of text on them.

Send them to potential stockists Spark the interest of potential stockists by sending them your images printed onto postcards.

Sharing on social media

Add a slogan or quote over your image to make it more sharable.

VIDEO

Photographs are not the only thing that can help you reach more people with your brand message; video is a fast-growing tool too. Not only have you got YouTube and sites like Vimeo but now even traditionally photograph-orientated platforms like Flickr and Instagram let you upload video clips. Plus of course Facebook lets you add video to personal or business pages.

You could use video to show customers behind the scenes, to show clips of you making your products, to speak directly to them (perhaps a welcome message on your site) or to share advice on how to use your products.

Visual marketing

Visual marketing is the use of images to communicate a message about your business. The images you use can come in a number of formats such as jpg files, video, PDF, slide or print, and can contain a wide variety of content – text, photographs, diagrams and icons – so the definition of visual marketing is actually a lot wider that it may seem at first. You can create visual content that suits you, your business, and your audience. The key is to get visual.

Why use visual marketing?

People are visual. Social media is visual. Visual content is highly sharable and resonates in a way that words alone often do not. Visual content adds variety to your marketing, creates brand recognition, and helps your business stand out!

The best way to get started is to take something that you already know resonates with your audience and make it visual. A quote, a helpful tip, a list, some instructions, something funny or entertaining – choose something that fits with your brand and will appeal to your audience. Use a free tool such as PicMonkey or Canva to create an image using that text. You can include a photograph or just use a plain background – the key is to keep it really simple, as simple images look the most professional. Brand your images using your brand colours, use a typeface that matches your brand vibe, and be sure to include your name or website address. Finally, share the image with your audience using all of your social media platforms – plus your blog and newsletter too.

INVESTIGATING VISUAL MARKETING

Karen Gunton from Build a Little Biz (buildalittlebiz.com) runs an excellent visual marketing course online a couple of times a year, and you can work through it at your own pace. There is also a free taster class and lots of useful articles on visual marketing on her site.

Etsy has a collection of useful guides to photography on its blog (etsy.com/blog) as do Craft Blog UK (ukcraftblog.com) and Folksy: (blog.folksy.com).

Many people teach craft photography. Try looking at your local craft class studio to see if they offer courses. In addition, many colleges and universities run general photography courses and classes, so have a look on their websites to see what is on offer.

Image sources

Good quality images are essential to your business, but sometimes you do not have the time or resources to be taking your own. Luckily there are many kinds of images available for you to use on your site or social media.

If you are writing articles for your site or blog, building your website, looking to create sharable images, or need images for adverts, there are several places where you can source images, some free and some that charge.

Stock image sites

Images on stock sites are usually taken by professionals and are high quality. The sites are easy to search and usually have hundreds, if not thousands, of images available for most keywords you search. They also have vector graphics available too. Stock image sites are mostly paid-for, either charging a fee per photograph or on a contract basis – usually monthly – which allows you to download a certain amount of images. I have listed some of the main stock sites in the links section.

The benefits of using stock image sites are that the images will be good quality, there is a huge range available (saving you time searching lots of sites), and you do not usually have to credit the image. Most stock images do not need to be credited to either the photographer or stock site; however, I have found that a few do, such as paparazzi photographs.

MAKING THE MOST OF A STOCK IMAGE CONTRACT

Monthly contracts can work out well if you use a lot of images, or if you are setting up a website and need lots of images at once. In the latter case, you could sign up just for a single month, download as many images as you think you will need and save them in a folder. You can then upload them to your site as you complete it, subject to the stock site's terms and conditions. They usually specify images must be used within a set period after purchase.

This approach can work out cheaper than the pay-as-you-go rate if you are looking for a large number of images in one go.

My preferred stock image site

Personally I use Shutterstock because I have found it has a good selection of craft related images, and works out cheaper than most other sites to download individual images. It has over twenty million images available in total. Shutterstock charges up front in batches of twelve images; but you can download them individually as and when you need them, so long as it is within twelve months of the purchase. It offers a monthly payment option, too.

The downsides of using stock sites are the cost, and the fact that other people could be using the same images as you, they are not unique. Also you can often find that the pictures have a distinctive 'stock image' look, which means some people can tell you are using stock images and not your own.

If you plan to use stock images, always take the time to read through the terms and conditions and the licensing terms. Some companies require you to purchase an enhanced licence if you plan to print their images on your products, for example. The terms can vary from site to site so make sure you read them for each site you plan to use.

Some stock image websites offer free trials, or allow you to download a certain number of images for free so this can be useful if you do not have a budget for images.

Look before you leap

Most stock photo sites allow you to search their database and view the images, with a watermark on them, before you join. Try searching a few to make sure they have the type of images you are looking for before you sign up.

Free image sources

There are also many places where you can get free images to use. Normally you are expected to credit and link back to the original source in exchange. A lot of the free stock photograph sites are funded by advertising for the paid stock sites. Do double check before clicking on an image or you may find yourself being transported off to another site and being asked to pay before you can download the image. They are indicated as being from a different stock site but on your first visit it can be a little confusing.

Creative commons sites

Flickr Creative Commons is a collection of images that people have shared under various creative commons licences. The exact licences vary so you need to read through before using the images. Some images are allowed to be used for personal use but not for commercial use. Others allow any use but require a specific accreditation and back link. The images are sorted by licence type and, once you choose a category, you can then search by keyword.

The benefits of Flickr Creative Commons are that there millions of images to choose from, and it is easy to find relevant images because a lot of crafters use Flickr. The downside is that you need to take the time to read and understand the different licences, and make sure you correctly credit the images.

Wikimedia Commons is a similar site with a large number of creative commons images available.

Free stock sites

There are many free stock images sites where you can download images at no cost. Most require registration and often have conditions imposed on the use of the images. These sites include:

Morgue File A free stock site, made by creatives for creatives. These images are intended to be used 'in the creative process' for artists or crafters creating their own work. Therefore you cannot use them as standalone images but have to adapt them or incorporate them into one of your designs.

Pixabay Pixabay allows you to download its images to use as you wish, whether altered or in their entirety and for commercial purposes. It does not require credit, but says it would appreciate a link back.

Stock Xchng A source of royalty-free photographs that can be downloaded to use as you choose, whether for commercial purposes or personal. There are some limits: you cannot sell or redistribute the image itself or use it as part of a logo or trademark.

Open Photo The licences on these photographs vary. All are free, but some require accreditation to the original photographer. It is clearly indicated under each photograph what the licence is and whether you need to credit the image or not.

Public Domain Photos These images require a hyperlink back to the page of the site where you downloaded the image if you are using them online.

Death to the Stock Photo If you sign up to this site you will get e-mailed ten free high-resolution stock photographs every month. The images are based around a different theme each month: 'technology', 'bricks and mortar', or 'coffee shop', for example. You do not need to credit the photographs, nor link back to the site, but the owners say they appreciate it if you do.

Stick to the conditions

When using any free stock images, always read through the licence and make sure that your usage of the image is within the licence.

VINTAGE IMAGES

Copyright on images expires a certain number of years from creation or publication, depending on the date the original work was created. This is good news for any small craft business. In the UK, all images are automatically copyrighted, and remain protected for seventy years after the creator's death; after which the copyright expires and the images enter the public domain, making them usable by anyone.

This means that there are many (though not all!) beautiful vintage adverts, drawings and photographs that are free for you to use. One website, thegraphicsfairy.com, has over four thousand predominantly craft-based vintage images free for you to download.

Individual owners

Another potential source of free, non-stock images are those you come across in online searches on individuals' websites. Those images are copyrighted to the individual owner, so if you see one you want to use you need to contact the person whose photograph it is and ask them for permission to use it.

The majority of individuals do not mind their image being used when it is promoting their product and sending people to their shop. Legally, however, they can insist you take the image down if they do not want you to use it, and in extreme cases you could find yourself being billed for having used the image without consent. As a result, it is best to ask permission wherever possible in order to protect yourself from potential problems in the future.

In reality, a lot of people will use photographs without prior permission, instead crediting the person to whom it belongs. For instance when bloggers write a post on 'my favourite handmade fox-themed products' they do not tend to contact the owner of every single image they are featuring and ask permission. They will take the image from their site or shop and include a link back to the relevant website or shop in the blog post.

Build your own image collection

The ideal solution is to start building your own stock image collection for use in your visual marketing. Keep a camera close to hand and take photographs whenever you can. When you are planning your website or blog content, think about what images would fit well with it and see if you can take those images before you write the post. Build up a collection of generic images of your craft supplies, your workspace, nature shots, office shots, pictures of your creative process and so forth. If all else fails see if you have any product photographs which vaguely tie in with the subject you are writing about and use those to illustrate your post.

BEWARE!

You could find that by taking an image from someone's site without consent you could actually be downloading a stock image.

Stock image companies regularly run image searches to see if anyone is using their property without permission. In this situation the stock image companies may end up charging you a lot more than the original purchase price of the image.

Combining promotion

While conducting marketing training for T&G Woodware (tg-woodware.com), a kitchenware company, I asked the employees to write a blog post with their ten favourite chicken recipes, which they would find on the internet. Rather than illustrating it with photographs of the food, from other people's websites, I suggested they used photographs of their own chicken tea cosies with a product link embedded in the photograph description. Not only did they not need to seek permission to use the recipe images, but they could also subtly promote their products too.

Creating other images

Of course, not all of the images you use in your visual marketing have to be photographs. If you are artistic you can draw or paint your own images, and even if you are not artistically inclined, there are several sites which will let you create your own graphics, adverts, infographics, and sharable images for free. These can all be used to spread your brand message, and if you create them yourself you are saving money too.

Images that you have created yourself have the advantage that they are unique and specific to you – and ideal for the purpose!

Use your images creatively

It is important to make sure you get the most possible use for your images, especially if you are paying for them. Do not limit yourself to only using the image once. Think of different places you can use it, such as your site, blog, social media platform, newsletters, flyers, or adverts. By altering it a little, you can use it in more places without people realising they are seeing the same image. Photo editing software can help you add text, graphics or special effects to the images; to change the colours; to combine or crop them; or any of a hundred other changes that will help to keep them fresh.

Keep your brand in mind

Remember that you want to keep your branding consistent, so consider this carefully when choosing your stock images. Do not just go for an image because it is free or cheap; it is worth paying to get something that is perfect for your visual brand.

Activity: Learning the tools for visual marketing

Trial and error can be the quickest way to learn. Take a look at some of the recommended sites overleaf and set aside some spare time to play with them. Experiment and see what you can make and which interfaces you find easiest and most rewarding to use.

Make sure you bookmark those sites – or write them down either below or in your notebook – in order to return to them in the future and create more great images for your business.

USEFUL LINKS AND FURTHER READING

Branding

The psychology of colour:
helpscout.net/blog/psychology-of-color

Colour meanings:
color-wheel-pro.com/color-meaning.html

Colour scheme designer:
colorschemedesigner.com

Design Seeds: design-seeds.com

Colour pickers: colorzilla.com; colorpicker.com;
iconico.com/colorpic

Wordmark, allows you to test fonts: wordmark.it

Free Fonts Database: freefontsdb.com

Font Park, over 70,000 free fonts: fontpark.net

Fiverr: fiverr.com

Useful branding site: bigbrandsystem.com

Free design and editing software

PicMonkey: picmonkey.com

Paint: getpaint.net

Picasa: picasa.google.com

Gimp: gimp.org

Pixlr: pixlr.com

Canva: canva.com

Commercial design and editing software

Photoshop: photoshop.com

Adobe Creative Suite: adobe.com

Logo Maker: logomaker.com

The Logo Creator: thelogocreator.com

Branding products

Moo: uk.moo.com

Avery: avery.co.uk

Vistaprint: vistaprint.co.uk

Photography

The Crafter's Guide to Taking Great Photos by
Heidi Adnum: book available from
searchpress.com

Image compression site: imageoptimizer.net

Image compressor: compressnow.com

Digital photography school, lots of useful tips:
digital-photography-school.com

Light tent tutorial: digital-photography-school.com/
how-to-make-a-inexpensive-light-tent

Photography backdrops:
creativitybackgrounds.co.uk

Daylight lamps or bulbs: uk.daylightcompany.com

Photography tips:
photography.nationalgeographic.
co.uk/photography/photo-tips

Advice for photographing art:
saatchionline.com/artschool

Craft photography tips: ukcraftblog.com/2011/10/
craft-photography-tips.html

Photography tips: picturecorrect.com

Visual marketing

Training and free resources: buildalittlebiz.com

Video platforms: vimeo.com; youtube.com;
flickr.com/explore/video; instagram.com

Commercial stock image sites:
shutterstock.com; gettyimages.co.uk;
istockphoto.com; bigstockphoto.com

Free stock image sites: flickr.com/
creativecommons; commons.wikimedia.
org; morguefile.com; pixabay.com; sxc.hu;
openphoto.net; publicdomainpictures.net;
deathtothestockphoto.com

Copyright free vintage images:
thegraphicsfairy.com

Image creation programs

Infographics: visual.ly; piktochart.com

Mindmaps: text2mindmap.com

Word clouds: wordle.net

Collages: picmonkey.com

Banner adverts: bannersnack.com

Moving adverts: ms-gif-animator.en.softonic.com

YOUR LINKS AND NOTES

You can use this space to keep a list of links to websites and services you find helpful.

SOCIAL

MEDIA

USING SOCIAL MEDIA

When you first start using social media to promote your business it can be hard to choose which platforms to use and to figure out how to promote your business in a manner which is not too promotional. When you only promote yourself on your social media channels, you risk people getting bored and no longer following you. The skill to using social media for business is to work out the perfect blend of promotional posts and non-promotional posts which are of use to your followers.

How to use social media to promote your business

When utilising social media to promote your business, the key thing to remember is that you are competing with thousands of other businesses to attract people's interest and convert them into followers. The best way to do this is to provide value and keep them engaged. This means providing something useful that will keep them coming back for more.

For craft or art suppliers the easiest way to give value is to share projects, inspiration and techniques. Show people how they can use your products, and give them ideas of what they could make with them. You do not have to relate these ideas directly to your product; just give them ideas and inspirations alongside occasional updates about your products in order to remind them to look at your site when they are ready to buy supplies. Becoming known as a good source of inspiration will naturally bring followers to you via word of mouth and social shares which means when you do post about your own products a lot more people will be seeing them.

Common mistakes

A common fear is that promoting other people's product will only hurt your own business. However, this can limit the posts you can share and, as a result, potentially prevents you delivering useful content to their followers. It can also mean your updates are few and far between; and that they contain a very high proportion of self-promotion. In turn, this will reduce the number of people who will want to follow you.

However, some people get so anxious about excessive self-promotion that they go to the other extreme and almost never promote their own business on their social media. This defeats the object of putting time and effort into building a social platform for your business.

Clarity is also important. I have seen several people who make handmade products sharing images of other crafters' products and promoting them, which is great unless it gets confusing to tell which products are made by the page owner and which are not. Try to make it as clear as possible which products are yours. Do not fill your account exclusively with other people's images as you are then failing to generate business for yourself.

In your interactions through social media, aim to strike a balance between promoting yourself and others, and also show clearly what products you make or service you provide. I recommend keeping self-promotional posts to a quarter of your updates or less – use the rest to give value to your followers, or to promote complementary businesses or events you think will be of interest to your followers.

Overcoming anxiety

One of the companies to which I gave social media training was too scared to share posts that showed people using their competitors' products.

Once I helped the company overcome this fear, its following grew much more quickly. In addition, it had a higher rate of interaction as people started sharing and commenting on its posts.

WHY PROMOTE OTHER BUSINESSES?

There are a number of advantages to promoting businesses that are complementary to yours, including:

- Helping other businesses, which may promote you in return.
- Giving value to followers by helping them find products that complement yours.
- Building relationships with other businesses – tag them so that the owners know you mentioned them.

Tagging

Tagging a person or business on social media normally involves putting @companyname in your post. This alerts them that you have mentioned them.

On most platforms typing the first few letters of the other business' name will automatically bring up the business, though sometimes you need to be following them already for this to work.

Providing value in your posts

If you teach crafts, give people a little taster of what they could learn in your classes: share a useful tip or a technique and add that they can book onto a course with you if they want to learn more about the subject. Share photographs of your samples, or show followers what people have made on previous courses in order to tempt them to make a booking.

If you make handmade products or art then show examples of how your products can be used or displayed in order to convince readers that the product will fit perfectly into their homes. People like to know the story behind your designs, so tell or show them what inspired you. Sharing a back story can create an emotional connection to your creation.

The process of making your artwork will also interest some of your followers. Share photographs of the making stages in order to build anticipation of the final design. If you take commissions, share pictures of the things you have been commissioned to make, and then let people know how to commission you.

Asking permission

Most will be delighted, but do get your students' permission before sharing photographs of them or their designs on social media.

What to include in your posts

Deciding what to talk about on social media can be tricky when you are just beginning to use it. This list of suggestions should help you get started:

- **Related products and services** If you sell fabric, then share projects and tutorials which show people what to do with the fabric they buy from you. Discuss sewing magazines, blogs, websites or books. All these things are complementary to your products and will help to engage your followers. If your followers like sewing, the chances are they also buy sewing magazines or books and read sewing blogs, so it gives you a common ground with them beyond your products alone.

- **Tips and 'How to' guides** People always appreciate advice. If you sell beads, tell people about different storage options or beading techniques, or write a tutorial to share with people. If you stock art supplies explain the difference between types of paint and when best to use each; demonstrate techniques; or interview artists to get useful advice to share with your followers.

- **Show who is behind the business** It is a lot easier to relate to a person than to a faceless business, and people like to know who is selling the products they buy. Consider profiling yourself and your staff on your blog, share pictures of the team at shows or in the shop. Let people know about the history of the company, celebrate milestones with them and make them feel a part of your business.

- **Industry news and events** Keep an eye on key industry sites and magazines so that you can share details of upcoming shows, new products and news about the industry with your followers. If you become a good source of information for people, they will keep coming back. If you will be at the event, let your followers know where they can find you. Even if you will not be exhibiting, shows are a great chance to build face-to-face relationships with people who have been following you on social media.

- **Your products and offers** Facebook, Pinterest or Instagram are ideal for sharing pictures of your new products. Blogs give you a place to tell people what is coming soon (or simply currently in stock).

   Tempting one-liners on Twitter will get people clicking to see more. Try something like: 'Wow! Look what just arrived...'

- **Promote others** As explained earlier, promoting businesses complementary to yours through your social media can pay dividends – besides being a nice thing to do! Often they will return the favour, therefore getting both of you new fans and hopefully new customers. For instance, if you sell quilting fabrics but not wadding you could tell people about a business you like that sells wadding. Hopefully when that business gets customers looking for fabric, they will send them your way – perhaps mentioning you on their social media in return.

- **General chat** Social media is all about being social: think about what you would discuss with someone you just met in real life – the weather, what was on television last night, or an interesting (and ideally relevant) news story.

Promoting yourself: the balance

Followers will expect that you will talk about your own products and offers through your social media platform – but it bears repeating that over-saturation may annoy or drive some people away.

Be professional — but friendly

Personally I think posts on business accounts or blogs are best kept mainly to business, but that does not mean there is no space for an occasional little bit of general chit-chat. In my experience, those kinds of posts tend to have a very good response rate too!

Which platform to use?

The key thing to remember when choosing which social media platforms to use is that your content needs to reach your target audience. It is much easier for you to go to them than to try to make them come to you on a platform they do not already use. It may take a bit of customer research to find out where your customers spend their time online.

The focus of this section will be on the most commonly used platforms: Facebook, Twitter and Pinterest because you are likely to find that your target audience will use at least one of the three, but I have included useful information for using other platforms such as Instagram, Google Plus and LinkedIn; and include links for more information on all those mentioned at the end of the chapter.

Due to the fast-moving nature of the industry, these platforms tend to update regularly, so you may need to reorient yourself occasionally in order to keep abreast of the latest developments.

Blogs

Blog is short for 'weblog', meaning an online diary or journal. They are sites that provide information, opinions and discussion. In the creative industries there are a lot of bloggers. Having your own blog can be beneficial for several reasons: It is a platform that you control, so you can set your own rules and limits – especially when hosted on your own site. This means, for example, that you have a lot more space on a blog than most other social media platforms, and are not limited to a certain number of characters or images. This can be useful for more wordy or picture-intensive posts such as how-to guides that rely on multiple photographs and steps.

Having your own blog allows you to interact with other bloggers on an equal level. People can comment and interact with you, usually when doing so they leave a link to their own blog so you can then interact with them too. You can also set most blogs up to e-mail you people's comments so you can start an e-mail conversation with them if you choose. I have made many great contacts this way. You can of course promote your blog posts through your other social media platforms too.

Content rights

Check the terms and conditions of each social media platform to see what you can and cannot do on said platform and what rights you are giving them over your content.

A note on updates

Check my website, craftacreativebusiness. co.uk, for any changes made to the platforms since this book went to print.

Facebook

Facebook is a very popular social media platform used by a lot of people – over one billion people worldwide, in fact! It allows you to share text, images, links and video updates. The company went public in 2012 which caused discontent, amongst business users in particular, as only a small percentage of page users see your posts unless you pay to promote them.

Despite this, many people still use Facebook, and the chances are that a large percentage of your target market will be on there. Despite the dwindling reach of posts it is still good for interaction and business. Of the platforms I use, Facebook sends me the second highest amount of traffic to my site. Alexa consistently places Facebook as the second most popular website in the world (after Google).

Alexa

Alexa is a site that measures the global traffic rank of websites.

Twitter

Twitter has about half the number of registered users as Facebook, but it is still one of the top social media networks. It is primarily text based, with updates limited to one hundred and forty characters or fewer, though you can also attach links and images. Being limited to so few characters can be a little frustrating and it is a fast moving network, but is great for making new contacts and your following seems to grow a lot quicker on Twitter than on Facebook. I find people seem to be a lot chattier on Twitter too. Twitter is one of the top fifteen most popular sites in the world according to Alexa.

Pinterest *Pinterest*

If you are in a visually-led business like the creative industries, Pinterest is a great platform to use. It is an online pinboard which allows you to collect useful links in a visual manner, rather than as text bookmarks. You group your pins into themed boards. The site has grown hugely in popularity in the last couple of years and is very popular amongst crafters.

My Pinterest

Pinterest has rocketed to the top of my social referrals list on my website analytics — even though I have significantly fewer followers there, it sends me more traffic than Facebook and Twitter combined.

YouTube

Ranked by Alexa as the third most popular site in the world is video-sharing site YouTube. It gets more than one billion unique users per month. It also ranks very well in search engines, which helps to attract visitors. Many people prefer to see visual demonstrations of how to do things than read about it.

As a result, this platform works particularly well for sharing craft techniques, projects and product demonstrations.

Vimeo

Vimeo is another popular video-sharing site, a competitor to YouTube. This platform has been becoming more popular within the craft industry. It may not attract as much traffic as YouTube, but do not be fooled into thinking it is a small site. It attracts over one hundred million unique visitors per month.

Like YouTube, you can use Vimeo to share instructional videos on how to use your products, clips of you making your handmade products or to share tips and techniques that you use.

Instagram

Instagram is a photo-sharing app that allows you to apply filters to your images to enhance them. It allows brief video clips too. Once you have added the Instragram app to your mobile phone, images can be shared from there, rather than from your computer. You can then comment on other people's images and tag people in conversations, which makes it a good way to interact with people using your products or to share what you are making.

Instagram is used by a lot of people sharing their craft purchases or what they have made; and as a result, it is another site that is growing in popularity within the craft industry.

Flickr

Another popular photo-sharing site amongst creatives. People with shared interests can form groups on Flickr to share photographs of what they are making. You can also comment on images and start conversations in the comments to build relationships.

Uploading photographs with a creative commons licence, giving other people permission to use them and link back to you, can be a good way of reaching more people with your brand/product images.

Google Plus

Google Plus, or Google +, is the second largest social media network after Facebook, with over half a billion members active at least once a month. The SEO industry seems to think that Google Plus will help influence site rankings so more people are starting to use it. You now have to have a Google Plus account to use many of Google's other services like You Tube or Gmail so more and more people are setting up accounts.

LinkedIn **Linked** in.

LinkedIn is not just a chance to share your CV: it is very good for networking within your industry. There are several good craft groups on LinkedIn where people share tips and advice. You can connect with people you meet at shows and events, build your network of contacts and keep them updated with news of your business.

Dos and Don'ts of social media

Whichever platform – or platforms – you choose to use, there are some general principles of using social media which carry across. Below is a summary of what I consider to be the unofficial rules of using social media for business.

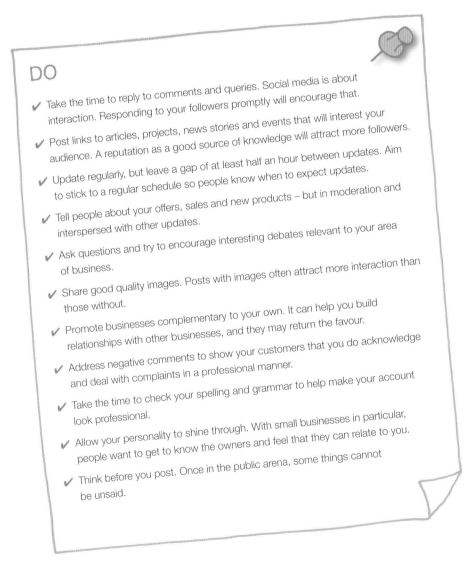

DO

✔ Take the time to reply to comments and queries. Social media is about interaction. Responding to your followers promptly will encourage that.

✔ Post links to articles, projects, news stories and events that will interest your audience. A reputation as a good source of knowledge will attract more followers.

✔ Update regularly, but leave a gap of at least half an hour between updates. Aim to stick to a regular schedule so people know when to expect updates.

✔ Tell people about your offers, sales and new products – but in moderation and interspersed with other updates.

✔ Ask questions and try to encourage interesting debates relevant to your area of business.

✔ Share good quality images. Posts with images often attract more interaction than those without.

✔ Promote businesses complementary to your own. It can help you build relationships with other businesses, and they may return the favour.

✔ Address negative comments to show your customers that you do acknowledge and deal with complaints in a professional manner.

✔ Take the time to check your spelling and grammar to help make your account look professional.

✔ Allow your personality to shine through. With small businesses in particular, people want to get to know the owners and feel that they can relate to you.

✔ Think before you post. Once in the public arena, some things cannot be unsaid.

DO NOT

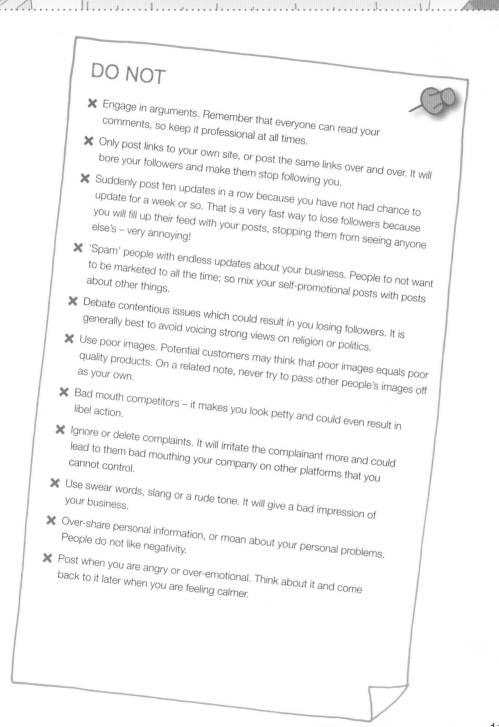

✖ Engage in arguments. Remember that everyone can read your comments, so keep it professional at all times.

✖ Only post links to your own site, or post the same links over and over. It will bore your followers and make them stop following you.

✖ Suddenly post ten updates in a row because you have not had chance to update for a week or so. That is a very fast way to lose followers because you will fill up their feed with your posts, stopping them from seeing anyone else's – very annoying!

✖ 'Spam' people with endless updates about your business. People to not want to be marketed to all the time; so mix your self-promotional posts with posts about other things.

✖ Debate contentious issues which could result in you losing followers. It is generally best to avoid voicing strong views on religion or politics.

✖ Use poor images. Potential customers may think that poor images equals poor quality products. On a related note, never try to pass other people's images off as your own.

✖ Bad mouth competitors – it makes you look petty and could even result in libel action.

✖ Ignore or delete complaints. It will irritate the complainant more and could lead to them bad mouthing your company on other platforms that you cannot control.

✖ Use swear words, slang or a rude tone. It will give a bad impression of your business.

✖ Over-share personal information, or moan about your personal problems. People do not like negativity.

✖ Post when you are angry or over-emotional. Think about it and come back to it later when you are feeling calmer.

Setting up your social media presence

The following pages explore the specifics of setting up and using some of the most popular networks. Ultimately you want to choose whichever networks will allow you to engage with your potential customers, and those that you are comfortable using. Do not try to do everything at once. Start by choosing one network at a time, allow yourself time to get to grips with it and start building a following before you add another one.

Engagement

You can get insights into the engagement rate through the number of followers 'talking about this' on Facebook; and the number of retweets and favourites on Twitter.

SOCIAL MEDIA TIPS

These tips are from Alex Veronelli, brand manager of Aurifil Threads (aurifil.com), an Italian company whose renown amongst quilters worldwide is largely due to its great internet marketing campaigns.

- **Be yourself** People prefer to engage with people rather than brands: it is much more personal. Profiles with a face, a name and a last name give better performance than those with logos. Once the relationship is established, it becomes easier to steer the audience towards the brand.

- **Listen** A regular search of the tags related to your brand is due in order to figure out what your product's users are saying about it, and to discover the content related to your products.

- **Promote others** Do not be selfish. The very best content for a brand's page comes from what the others say about it. Of course we say great things about our own brand, but it means much more when others say it. Do not let the voice of your customer be left by the wayside, but instead share and highlight it. They will be also grateful to receive traffic and readers coming from your page.

- **Pay attention to engagement** Do not measure your social marketing performance purely by the number of followers but by how they engage with your business.

- **Always on and everywhere** Social networking does not stop for breaks, weekends or holidays. Answers should be always given, ideally within twenty-four hours.

SOCIAL MEDIA MANAGEMENT

Your business' social media duties can grow to take up a great deal of time, particularly if you use more than one network. Social media management programs such as Hootsuite, TweetDeck and Buffer can help to make administration much simpler, which will save you time and energy. These programs allow you to connect several social networks into one place, so you can see the content on each platform and schedule new material to go onto your profiles. Some also support complementary mobile apps, so you can check your accounts on your smartphone.

My preferred program, Hootsuite, allows up to five different social media accounts on its free service; so I can administer both my Facebook and Twitter from one location, which helps to make sure I do not duplicate or miss out information I send to my followers.

Some of these programs also allow you to administer more than one account within a social network without having to log in and out between them, which is very useful. For example, Hootsuite allows me to have up to four Twitter streams visible at the same time, so I can look at the activity on my @sewingdirectory stream and my @craftabiz stream at once, and hop between them as I add or schedule new material. For comparison, if I want to tweet the same information to both streams directly on Twitter, I have to log out of one account before logging in to the other to so do.

These social media management programs make it easier to look through people's responses to your posts and quickly pick out those you want to share or to which you want to respond

Hootsuite, Twitter and Facebook

Hootsuite is the social media management program I use. Hootsuite shortens any long web address links (URLs) in the post, which makes it ideal for Twitter as it saves precious characters. I then cut and paste the update over to Facebook, where I add an image and schedule it for the same time and date as I did on Hootsuite.

As Facebook posts have a longer character limit than Twitter, I will often expand on the text; and also tag anyone I have mentioned before saving the update. This does take a little longer than asking Hootsuite to send the same update to both Twitter and Facebook, but a little customisation is worth it to reach more people.

Facebook ⓕ

Setting up

As the largest social media platform, Facebook tends to be where a lot of businesses start their social media marketing. Many people already have personal Facebook accounts, familiarity with which will make setting up a business page quick and easy.

The easiest way to set up a Facebook page for your business is to visit an existing page (you can find mine at facebook.com/thesewingdirectory) and look for a box with an ellipsis mark (...), to the right of the page name. One of the options that comes up when you click on that is 'create a page'. You can then choose your business type, pick a category and then give your page a name.

Keeping it Personal

If you do not already have a personal account, you will need to set one up (visit facebook.com and follow the sign up steps) before you can start a business page. Do not worry; your page fans will not be able to see your personal account, only what you post on your business page.

My business page on Facebook. Note the button with the ellipsis mark (highlighted).

It is hard to change the name once selected so do be careful with your name choice. Think about what people would type into the search box to find your page. Choosing a long name that includes a description of your business – 'Crafty Cat – quilting supplies and haberdashery', for example – seems like a good idea, but if someone wants to tag your page (see page 124), a long name will take up a lot of space in the text box which could put them off doing so. Weigh up whether the SEO (search engine optimisation) benefits of having keywords in your page name are worth the risk that people may be reluctant to tag your page because of the length of the name.

Before choosing your page name, check if anyone else is already using it. Do this by using the search box on the blue bar at the top of the page. If there are several pages with the same name as yours, use a different name to avoid people following the wrong page when they are looking for you, or tagging the wrong page and promoting someone else. One way of making your page unique is to add a location to the name. 'Crafty Cat Cardiff', for example, would let your customers know they have the correct page.

If you do not sell in a fixed location, add a descriptive word to differentiate yourself from other similarly named pages: 'Butterfly Jewellery Designs' rather than simply 'Butterfly Designs', for example.

Before going live

Now you have created your page, there are a few things you should add before making it live:

Avatar An avatar is the picture which appears next to your page name. A good avatar is something that represents your brand: it can be your logo, it could be you, or it could be a photograph of one of your products. Ideally you want this image to be 180 x 180px. You can use a service like PicMonkey to resize pictures to the correct dimensions. Facebook will shrink many images to fit.

Cover photograph This is the large image across the top of your page. As the first thing people see when visiting your page, it is important that it fits with your branding, shows people what you do and attracts their attention so they want to see more of your page.

You can experiment with your cover image and change it around every few weeks to see what people like best, or to showcase your latest creations or products. Collages tend to work well as they allow you to show several things at once and combine text with photographs. The default dimensions for a cover photograph are 851 x 315px. Many image-editing programs, such as PicMonkey, will have a default Facebook cover setting which will make it the correct size for you. Facebook itself advises you to use a PNG file to get the best image quality.

Apps Facebook apps (short for applications) are the little boxes on the left-hand side of the page, under the 'about' section. Here you can add things like a newsletter sign-up button, links to other social media accounts, a direct link to your shop, a location map, or an events section. If you are unsure of what to add, take a look at the pages of a few similar businesses and see what they have on their pages.

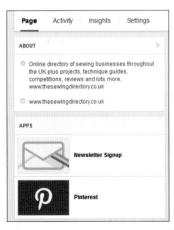

The Facebook sidebar, showing the 'about' and 'apps' sections. Only three apps will show by default.

About Part of creating your page involves filling in the 'About' section. Before going live, preview it and make sure the most important information about your business is in the first three lines as these are visible to viewers without having to click to see more.

Do take the time to fill out all your contact details, website, location and opening hours, if you have premises. It makes it much easier for potential customers if they want to get in touch to find out more. The more steps people have to take to find information, the more likely they are to give up.

Add content Going live with an empty page will not entice people to come and follow you. Before you go live, write an introductory post explaining who you are, what you do and what people can expect to see on your page. Add another post with your website details, blog, social media, and similar links. Finally, upload some images of your products, your premises, and features on your website so that there are some eye-catching images for people to see when they join your page. If you have the time, do a few posts over two to three days so that it does not look like a brand new page when people see it. This will give people a taster of what they will get if they join your page.

Altering the About section

You can alter the 'About' section at any time by clicking on the pencil icon that appears on the top right of the 'about' box on your page.

ADMINISTRATION

At the top of your page above the cover image you will find your administration (or admin) controls. This contains the 'settings' option. Click on that and check all the settings are as you want them to be.

For instance, have you set it so people can comment, post or send you messages through your page? You also have the option to add other people as administrators so that they can help share the responsibility of looking after the page with you. You will also find the option to make your page live here.

Activity: Going live

You are now ready to put your page live. If you use any other social networks, add a post to tell people they can now find you on Facebook.

Mention the launch of your new business Facebook page in your newsletter, or blog about it. Do not forget to add a Facebook button to your website which links to your page.

Why not start by inviting some of the friends from your personal profile to your page to get your first few page fans?

Basic actions on Facebook

Now your Facebook page is designed and up and running you will want to know how to perform some basic actions. We start by looking at what kind of content you can share on your page.

Text update You can type a status update of up to 63,206 characters. Only the first few lines will be visible and people will have to click 'view more' to see the rest of it. To encourage engagement why not ask a question?

Images Images on your timeline will show at around 400–500 pixels square, and will enlarge when clicked upon. When sharing images of your products, include a link of where to buy the product, along with a price and brief description. This saves people time and makes things easy for them – if they love it they can click straight through and buy.

Video You can either upload video directly onto Facebook, or share a link to a video which is hosted elsewhere (such as YouTube). The maximum file size for a video is 1024mb and a maximum running time of twenty minutes.

Links You can add a link to an external site by copying the web address (URL) into the update bar. A thumbnail image will automatically be generated from the images on the page to which you are linking. If you do not like that image you can click to select another from the page or upload your own.

Milestones You can add milestones to your page, which can be backdated. These are things you want to celebrate and share with your page fans such as your one year anniversary of trading. Set a new milestone by clicking on the offer/event tab at the top of the status box.

Offers You have the option of adding special offers to your page which people can claim by clicking on it. These can be set up to automatically e-mail a special offer code to claimants. You access this option by clicking on the offer/event part at the top of the status box on your homepage.

Events Clicking on the offer/event tab will give you the option to add an event to your page. Fill in the details of where and when the event will be and then invite people to come. This sets up a separate page for your event where people can comment, find out more details and confirm whether they are coming or not.

A lot of people use this to add details of classes they are running, or craft fairs they will be attending.

A NEW ADDRESS

Once you have twenty-five Facebook fans you can set up a custom URL (uniform resource locator, also known as a 'web address'). This a tidier, neater link than the one you get by default, which will be something like 'facebook.com/2568221713981-Crafty-Cat'. When you set up a custom URL you could change this to: 'facebook.com/CraftyCat'.

This is much easier to remember, and therefore easier to share with people. To find out how to change the URL, search 'custom URL' in the Facebook help section. Choose carefully – once set, you cannot change it again.

REACH

Most Facebook users follow hundreds of people and pages, so if every single update were shown in their feed, users would be overwhelmed with an average 1,500 updates per day, according to businessinsider.com. Instead, Facebook uses an algorithm with a huge number of criteria to decide which posts people should see in their feed.

The main thing to understand is that not all of your page fans will see your updates, just as not all of your friends on your personal Facebook page see every post you make. Only one to fifteen per cent of your followers will see the posts on your page. A note at the bottom of each post (and in your admin panel) will tell you how many people have seen each post. If you pay to promote a post – which is course is what Facebook are hoping you will do – you will get a higher reach. Pinning posts to the top of your page or highlighting them can help you reach more people.

Spreading the word

Once you have created one of the post types explained on page 121, there are a few things you can do to bring it to the attention of more people. If you hover your mouse over the top right-hand corner of the update, you will see a little arrow appear. Click that to get more options to help expand your reach.

Pinning Pinning a post to the top of the page means that it will not be bumped down by subsequent updates, instead remaining at the top of your feed. As a result, it will be the first post that any visitor to your page will see. This is worth doing with special offers, sales, new products or any quality content you want to highlight. Just do not forget to unpin it after a few days or it will be at the top forever!

Edit This allows you to alter your post once you have put it live.

BOOSTING

You can pay Facebook to promote your post, making it appear in more people's feeds. You can choose whether just your page fans see it, or the friends of followers too. Normal, unboosted, posts are only seen by a small percentage of your page fans, so the paid option is a way of reaching more people. The 'boost post' option sits on the bottom right of your update. Click on it to find the options and prices for promotion.

Using a mix of different types of posts is the best way to go when starting out, as it allows you to check the reach of each type and see which sort gets the best response from your fans. In my experience, posts including images work better than plain text; but the occasional text post, particularly a question of some kind, will also reach a lot of people. The more people that interact with a post the more people Facebook will show it to. It reasons that a post must be important if lots of people are commenting on it, liking it and sharing it; so once you get those first few interactions you will find your post reach suddenly grows.

Do not be upset about the fact that so few of your fans are seeing your updates. This is likely true of most social media networks – it is simply that they do not give you the statistics. For instance, think how fast-moving Twitter is, if people do not see you tweet within a few minutes there will be lots more popping up above yours in people's feeds and yours will sink down to the bottom.

ANALYSIS TOOLS

The admin panel (see page 120) at the top of your page allows you to get statistics about your posts, page fans and the level of activity on your page. A page needs thirty fans before you start to see insights, which include:

Post statistics

This shows your last few posts along with the number of people they reached and how much engagement they got. These statistics are a good place to start analysing why a particular post was popular.

Notifications

This will let you find out if anyone has commented on your posts, liked your posts, shared them or posted onto your page. Click on the notification to view the original post with the comment/like/share.

Insights

There is an option at the top of your admin panel to 'see insights'. This gives you figures and graphs to show variation in the number of page likes, level of engagement on your page, post reach, post clicks and more. There is a guided tour option to explain these in further detail.

You can also get data on your page fans such as gender, age groups, and location. You have the option to export this information for your records.

Changes

Facebook changes its reach algorithm quite frequently and there is no hard and fast set of rules which will guarantee that lots of people will see your posts. If you put 'Facebook algorithm' into a search engine, there will usually be several articles telling you what types of post are currently proving most popular on Facebook at the moment.

Messages

If anyone sends you a private message, this will also appear in the notification part of your admin panel, where you can read and reply to it.
Note that your reply is also private, so other page fans will not see it.

Good use of your Facebook page

The big advantage Facebook has over other social networks is that it combines several types of media – text, images and video – so you are not as limited as you are on other networks. Your Facebook page is a place where you can interact directly with your customers, potential customers and people with similar interests to you. It is the perfect place to ask questions, show photographs from behind the scenes, and to establish yourself as an expert in your area by dealing with queries or sharing useful information. It also offers a great position to tell people about your business, share your new products or offers, notify people of events you will be attending or simply to talk about what is coming up in your particular niche of the craft industry.

The more people feel a part of what you are doing, the more loyalty towards your brand they will feel. Try to be consistent so your page followers know when to expect updates from you. You do not have to post daily, but if you leave several weeks between updates you risk losing people's interest. Invite people to get involved and feel a part of your business. Share a few ideas you are considering and ask people for feedback. Ask them what you could do to improve your website, shop or product range.

As well as reaching your customers, Facebook is also a good place to engage with other businesses, whether cross-promoting or simply networking. Tagging someone on Facebook embeds a direct link to their page, which is great for recommending a complementary business. To do so, type your update about them, then type '@' followed by the first few letters of the name of their business page. This will bring up a list of names as you type. Select the one for the business you want to tag and it will turn that word into a link to their page. This will also notify the business that you have mentioned it, as well as allowing your page fans to click through to its page. In this way, tagging allows you to quickly and simply cross-promote.

Be genuine – and fair to yourself

Facebook should be used to network and build online relationships organically. I regard self-promoting posts added to my page like 'Popping over to say hello from @Crafty Cats' as unwelcome spam. The poster is sneaking in a link to their own page in the hope of picking up some new fans, without offering anything in return. Such posts do not join in with the page or make a genuine interaction. Many business page owners delete such posts and ban the users.

The people I am most likely to like back, and promote in the future, are those who have something relevant to say; those who join in conversations on my page and share their advice or viewpoint; those who share my posts onto their pages without feeling the need to notify me publicly every time they do so, in the hope I will do it back. It does not take long to get wise to distinguish your real fans from those only out for some promotion from you.

Another way to engage with other businesses on Facebook is to click the arrow on the top right of the page and select 'use Facebook as your business'. Next, interact with other pages by sharing their posts, commenting on their posts or pages and liking their updates. Good pages to look at are those for magazines in your part of the industry, key bloggers or websites and complementary businesses in your area. They will then see your business name and can click through to your page. When done in the right way, this can help form friendships which could lead to working together in the future.

You will be spending months, and eventually years building up your fanbase on Facebook, so do not let others piggyback off your success and hard work. You do not have to share anything you do not want to – keep your page genuine and true to you and your brand, rather than feeling you have to give in to pleading requests. The bigger and more popular your page gets, the more requests you will get to promote things for other people.

PROMOTING YOUR BUSINESS WITH FACEBOOK

These tips are from Mat and Monica from the fabric shop Frumble (frumble.co.uk), which has a great mix of photographs and questions that get a good interaction rate on their Facebook page.

- **Post regularly** Try to post a little bit every so often, but be careful not to get carried away and let Facebook take all of your time. Our favourite kind of posts are the ones that engage our fans in a way that lets them continue the conversation with their own momentum, bouncing ideas off each other. This way the interaction builds up more reach for the post.

- **No hard sell** One of the main reasons most businesses have a Facebook page is to sell more things, but you have to be careful not to always be pushing your latest items onto your fans. Try not to always talk about your own business, but make sure you engage people too. Not all posts should be business related – mix them up with posts that reflect your page's personality to show that you are a person running a business and not a business chasing the sale.

- **Share the love** Facebook is a social network that thrives off sharing. If you have fans whose work or posts you appreciate, make sure you share them with your fans. This will add something different to your page and also often help out the other pages too.

- **Did you get the picture?** When you add a picture to Facebook it appears in your fans' newsfeeds along with hundreds of other updates and photographs. An original, good quality, eye-catching image is the best way to get noticed. Consider investing in a good camera and a photography course to enhance your skills if you do not feel very confident behind the lens.

GIVEAWAYS

Many people run 'sharing' promotions on Facebook, asking people to share a post or image to enter a giveaway which is (at the time of writing this) against Facebook's guidelines and has been for years. Facebook does not want people to be filling their feeds with competition entries which might annoy their friends; and the site has strict rules about running promotional giveaways through their site. However, running your giveaway off-site and using Facebook to promote it gives you a lot more freedom and is within the rules.

If Facebook catches you running a promotion against its guidelines, it can remove the giveaway, or close your whole page down, without warning. Clearly many people think it is worth the risk and continue to get away with it. It is up to you to weigh the risks against the benefits. Personally, I do not feel it is worth the risk. You might gain a hundred or so new fans, but you risk losing all of them and having to start again from scratch.

If you do go ahead with such a promotion, bear in mind that many people will like a page simply to enter a giveaway and then unlike it again after the winner has been drawn. Even if they continue to like your page, they may have only liked it for the giveaway and not because they would ever be interested in your products or services. Your page is most useful to you if it is built on a group of page followers who want to be there because they like you, your products, your website and your brand – genuine fans. They are the ones who are most likely to buy from you in the future, not those hoping for a freebie.

Facebook's promotional rules

Facebook change their promotional rules from time to time. To check the current guidelines see search for 'promotion guidelines' in the Facebook help section.

Scheduling updates

You do not have to be tied to Facebook posting regular updates to keep your fans engaged. You can preschedule them in advance to go live at a time and date you specify. This is a great time saver and frees you for other tasks. Prescheduling gives you much more freedom than having to log in and manually post updates every day.

To preschedule an update, type your post and upload your image or add your link. Instead of pressing 'post' when it is ready, click on the clock just under the update box. This allows you to give a date and time you want the post to go live. You can also backdate posts if you want to add a milestone to your timeline for instance.

Double check

Even if you use prescheduled posting, check in every day or two to reply to any queries on your page and ensure nothing has gone wrong. Occasionally posts do not go live when they should, or you might accidentally schedule it for midnight instead of noon!

To view the posts you have prescheduled, click on 'activity' at the top of your page and you will see the scheduled posts option on the left. The first four prescheduled posts will be shown, and you need to click 'show more' to see the remainder. Hovering the mouse over any prescheduled post will bring up an arrow on the top right. Click on that to change the time of the post, edit it, delete it or put it live now.

There are several social media management programs and apps, such as Hootsuite, which allow you to preschedule Facebook updates away from the site (see pages 117 and 136 for more information on social media management programs). However Facebook tends to rank them lower than updates directly scheduled on Facebook so you will reach fewer people this way. If you want to experiment try using an third party app, check the reach of those posts compared to the reach of posts you scheduled or posted live on Facebook and decide what works best for you.

FACEBOOK ETIQUETTE

While these are not hard-and-fast rules, some behaviours are frowned upon and seen as impolite by most Facebook users. The following points are my advice to avoid annoying your fans and other businesses.

- Do not post self-promotional posts on other people's Facebook pages just to try and get more page fans. Be genuine and engage and contribute to their page instead.

- Do not take part in 'ladder' or 'bus' schemes where you tag loads of pages and tell all your fans to like them in exchange for them doing the same for you. This is not how you go about attracting genuine fans and is very annoying for your page followers. If you have someone you really want to recommend to your followers, write a proper post that explains why you like them and why you think your page fans would like to follow them. Remember – your followers are people, not sheep!

- Public complaints – about Facebook, or how few people are seeing your posts – and asking if people saw a post you made earlier that day, are tiresome. If an important post got a low reach rate, leave it a day or so and post it again. Maybe it was not engaging enough or was simply badly timed. Try using a different image, or phrasing it a little differently when you repost.

Twitter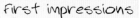

Getting started

Twitter is a social network which allows you to interact with others using one hundred and forty character messages known as tweets. If you are not already a member, visit twitter.com to set up a profile.

Twitter is a fast-moving network; and as a result users will rarely take the time to look up your Twitter name, instead simply typing in what they think it would most likely be. For this reason, try to pick a name as close to your business name as possible.

Similarly, people are unlikely to click through to your profile page to find out who you are, so take the time to put some information about yourself in your bio (short for biography), as this is immediately visible. Many people want to know a little bit of information about the user before following them. If there is no information, no photograph and no tweets on a profile I do not follow it and I suspect many other people are the same. For this reason, it is a good idea to write a few tweets before following people so that people who come to look at your business are reassured to see your account is genuine.

If you run a fairly large business with several employees, it is nice to let people know with whom they are interacting, by putting their names in the profile – 'tweets by Nicole and Kim', for instance.

Do add an image to your profile. Some people use their business logo or avatar while others use a picture of themselves. There are advantages to both of these: using your logo helps to build brand awareness; while using a photograph helps people to relate to you as an individual. Neither is right or wrong; go with whichever you feel most comfortable using.

Include a web link (URL) in your profile. People are unlikely to trawl through your tweets to find a link to your site, so including it in your bio makes it easy to find and more likely to be clicked.

Finally, while you are signing up, pop into the settings tab and check the e-mail notifications setting. Let them know when you want notifications otherwise you could end up getting a lot of unwanted e-mails.

Attracting followers

Once you are up and running, the next step on Twitter is to get followers. Followers are people that want to see your updates and will see all your tweets on their homepage. You want to build an ever-increasing number of quality followers – i.e. those who share interests with you, would potentially buy your products, or with whom you could build a business relationship.

unfortunate name choice

Pick your name carefully. A teacher named Natalie Westerman chose '@natwest' as her Twitter name. Unfortunately, when the NatWest bank had IT problems that resulted in a lot of people not receiving their pay, she received lots of angry tweets intended for the bank!

First impressions

Your Twitter profile gives you space to describe yourself in more detail, while your bio is limited to one hundred and sixty characters, but is immediately visible. I get around thirty or so new followers a day so I do not have the time to visit each of their profiles; instead I scroll down the list of new followers reading the bios and follow those that I think sound interesting.

There are several sites that offer to get you thousands of Twitter followers, usually for a price. However, the chances are they are not people who are at all interested in your business and what you have to say. Several people try running giveaways to get new followers, usually with the condition that you have to follow them and tweet about the giveaway to be entered, but that often results in a lot of people following you just for the competition and then unfollowing you once the competition has ended.

It is not the number of followers you have that counts, but the quality, so do not get caught up worrying about numbers. There are a few activities to work through below which will help get you up and running on Twitter in no time.

No link?

If a business does not have an immediately apparent link on its site, use the search box on Twitter itself to see if you can find its account that way. Alternatively, if you are able to find it on Facebook, you could post a comment asking if the business has a Twitter account. Finally, try running their company name and the word Twitter through a search engine and see if anything comes up.

Activity: Find your first followers

When you follow someone they get notified in their @connect section of Twitter. The aim of this exercise is to get a few of them to follow you back.

Brainstorm and use your notebook to write down the names of twenty magazines, blogs, websites, suppliers or television programmes that are relevant to your business: those that cover subject matter that would interest you and your customers. If you sell paper and papercrafting supplies, for example, look at the profile of papercraft magazines. Their followers are likely papercraft enthusiasts and may be interested in buying supplies from you in the future.

Visit the website of each company you have noted down and see if it has a link to a Twitter account. If it does, click on the link and follow it on Twitter, ticking the company off your list as you go. To follow it, click on the box that says 'follow' on their profile below the image.

Once following them, view each of their profiles in turn and click on the list of people that they are following. Work your way down the list and follow the ones that are relevant to you. You can also do the same to the list of people who are following them.

Who to follow?

Friends, customers and businesses/people that you already know 'offline' are a good place to start; particularly as they are more likely to follow you back.

If you sell handmade products it is probably worth following the accounts of big handmade platforms such as Etsy, Folksy, MISI, and Not On The High Street. Not only do they often share selling tips which may be useful to you, but they often tweet about products on their sites which can help you with market research. It is also worth following the magazines that cover your art or craft as you may find opportunities for editorial coverage – some magazines use Twitter to say they are looking for certain products or content for features.

Repeat the brainstorming exercise every so often, and aim to build your numbers slowly over time. If you are following hundreds of people and no one is following you, it can make your account look like a spam account and turn potential followers away.

You do not need to tweet every single new person that you follow, in fact it can look pretty fake if you do. Try to find one or two you could contact each time you add a batch of new people to follow to your profile. It is a good way to get people interacting with you, and often you will find that once you speak to them they will follow you back.

Click through to their site or blog and take a look at their latest posts. Finding something that will allow you to start up a conversation will result in a more interactive relationship with your followers.

Twitter terms

This is a guide to some of the common jargon and abbreviations used on Twitter.

- **TL/Time line** This is your home page, the one which shows all the tweets from people you follow on Twitter.

- **#/hash tag** If people in a group discussion use the same hash tag at the end of their tweets, the whole conversation can be viewed by clicking on that hash tag. For instance the Craft Blog UK Twitter chats use the hash tag '#CBUK'. Hash tags can also be used to give more information about the subject of your tweet or to show you are talking about a particular topic: e.g. 'press all seams as you go for a professional finish. #sewingtips'. Anyone wanting to find tips on sewing could type the hash tag into the search box at the top of the page and read more tweets with the same hash tag.

Take your time

You do not need to work through all of the followers of all the businesses you noted down at once. Start looking through likely followers of one business, then pick another business the following day.

By doing a few at a time you can take the time to look through their timelines, and read their last five to ten tweets. Is there anything you could comment on to start interaction between you and them? Have they asked a question you could answer, or shared something interesting you could retweet?

- **RT/retweet** When someone shares your tweet with their own followers, it is called a retweet. The more you get retweeted the more people you reach. You can retweet someone else by clicking the 'Retweet' option under their tweet.

- **MT/modified tweet** A paraphrasing of someone else's original tweet, this is often done when the full original tweet will not fit into the character limit when being retweeted – if the retweeter wants to add a comment or observation to the original, for example.

- **TT/top trends** These are popular topics currently being talked about on Twitter. You will find these on the left-hand side of the timeline. Click on them to see tweets on that subject.

- **@** Putting the @ symbol in front of someone's Twitter name makes the tweet show up in their 'mentions' so that they know you are talking to/about them. If you forget to add the @ symbol in front, they may not spot your comment.

- **#FF** This hash tag means Follow Friday. Followed by a mention of a twitter name (i.e. with the @ in front), this is used to recommend other tweeters to your followers. Being mentioned in someone's #FF's can help you get new followers if people act upon that recommendation. Some people simply list a lot of names when doing this, others will give reasons for their recommendation, e.g. '#FF @thedesigntrust for great craft business tips & advice'.

- **FB** An abbreviation for Facebook.

- **DM/direct message** This is a way of sending a private message to an existing follower so that only they, and not all your followers, will see it.

- **Favourite** If people like your tweets and want to save them or come back to them later, they can favourite them. You get notified of this by seeing a little star and your tweet in your @ feed along with the name of the person who favourited it. This helps you see what content is popular. You can favourite tweets yourself by clicking on 'favourite' at the bottom of the tweet. Find your favourites by clicking the 'me' option at the top of the screen and then selecting favourites.

where is it?

If the retweet option is not immediately visible, hold your mouse over the tweet and it will appear. This is also the method for making the reply option – used to respond to a tweet – to appear.

Mentions

Click on '@ connect' at the top left of your timeline to see who has mentioned you.

Twitter lists

When you are following thousands of people it becomes hard to keep up with all the tweets on your home page. Splitting your followers into Twitter lists based on categories – magazines, websites, selling platforms, people who sew, people who knit, blogs I like, businesses I love, friends and family, and so on – allows you to view the updates from a few key tweeters at a time.

You do not need to put all your followers into lists, but organising the ones you look at the most into lists means you can easily find them again in the future, and can keep up to date with their news.

The earlier you start putting people into lists the easier it is. You do not want to have to split five hundred people down into groups. Ideally, do it before you pass the one hundred mark. You can always add more lists at a later date.

To create a list, click on the cog on the top right of every Twitter page, then select 'lists'. At the top you have the option to 'create list'. Click on this, then write down one of the category names and brief description from the exercise above. You also have the option at this stage to make your list private if you want, which means only you will be able to see your list.

To add someone to one of your lists click on their name so that it brings up their profile summary. Click on the little head icon next to the words 'following' and select 'add or remove from lists…' from the drop-down menu. This will bring up all of your lists; tick the list to which you want to add them. You can also untick a box to remove them from a list. New lists can be created from here, and people can be added to multiple lists if you want.

To view your lists and the updates from members of your lists, click on the cog at the top of the screen and select lists as before. The names of all your lists will appear. Click on the list name that you want to view and it will load a page of the latest updates of people from that list.

Names, not numbers

You cannot start a twitter list name with a number written as a figure. If you need a number at the start, write the number out as a word.

Privacy

I keep my friends and family list private, but leave my other lists public so other people can see them and subscribe to them. People subscribing to your lists will have your list in their list section and can see the updates from all the people on that list. You can of course subscribe to other people's lists too. It saves you from having to build so many yourself.

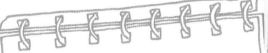

Activity: Twitter lists

Once you have around fifty to one hundred people in your 'following' list on Twitter, it is time to think of ways that you can categorise them. Write down some categories in your notebook and put the names of a few of the people you follow next to the relevant category. For example:

List name: Publications

List description: Sewing and craft magazines

Twitter user: *CraftyCat*; *Crafty Focus*; *Sewing World*, etc.

Using Twitter on a regular basis

In your first month on Twitter try to make a point of logging in two or three times a week and finding five new people to follow, using the methods explained earlier. (You will find that Twitter suggests people you may want to follow on the left-hand side of your screen.) Post an update each time you are logged in and interact with at least one person while you are there. That person could be one of the new people you follow that day, or one of the people you are already following. Make sure you reply to any tweets directed at you (click on the @ symbol at the top left of the page to see them). You can also check any direct messages you have been sent by clicking the envelope at the top of the screen.

Building this routine will help you get used to using Twitter on a regular basis, keep your follower numbers growing and ensuring you interact with new people. If you do not have the time to update two or three times a week read the prescheduling section on page 136.

Twitter's help

Twitter has a section of useful advice and tips for businesses using Twitter in their help section. It even has downloadable guides too. Find the help section by clicking on the cog symbol and selecting 'help'.

Activity: Tweeting

If you have followed the information on the earlier pages, you will have some followers who are sorted into lists so you can easily find them and you are logging in three times a week to interact with people and post an update.

The next step is to begin to write tweets – which leads to the question 'what on earth should I say in my updates?' The start of this chapter gives lots of ideas on topics to talk about, and the following ideas may spark some inspiration.

- Study what other businesses in your industry talk about.
- Try different types of tweets to find what gets the best response.
- Post at different times to see if there is a day of the week or time of day which is best for reaching your followers.

Tell people you are on Twitter

This may seem like stating the obvious but do not forget to let people know that you are now on Twitter.

- Include links to your Twitter account on your site, blog and other social networking sites.

- Include your Twitter name on your business cards, flyers and other stationery.

- If you have premises, put up a poster saying 'find us on Twitter', followed by your Twitter name.

- Tell your customers when you speak to them.

- Put a link to your Twitter account in your e-mail signature and on your newsletters.

- Mention that you are on Twitter in any press adverts you do. This can be done by adding your Twitter name or the Twitter logo.

Activity: Planning ahead

Set aside some regular time – perhaps one afternoon a month, or an hour or two a week – to plan your Twitter content for the coming period.

What new products or offers do you want to tell people about? What upcoming industry events could you share details of? Have you seen any good tutorials or tips that will help your followers? Have you read an interesting industry relevant news story you could share? Jot down as many ideas as you can in your notebook.

Create a list like the one below to help you plan your content.

Week one

Self-promotional post: _

Industry news or event: _

Useful tip or technique: _

Tutorial: _

Complementary business to promote: _

Other: _

After that first month

Once you have managed to get some followers, you need to keep up the momentum. Try to stick to a regular posting schedule and take the time to follow new people. Keep up a good mix of self-promotional tweets with useful advice or links for your followers as well as engaging in conversations and replying to tweets. When you are looking for things to share, click on your lists and take a look at their recent updates. If you are following the right people – those of interest in your industry – there will almost always be something worth retweeting in there.

Take the time to check through the list of people following you and pick a few to follow back. This is an easy way to find people to follow; they are interested enough in what you have to say to have sought you out so the chances are you will have things in common with them.

Be ruthless with your followers. Streamline your Twitter feed by removing people whose tweets turn out not to be of interest to you. This ensures you are only seeing the updates you really want to see.

It becomes a lot easier to update on a regular basis if you know you have the content ready. If you have to take the time to find something to post about you are less likely to do it. If you come across things during the month that might be useful for your next month's posts, save the links in a document or pin them to Pinterest so you know where they are when you do your planning session.

Keep an eye out for things to tweet about. While you do not want to be constantly posting links to your own site and talking about your own products all the time, it is also worth thinking about alternative ways to present your products when you do tweet about them. How could they help satisfy a customer's need? Can they fix someone's problem? Are they relevant to an upcoming seasonal event?

Follow me

Don't forget to come and follow me on Twitter: @craftabiz or @sewingdirectory

Spam

I would advise against automatically following back everyone who follows you, as you will likely find many are spam accounts. Spam is still a common problem on Twitter.

If you do get followed by spammers or get tweets from them you can report them to Twitter by clicking onto their profile and then clicking on the little head next to the follow button and then 'report for spam'.

Generating loyalty and enthusiasm

One good way to get or keep people following you on Twitter is to reward them for following you. Note down a few ideas below as to special offers, discount codes, giveaways or exclusive Twitter deals you could offer your followers. Do not forget to measure the level of response you get to see what kind of offers your followers like best, and make sure you promote it more than once.

Remember, Twitter is very fast-paced. People may not see your tweet the first time around. Do not get disheartened. If it is important you may want to tweet the post again a couple of days later.

Prescheduling

Prescheduling is a great time saver when it comes to Twitter. It means you do not feel tied to your computer and can schedule several days or weeks of content at once. I schedule my week's content on a Sunday or Monday, which leaves me free to focus on other tasks during the week.

Discount code

If you give a discount code make it exclusive to Twitter, use a different code if you are doing the same thing on Facebook or in your newsletter. This will allow you to track how many sales came from each different social network.

PRESCHEDULING WITH SOCIAL MEDIA MANAGEMENT PROGRAMS

As with general administration, social media management programs can help with prescheduling. Once you have connected your Twitter account to the program – for most, this is done as part of the signing-up process – you can preschedule tweets. On Hootsuite (see page 117), the program I use for prescheduling, you do this by typing your tweet into the box at the top which says 'compose message' and picking the network where you want it to be posted (Twitter, in this example, but it is likely that you will have multiple social media networks connected).

You can then either post the message straight away, or click on the calendar to pick a time and date for your tweet to appear on Twitter. Hootsuite allows you to view or edit any already-scheduled tweets by looking on the pending stream. This allows you to make sure you do not schedule tweets too close together, or at the same time.

TWITTER ETIQUETTE

Like Facebook, there are some things that are not against the site rules, but that are likely to antagonise or irritate other users.

- Do not put 'please RT' at the end of every tweet! If people think your tweet is worth retweeting they will retweet it of their own accord. If it is something you really want retweeted then do ask, but only very occasionally. Then people are much more likely to pay attention.

- Do not tweet people and ask them to follow you or retweet things for you. The best way to get someone to follow them is to genuinely interact with them – not begging for follows or retweets. You would not just walk up to a stranger in the street and ask them to promote your business so do not do it online either.

- Posting lots of updates in close succession fills up people's feeds with your tweets so please try to space it out a bit. Twitter moves so fast that just waiting a few minutes between tweets can stop them all appearing as a big block of updates.

Press opportunities

Typing #journorequest in the search box will bring up tweets from journalists looking for people to feature in articles they are writing. You could find some useful press opportunities for your business this way.

Pinterest *Pinterest*

Getting started

Pinterest consists of a series of user-created pinboards: users 'pin' images from a site along with their own description or comment about the image. A pinned image retains a web address (URL) link to the original site, so users can view the image and description on Pinterest, or click on the image to visit the original web page.

To set up a business account, visit pinterest.com and select the businesses tab. Signing up as a business allows you to link your web address to your account and it also gives you access to free analytical tools (also called analytics).

Once signed up, you can create boards with themes of your own choosing. Users install a 'pin it button' in their toolbar so that when they spot something they like while browsing the internet, they can pin it and return to it later. In that respect Pinterest works in the same way as bookmarking a page on your browser, except that instead of simply seeing the name of the link you have an image and description too.

The social side of Pinterest is the critical difference, as it means people can follow other users on Pinterest, or choose to follow particular boards that they like. They will then see anything new the owner pins to those boards in their home feed, plus they can like your pins, share them with others and comment on them. This makes it a poweful platform that can benefit your business.

Pinterest is proving hugely popular amongst creative people. There is so much visual inspiration available there – you can find tutorials, projects, items to buy, tips and tricks and inspiration for your designs as well as business advice.

Pinterest principles

To get you started, let's looks at a few basic principles about using Pinterest. The following instructions assume you are on the Pinterest homescreen.

- **The 'Pin It' button** Add the 'Pin It' button to your browser's toolbar by clicking on your name (top right) and go to 'your profile and pins'. There you will see a 'get started' tab which lets you install the pin button.

- **Your profile** Set the account up in your business name if possible, so people see it on every single one of your pins – this will help with brand recognition. Make sure you include a link to your website in there and your business name.

- **Settings** Click on your name at the top right, then select settings in order to choose when you want to receive e-mail notifications and to link other social media accounts.

> ### updating your profile
> If you ever want to update your profile, click on your name and then your profile and pins to update it.

- **Searching** There is a search bar at the top left of the page where you can type in keywords to find pins that interest you.

- **Finding friends** Use the drop-down menu under your name and select the 'find friends' option to find friends from other social media networks who are also on Pinterest. You need to have connected other networks with Pinterest to do this.

- **Creating boards** Click on the '+' symbol on the top right of the page and select 'create a board'.

- **Editing boards** Click on your name to get the 'your profile and pins' option, which lets you view your current boards. Click on the board itself to see the pins on it, and click on the edit button underneath the board to make changes. Add a keyword-rich description to each board to help search engines pick it up (see pages 180–181 for more information on SEO).

- **Changing board cover images** When viewing your boards, hold the mouse cursor over the image that is largest and above the others (this is the cover) and you will see a 'change cover' option appear.

- **Editing pins** Put your mouse over a pin when viewing your boards and a pencil will appear in the top right-hand corner. Click on that to edit or delete a pin. You can also find all your pins by looking on the pins tab in the profile and pins section.

- **Uploading a pin** Click on the '+' symbol on the top right of the screen and select 'upload a pin'. You will be asked to choose an image to upload from your computer. You can give it a description too.

- **Social share** When you are adding a pin, tick the boxes under the comments if you want to share your pin on your other social networks. To share one of your older pins, or to share someone else's pin, click to load the image full screen. The share options (a box with an arrow on it) will be at the top right.

- **Recent activity** Keep track of people commenting on your pins, re-pinning your pins and following your boards by viewing the recent activity updates on the top right of your screen. The number that appears tells you how many notifications you have.

Important note

Unlike pinning from a website, uploading a pin from your computer does not add a link, so once saved you need to edit the pin and add in the web address (URL) manually.

Using Pinterest to find useful content

When used correctly, Pinterest can generate a continual stream of useful content – such as techniques, fun projects, key posts and industry news – which you can then share on your other social media networks. If you are prescheduling your social media content in advance, a well-kept Pinterest account will mean you can spend an hour on Pinterest and find enough content to schedule a few weeks posts in one go.

However, you need to make sure that you are following the right people, and only the relevant boards. You do not want to have to pick through hundreds of pins to find the ones you want.

Once you have your Pinterest account set up and have experimented with the basics (see pages 138–139), start by looking for key magazines, websites and bloggers in your sector, or by asking your followers on other social media networks who they recommend on Pinterest.

You can use the Pinterest search bar to look for people by name and then click 'pinners' in the search results to find their boards, or visit their website and see if they have put a link to their Pinterest account on there. Such links are usually found in the sidebar or across the top of most sites or blogs.

Once you have found the Pinterest accounts you want, start looking through the names of their boards and follow only the ones that are relevant to you. If you follow the person rather than individual boards, you will see all the users' pins, no matter which board they pin them to – most people's boards cover several different interests so you probably will not want to follow them all. You can also click on the boards to view the pins and see if there are any you can re-pin to your own boards.

Keep your friends close...

It is a good idea to follow some of your competitors to keep an eye on what they are doing.

MAINTAINING YOUR PINTEREST

If you start to find some of the content in your home feed is not relevant as time goes on, click on to the board and unfollow it. This will ensure that only the best content is there waiting for you on Pinterest when you need it.

Checking and editing the boards you follow as your business grows will save you time and energy and ensure you always have a wealth of relevant content for your target market.

Videos

You can pin video onto Pinterest but, at the time of writing, not many people seem to have caught on to this yet. Make your boards stand out by pinning video content to them.

Another way to find relevant content is to use the Pinterest search bar to look for boards or pins on specific subjects. If you type in 'bead embroidery', for instance, you will find lots of boards devoted to the subject, as well as individual pins. If you wanted to put a post on Facebook about bead embroidery because you sell beads and want to give your followers some ideas of what to do with them, you will be spoilt for choice for tutorials and projects to post.

By following lots of relevant boards and accounts, you should start to find that every time you visit Pinterest there should be lots of great content on your homepage for you to share on other networks. This content can be used as-is, but it is also perfect to use as the basis for a blog post or article on your site.

Remember, you can use this content on your other social networks, but it is important to make sure that you re-pin them to your own Pinterest boards – over time, this will help you become a great content curator in your niche, which will mean people will come to you for the latest news, products and projects.

Round-up

One fun idea is to do a round-up style post: '20 brilliant things to make with beads', '30 creative necklace tutorials', or '100 great Christmas card projects', for example.

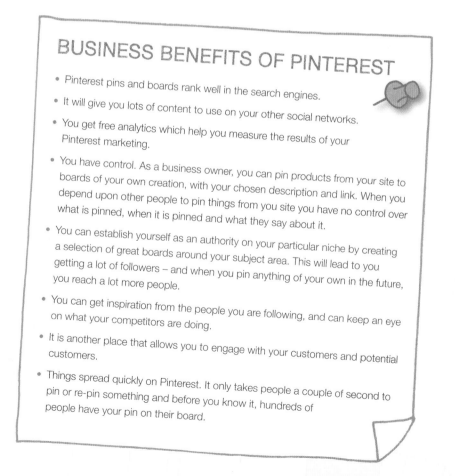

BUSINESS BENEFITS OF PINTEREST

- Pinterest pins and boards rank well in the search engines.
- It will give you lots of content to use on your other social networks.
- You get free analytics which help you measure the results of your Pinterest marketing.
- You have control. As a business owner, you can pin products from your site to boards of your own creation, with your chosen description and link. When you depend upon other people to pin things from you site you have no control over what is pinned, when it is pinned and what they say about it.
- You can establish yourself as an authority on your particular niche by creating a selection of great boards around your subject area. This will lead to you getting a lot of followers – and when you pin anything of your own in the future, you reach a lot more people.
- You can get inspiration from the people you are following, and can keep an eye on what your competitors are doing.
- It is another place that allows you to engage with your customers and potential customers.
- Things spread quickly on Pinterest. It only takes people a couple of second to pin or re-pin something and before you know it, hundreds of people have your pin on their board.

Using Pinterest to promote yourself

When done correctly Pinterest is a very effective marketing tool – I now get more traffic from Pinterest than from all the other social networks combined – and it also takes a lot less effort than other platforms.

To achieve this, you should first make sure that your boards do not sound self-promotional. If all your boards are about you and no one else, only your die-hard fans will follow you. The trick is to have a wide selection of boards (each of which covers an area that relates to your business) to which you can pin content; some from your site, but also lots of good quality content from outer sites. If possible, you want some overlap between your boards so that you can re-pin your content in the future onto a board that is related but has a different focus.

For instance, I have a 'sewing for beginners' board, a 'sewing projects' board and a 'sewing tips and techniques' board. I will often have one article on my site which can fall into two or all three of those boards. I will pin the article to one of the boards, then add it to another a few weeks later. A few weeks later still, I will pin it to the third. This approach increases the chances that people who were not following the initial board, or who simply missed it, will spot it at a subsequent date.

THEMES FOR BOARDS

A business that sells hand-painted mugs could have a board that showcases their own products, titled 'my hand-painted mugs'. In addition, the business could maintain a few themed boards. These might be themed around style: 'vintage chic', 'country style kitchens', and 'modern kitchenware', for example. Relevant mugs from the business could be pinned onto these other boards, along with other items – found elsewhere – which fit those themes.

Content is another way to theme a board. Floral mugs could fit in a floral board, which could have anything from floral paintings to floral clothes. Boards themed around seasonal events like Christmas or Easter are popular too. If a company produces some mugs aimed just at men, it could set up a 'gifts for men' board and fill it with a few of its own mugs in alongside other gifts for men. Boards could be themed by colour – a board filled with lots of beautiful handmade red products, including of course some red mugs.

Try to work out where your products can fit – and remember that items can be pinned to more than one board. A mug with red flowers would fit into both the red board and the floral board.

I also have only one self-promotional board, clearly labelled 'From The Sewing Directory' so people know that everything on that board is from my site. If people want to see content from my site and my site only they can look there and follow that board. If they want a mix of ideas and inspiration from a big selection of sites and blogs, they can follow the other boards that interest them. Most of the content on that board is also on at least one other board too.

When it comes to pinning your own content in the description box, the aim is to entice people to click through to your site. Give a good summary to help viewers understand what it is that they are clicking through to: post a picture of a finished item along with 'find out how to make this in just one hour' if you are promoting a tutorial. Alternatively, try intriguing them: 'Look what I made in one hour, with just this block of wood'. Posting a picture of the original block of wood will entice them to click through to your site to see what you made.

Quick notes

If you highlight text on a page before pressing the 'Pin it' button, that text will carry over into your pin description box.

Activity: Creating your first Pinterest boards

Look at the products and content on your website and write down a list of board themes to which you could pin them. Try to make sure that the themes are broad enough that most items from your site could be pinned to more than one.

Next, write down a few ideas of where you could find things other than your own to pin to each board. Make sure they also fit the theme.

Create those boards one at a time (not necessarily all at the same time) and begin to pin items to each. Aim for at least ten pins on each board. Space out self-promotional pins so people do not just see several of your products or posts from your site in a row. Add a pin from your site followed by a couple of pins from other sites, then visit Pinterest and re-pin a few pins too so that people will see a good mix of pins from you and from others.

When adding your pins make the most of the pin description option. Get some keywords in to help with SEO (see page 182) and for when people are searching Pinterest or Google for particular things.

Pinterest's social side

It is important to remember that Pinterest is a social network. Do not forget to look at other people's pins and boards and re-pin them, comment on them, like them or share them on other social media platforms because this will help you network with other businesses, build a following and increase interaction on your boards. You could even set up collaborative boards and invite a few people to create the board with you. You can do this in board settings, click on 'edit board' and then invite people by e-mail or Pinterest user name to start pinning to the board.

The social aspect also means that it is important to make your boards useful and keep them well maintained – stay on top of your housekeeping to make sure visitors enjoy their experience of browsing your boards for best results. Make sure all your boards have relevant descriptions and names. Check back periodically to make sure the links on your pins still work, and that they have relevant pin descriptions. When your boards get too large and unwieldy, break them down into smaller sub-topics so that they are easier for people to browse. This has the added benefit that it gives you another board to which you can re-post your own content.

Whenever you are writing content for your site, keep at the back of your mind that you want to make it sharable on Pinterest. Make sure you use good sharable images, and include your brand name on the image somewhere so that if someone else pins it people can still see that it comes from you (see pages 70–77 for more on branding). I have tried to make it a habit that I create at least one really good sharable image for each article I write, and as soon as I put the article live I pin that image to start it generating traffic for me.

Getting your material re-pinned

You can encourage pinning by running a contest on Pinterest. You can ask people to create boards around set themes or featuring your products to enter. Or you can ask them to re-pin something from one of your specified boards, or from your site to enter. Like Facebook, Pinterest does have rules about contests, so check them (see Pinterest's helps section) before planning your giveaway.

Do not forget to tell people you are on Pinterest. Share the link to your Pinterest account on your site, blog, other social media platforms and newsletter. Build engagement by asking your followers what they would like to see you pin more of, or what boards they would like you to create.

> ### Tagging on Pinterest
> As with other social networks you can tag other people in your pins by using '@[username]'.

> ### Pin it!
> Encourage people to pin your content by adding 'pin it' buttons to your site and blog.

Secret boards

Pinterest allows you to have secret boards; boards that only you and people to whom you give permission (by inviting them to pin) can see. What could you use private boards for?

- **Shopping lists** We happily share boards of all the pretty handmade items and craft supplies that we want to buy with everybody. But there are things you want to buy online that you do not necessarily want to share with everyone – if you are looking at boring things like a new desk lamp or wastepaper basket for your home office, for example. A private Pinterest board is ideal for keeping such things away from your followers, because it allows you to view different types at a glance, or different places to buy, and to save them all until you make your choice.

- **Research** When researching ideas for blog posts, website articles and so forth, I do not necessarily want other people to see what I am working on, in case they decide to write about the same thing after seeing my pins. Then I would have done their research for them! By creating a private board, I can keep such research in one place so I do not have to scroll through a huge bookmark menu and try to remember what is what. On a Pinterest pin you can write a description that fits in more information than you could if you were saving something as a bookmark.

- **Limited sharing** You could use a private board as a way of sharing photographs of your paintings with the rest of your art class. They can also add their own pictures so you can have them all together in one place to share and discuss without having to show them to the rest of your followers. Similarly, if you have a few people working for your business, you can all share ideas and inspiration on a private board without your competitors being able to see it.

- **Separating hobbies and interests** You may have a big collection of craft boards and all your followers are crafters but you could also be really into Star Wars or football. If you are worried that posting loads of pins about your other interests will result in people unfollowing you, then pop them on a private board instead. You can still see them whenever you want but they will not come up in people's feeds.

- **Preparation** If you have an idea for a board but do not have the time to add lots of pins at once, or want to gather pins over time, set up a private board so no one else can see what you are doing. You can then change it to a public board so everyone else can see it when you are ready.

Measuring the results

As mentioned earlier, business users of Pinterest get access to free analytics. I have found these to be a little hit and miss – sometimes they just will not load the data for the period specified – but when they work you can get some very useful information from them.

Click on your name in the top right corner and then select 'analytics' to access the information. You will be shown a series of graphs with data from the last couple of weeks, showing how many people have pinned from your site each day, how many of your pins have been re-pinned or seen by others and how many people have clicked through to your website from Pinterest.

Select the 'most recent' tab on the top middle to see all the most recent pins from your website, who pinned them and to which boards. This is a great chance to interact with people, or thank them for pinning. It also lets you see which of your content is currently proving most popular. It is worth seeing if there are any trends you can identify here – a particular type of content that is more popular, or a particular style of image that people prefer – as identifying such trends can help give you ideas for future content.

The next tab across the top is 'most re-pinned'. This can show you the content that is going viral and spreading around Pinterest. If you click on one of the pins in the top left-hand corner it will tell you how many times the pin has been re-pinned. Again use this information to help plan future content.

You can also see the 'most clicked' content on the last tab across the top. This is very important because ultimately the main aim of using Pinterest is to get people visiting your site and hopefully buying what you are offering. It is worth keeping an eye on this to try to emulate the content in the future to bring even more traffic to your site.

Find, then follow

You can, of course, also identify who is pinning from industry websites or competitor's sites and follow them. If they are interested in sites that offer the same content or products as yours, hopefully they will be interested in your site and may follow you back.

To see the popularity of a particular pin, click on it to view it full screen, then check the top left-hand corner for the stats, as shown below.

This figure shows how many times the pin has been repinned.

This shows how many people have liked this pin. It will show in the 'like' section of their profile.

Pin it 535   ♥ Like 41   Visit Site

The Most Useful Sewing Links Ever

Activity: Finding what's popular

Use the link below, replacing the part in **bold** with your own web address (URL), to reveal what people are pinning from your site:

- pinterest.com/source/**thesewingdirectory.co.uk**

Note this down, then try replacing the part in bold with competitors' websites to see what people are pinning from their sites. Do the same with other sites or blogs in your industry to gauge what types of content prove most popular on Pinterest.

PINTEREST ETIQUETTE

- Attribute your images by linking all images back to the site(s) you found them. You can also give more details as to the image source in the comments box.

- Do not pin only things from your site, or just from a couple others. Variety is the key to Pinterest success – share inspiration from all over the internet.

- Try not to pin for hours on end because then you will fill people's feeds with your pins. Little and often is a better technique.

- Do not spam other pins by adding comments with links to your own site.

- Treat Pinterest like other social networking sites: be friendly, share and interact with others.

Online communities and content marketing

Content marketing and online communities are big buzzwords in online promotion. You can do both on your own site, or can host them elsewhere. These are long-term investments in terms of both time and money, but can result in your having access to a large number of people who are your target audience and who are loyal to you and your brand.

There is also a great sense of satisfaction knowing that you have brought so many people together!

Online communities

Building an online community is creating a place for people with similar interests to gather and interact. You can build a community around your site, through your social media, through your blog and by e-mail. I have built a great community around The Sewing Directory and after a few years of interacting online, I have now started to hold sewing meetups which give people a chance to get together face to face to sew and chat about sewing, fabric, and industry gossip. There are many people who have followed The Sewing Directory from the start and have now connected with not just me but each other as a result.

Another great example in the sewing industry is the American website Sew Mama Sew (see the box on community building, opposite), which has built a great worldwide community of sewing bloggers who participate in sewing challenges, worldwide giveaway days and in 'sew-along' events and swaps.

One of my customers, Minerva Crafts, recently set up its own online community called Look What I've Made, which is designed to encourage people to show off the items they have crafted. It also lets people comment on other people's makes and like them.

Building an online community has many benefits, it shows people that you care about them and their interests. It helps them to see you as a valuable resource and the lynch pin to the community. You bring people together and build a loyal following around you and your brand. It also establishes trust and helps you build relationships with potential customers.

I have put links to all the mentioned sites at the end of this section. Visit them and think about whether you could create something similar around your business. Even if you decide not to, if there is already an online community in your part of the industry, consider becoming a part of it in order to help raise your brand profile, to network and to keep up with what is popular in your industry.

PURELY ONLINE COMMUNITIES

You could set up a site dedicated solely to creating an online community. A great example of this is the Burda Style site where users can share patterns, projects and photographs of what they have made, as well as comment on others' projects.

Ravelry is a knitting community site based around a forum layout. In addition to the chat forums, it lets members sell their products through the site too.

Content marketing

Content marketing involves creating great quality content that will attract visitors to your site and help build awareness of your brand. The majority of the content should be on your own site and blog but you can also use it to guest post on others in order to establish yourself as an expert in your area and send traffic to your site.

The key to creating good quality content is to identify what specifically your customers want and is hard to find elsewhere. There is no point writing something that has been covered elsewhere unless you can put a unique spin on it or cover it better than has been done anywhere else.

Your content needs to be compelling, to help people and to be sharable. You want people to read it and think 'this is great, I must tell so-and-so about it, or share it on my social media'. Good quality content will encourage the reader to read more of your content and look through your site. This will hopefully lead to them signing up to your newsletter, following you on social media and eventually purchasing whatever you are selling.

Want more?

There is more on creating good content below in the blogging section and in the SEO part of chapter 5.

COMMUNITY BUILDING

These tips come from Kristin Link from the popular community site, Sew Mama Sew (sewmamasew.com).

Community is the name, reciprocity is the game. When we re-launched our site in 2013, we sent a letter to our contributors that included this slogan. Although the cheer-inspired sentiment may sound corny, they are words we really do try to live by. Being part of an online community is a lot like being part of a family, so it is important to be mindful of what you can give and not just what you can get.

- Participate in social media. Follow it, pin it, like it, comment on it, favourite it, and share it. Most of the social channels make it easy to give people a virtual fistbump, which you should do every day.

- Invite guests to your blog and sing their praises! Even if they are not business owners or for-profit bloggers they will appreciate being appreciated.

- Take advantage of opportunities to meet people in person. Connecting faces with online handles is good for your community and your soul.

- Always respond to requests for interviews, guest posts and blog hops. Graciously oblige whenever possible.

By paying attention to how you can help other people grow their businesses or their blogs, you are sure to get plenty of respect in kind.

Blogging

Your blog is a platform to tell people more about you and your business: what you make, what you love; and also to share advice, tutorials and inspiration. Unlike most social networks you are not limited to just a few lines or one image. This is where you can create great content that shows off your expertise as well as your creations.

On-site or off-site blog?

You have two choices when setting up your blog. You can make it part of your website or you can host it separately to your website. This decision will depend on what you want from your blog. There are many sites which will host your blog for free including Blogger, WordPress and Tumblr.

The obvious downside to having an off-site blog is that an on-site blog is easier for people to find – I am sure there are many visitors to my website who do not realise I have a blog; and it is for this reason that I make sure the link to the blog is prominent on my website and social media. I chose to host my blog separately, on the hosting site Blogger, for a variety of reasons.

Search engine optimisation From an SEO point of view, I knew Google would index my blog before my website, so separate hosting would drive traffic to the site via my blog while I waited for my site to rise in the rankings.

Backup If there is ever a problem with my website, my blog is still usable. I once had a big competition ending, and server problems with my site which meant it was down for a few hours. So I posted the winner of the competition on my blog and shared that link on social media. Once the site was live again I copied the details over to there.

The personal touch Around half of my posts on my blog are about The Sewing Directory and sewing, but the remainder are about me: my goals, hobbies and news. I shared the process of writing this book on my blog, I shared the progress of converting my garage into an office, the sewing projects I have been working on and my business goals each year.

Communication Hosting my site on Blogger means I have a Blogger account which makes it easier for me to comment on other blogs, and it includes an automatic link back to my blog in those comments.

My blogs

I started on off-site blog for The Sewing Directory while my website was being built in order to build some early followers for the site. I did the same with my social media too.

For the site that accompanies this book I use an on-site blog – neither is inherently better, so experiment to see which you prefer and which works best for your business.

A friendly place

I feel like I can be both more relaxed and personal, and less corporate, on my blog than on my website.

Creating your blog

Once you have chosen where you blog will be hosted you will be thinking about the design of the blog. Your blog should:

- Be uncluttered and use white space (see page 177 for information on white space).

- Be easy to navigate and easy on the eye.

- Have a biography to tell people who you are and what you do. You could add a strapline into your header image to do this.

- Include social media links.

- Include a newsletter sign-up link.

- Include a link to your main site, or shop if hosting off-site.

- Include options for people to follow or subscribe to your blog.

- Have popular topics or posts on the side to encourage people to look at other posts.

- Have branding that fits with the rest of your business.

There are many blog templates available for most blogging platforms; most of them are free too. Your blog should be an extension of your company even if it is hosted off-site. Stick to your branding. Use a similar colour scheme and the same logos and avatars – that way people will know it is part of your business.

You can search for widgets to add to your blog which do things like track visitor numbers, show what countries people visit from, allow you to showcase products in your online shops, adding social media feeds, and more. Most can be added by copying and pasting an html code onto your blog – you do not need a lot of technical knowledge to do that!

Most blogs have the option of adding a blog header across the top. This is a great place to show your logo, include a link to your site or shop (if your blog is off-site), showcase some of your products and tell people what you do. You can add a text motto or strapline into the image to communicate more information. This header image is the first thing people will see when they visit your blog, so make it count.

Make it easy

Make sure the 'follow' options are near the top of the page to encourage people to subscribe to your blog.

Design tips

The information on setting up a website on pages 168–179 includes tips on design. These principles can be applied to your blog, too.

Activity: Blog design

Analyse the popular blogs in your part of the industry and think about what elements of their design and layout you would like to incorporate into your own.

- Do they have a great breakdown of the content on their sidebar?

- Have they got a bold header image which tells people what the blog is about?

- Do they make good use of white space?

- Are their images outstanding?

- Are their blog posts really easy to read and digest?

Look at blogs outside of your industry for design inspiration too.

Writing blog posts

Cornerstone content

Once your blog is designed and live, start filling it with great content. It is good to have a mixture of different kinds of posts on your blog. The main thing you will need to put time and energy into is the what is called 'cornerstone content'. These are the really good articles which make people come back for more and attract traffic from search engines; and they form the foundations of your blog.

Craft blogs often include how-to guides, great projects or some really in-depth expert advice, such as how to choose a sewing machine, for example. Cornerstone content does not represent the kind of posts you will be writing every week. They take more time, more research and a lot of effort.

However, if you can create one of these killer pieces of content every few months, it will encourage people to subscribe and help grow your blog. After you put so much into writing these posts you want to make sure you promote the hell out of them! Promote them on social media every few months, highlight them on the sidebar of your blog, modify them to offer as guest posts on other blogs, mention them in your newsletter, update them regularly for SEO purposes. Keep them working for you for years; do not just view them as a one-off. I have a few articles on my site which each get several thousand hits a month. When you get a single piece of content bringing you over 50,000 hits a year you will realise it was time well spent.

Play to your strengths. If you are really good at choosing colour combinations for the craft supplies you stock, write an in-depth guide to colour theory and how to choose colours which work well together for your craft projects. Of course you can research and write about subjects you do not know well, but if you already have a certain amount of knowledge it will save you time.

Short and sweet

Try to create a short descriptive web address (URL) for your cornerstone posts, this makes them easier to share. Look at the length of the links in the blogging tips links section on page 159 to see what I mean.

Let people talk

Make sure you have activated the comments section so people can comment on your blog.

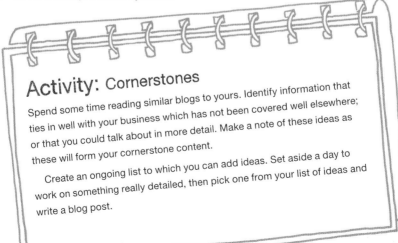

Activity: Cornerstones

Spend some time reading similar blogs to yours. Identify information that ties in well with your business which has not been covered well elsewhere; or that you could talk about in more detail. Make a note of these ideas as these will form your cornerstone content.

Create an ongoing list to which you can add ideas. Set aside a day to work on something really detailed, then pick one from your list of ideas and write a blog post.

Other content

Other content you can share on your blog includes:

Your business news Share information such as new stock coming in, opening hours, staff, events, or changes to the business. This goes back to letting people know who they are buying from and helping them to form a relationship with you.

Your projects Sharing your own craft projects and challenges work well. Show people what you have been making, what you plan to make, and even what you are struggling with. If you find you are working so much you do not get much time for making, then share pictures of your supplies, of your workspace, what you have been buying recently or what you plan to make in the future.

Inspiration Ideas are another good topic for blog posts. Share the source of your inspiration. Tell your followers about some really great blogs you want to recommend. Are you a Pinterest addict? Is there a particular magazine you find always gets you fired up? Write about these things, share them with your followers, and ask them where they get their inspiration.

Personal posts Posts about my business and sewing make up roughly half of my blog, but I do write some personal posts too. These posts help your followers relate to you; and sometimes there are things you just want to share that have nothing to do with work.

> ### Help!
> Asking for advice or showing you are struggling with something really makes people relate to you. They can see that you are just like them and it gives common ground. It also has the benefit that it will encourage more interaction as people reply.

TOO MUCH INFORMATION

Be wary of 'over-sharing' – giving away too much personal information. One craft blogger told me someone turned up at her children's school one day to meet her because they had worked out which school it was from her blog posts!

Remember that anything you put on your blog, website or social media is entering the public arena, where it becomes impossible to control. As with all places that you use for business, keep negative posts to a minimum. Using your business blog for a big rant about your interfering mother-in-law or noisy neighbours is bad form – and, needless to say, never use it to bad mouth your customers or suppliers.

Quick tips and techniques These are different from your cornerstone content as you may just want to cover something brief and not write a huge in-depth article – perhaps a new technique you have learnt or think your readers would benefit from, or a useful crafting tip you have come up with.

It is handy to draft some of these posts and keep them ready for when you do not have time to write anything fresh as they are not time sensitive and do not have to go live straight away.

Lists These work well as blog posts. Collect information from several places and combine it into one post. For example: 'Twenty ways to drive more traffic to your Etsy shop', 'Five simple tips to speed up your card making', or 'Eight essential tools for jewellery making'. These kinds of posts always appeal.

Interviews Sharing an expert's talents, advice and views is a great way to attract new followers to your blog. The interviewee will often tell their own followers about it, which sends extra traffic to your blog. If you are worried about over-promoting your own business, conducting an interview will both give useful advice to your followers and mean one less post you are writing about yourself.

Reviews Reviews can form great blog posts. There is now so much choice when it comes to craft magazines, books and supplies, that any advice you can give to help people choose will be appreciated. Contact publishers and ask to review one of their books on your blog – most are glad of the publicity and many will send review copies for free.

Scheduling

Some blogging platforms allow you to schedule your posts. If so, write a batch of posts and schedule them to go live on different days.

KEY INGREDIENTS OF A POPULAR BLOG POST

- Substance: something really worth reading.
- A catchy headline.
- Great images.
- Subheadings and bullet points to break up the text.
- Good promotion of the post.

Promotion

There is no point writing a post and not telling people it is there. Put a link on your social media, mention it in your newsletter, tell your customers face to face... just let people know!

Sharable images

A really good sharable image to use on social media and Pinterest will help your blog post spread more quickly. Include the name of the blog post and the link to your blog in the image. Here are a few examples of the sharable images I have created for my posts.

BLOG READERS

Running your own blog means being involved in the blogging community. Most of us do not have the time to spend hours reading and commenting on other people's blogs and looking for trends, and this is where blog readers come in useful. They stream the latest updates from your favourite blogs into one place so that you do not need to hop from blog to blog – you just load one page and find all the updates there.

Blog readers are very useful when it comes to looking for content to share on social media. You can sort the blogs you follow into categories: separating business blogs from sewing blogs, and your customers' blogs from other blogs. Once split into categories, you should be able to easily find relevant posts on any topic you wish; which you can then use to help write your own blog posts.

See the links section on page 159 for some popular blog streaming programs you can use.

Feedly

I use the blog reader Feedly. Its magazine-style layout makes it feel like reading a big free craft periodical full of ideas and inspiration; and it also synchronises with smartphones and tablets.

Attracting followers

Once your blog is live, encourage people to read it and – ideally – subscribe so that they see all your posts. Part of getting new followers is promotion. As with social media, when you set up a new account or blog you need to let both existing and potential customers know that it exists.

Enticement to click When promoting your blog post, make sure you include an enticement to click through to read the full post. Perhaps share a quote from the post, or ask a question and say 'to find out the answer, click here'.

Reach out You can reach existing customers through e-mail, social media, your site or face to face when they are in your shop. Using online advertising such as Facebook adverts or blog adverts on other relevant blogs is a good way to attract a new audience.

Interact Another great way to get followers is to interact with other blogs. Follow other craft blogs and interact on a regular basis. Read their posts and comment on their posts in a thoughtful, genuine way where you can. Share posts you enjoy on social media, and tag the blogger so they know you have done so. Interact with other bloggers on social media to start to build relationships. There is a really active craft blog community – get involved and you will start attracting people to your blog in no time at all.

Guest blog Guest blogging involves writing a blog post for another blog or website. In return, they credit you and include a link to your site. Ideally you want to use your best content for guest blog posts – if the post is brilliant, you are less likely to be turned down by the site to which you offer the content; and you want to impress people so that they click through to your website.

BECOMING A GUEST BLOGGER

When deciding where to guest blog, aim for blogs that are a little bigger than yours but have a similar target demographic. Ideally you want to build a relationship with the blogger in advance before approaching them to offer them the guest post. You can do this through interaction on their blog, on social media or by responding to their newsletters and by sharing their content.

When you approach them make sure you let them know the benefits for them, why you think their audience will enjoy your content and why they should give you space on their platform. Make the content as useful and engaging as possible, not self-promotional.

BUILDING A BLOG AUDIENCE

Tilly Walnes from Tilly and the Buttons (tillyandthebuttons.com), has been featured in the Guardian *and* The New York Times, *teaches sewing workshops around London, and has given talks for the likes of Folksy and Enterprise Nation. Here are her tips on building an audience for your blog.*

- **Be niche** Be clear and very specific in choosing what your blog is about and who it is for, otherwise it will most likely drown in the vast ocean of the Internet. If you try to appeal to everyone, you are going to struggle to appeal to anyone. Decide who your niche target audience is, write your blog to speak to those people directly, and you are much more likely to develop a loyal following.

- **Be purposeful** It is tempting to write about whatever pops into your head that day, but it can make for a random-looking blog. Potential subscribers will have no idea what to expect in their inbox if they click 'follow' so probably will not risk it. Instead, work out the purpose of your blog, what you are trying to achieve with it, and develop content that reflects your objective. For example, Tilly and the Buttons aims to help and inspire young women to start making their own clothes, so I write posts with this mission in mind.

  Develop regular strands to make your blog more considered, and showcase previous posts in these strands on dedicated pages so that they do not get lost in your archives but instead can be read and re-read for years to come.

- **Be social** Blogging is about having a conversation, so get friendly with other bloggers, by chatting on Twitter, contributing to group blogs and blogging projects. Moreover, be social on your own blog too. Being social is not only about talking, it is also about listening, and people want to be heard – so ask your readers questions, have a discussion, and use their input to help you write your blog. This will make your blog much more engaging for everyone.

Encouraging interaction

The key to courting interaction is making sure people read your post. Use a catchy title to tempt people to click to read it, and promote it on your social media too. Include questions in the post to encourage responses in the comments. Writing engaging content will make people want to join in and comment. Giving a new twist or alternate view on something is likely to encourage debate. Take the time to respond to commenters so they know their comments are being read and are appreciated.

Consistency is critically important. Produce regular good quality content to keep people coming back for more. Try not to set impossible standards. Promising an in-depth blog post every day is something you may well come to regret. One really good post a week is better than writing five low-quality rushed posts.

It helps to do some advance planning and draw up an editorial calendar for your blog. This helps ensure you do not find yourself short of content, and you can plan a regular schedule of different types of post. Put aside a couple of hours a month to read through other blogs in your industry for inspiration, brainstorm post ideas for your own blog and then schedule them on your calendar. Schedule when they will go live (remember that most blogging sites allow you to schedule those posts to all go live at different times) and also when you plan to write them too. Many people find it quicker to write in batches, and setting aside some time means you can turn off all distractions like social media and really focus on your writing.

Give back

Leaving comments on other blogs encourages people to take the time to leave comments on yours too.

Series

A lot of bloggers run a regular series. Many bloggers take part in Wordless Wednesdays, for example, where their posts contain no words, only a photograph; the idea being that the image says it all.

CAPTCHAS, SPAM AND SECURITY

Dealing with spam is an unfortunate reality of running a blog. Captchas are one system of preventing spam. They generate random combinations of words and letters that readers have to type into a box before they can reply to a post.

Although they rule out computer-generated spam, they can put people off. I have found disallowing anonymous comments got rid of nearly all of the spam from my blog without requiring people to complete captchas.

USEFUL LINKS AND FURTHER READING

Social networks

Facebook: Facebook.com

Twitter: twitter.com

Pinterest: pinterest.com

YouTube: youtube.com

Vimeo: vimeo.com

Instagram: instagram.com

Flickr: flickr.com

Google Plus: plus.google.com

LinkedIn: linkedin.com

Social networking tips

Instagram tips: hernewleaf.com/2012/04/11/instagram-tips-and-tricks

YouTube tips: gigaom.com/2009/07/28/34-ways-to-use-youtube-for-business

Google Plus tips: copyblogger.com/art-of-google-plus

Advice for using Flickr: flickr.com/bestpractices/

Facebook etiquette: contemporaryhandmadealliance.blogspot.co.uk/2011/07/facebook-etiquette.html

Getting interaction on Facebook: buildalittlebiz.com/blog/how-to-get-more-interaction-on-your-facebook-page.html

Facebook's advice for businesses: facebook.com/business

Pinterest marketing: copyblogger.com/pinterest-marketing/

Pinterest tips: socialmarketingwriting.com/20-pinterest-tricks-and-tips-you-might-not-have-discovered/

Social Media Management Apps

Hootsuite: hootsuite.com

TweetDeck: tweetdeck.twitter.com

Buffer: bufferapp.com

Examples of online communities:

burdastyle.com

lookwhativemade.com

ravelry.com

sewmamasew.com

Social media tips and advice

Useful social media tips: everythingetsy.com/2013/02/10-social-media-tips-to-make-you-a-rock-star

Social media scheduling apps: authormedia.com/how-to-put-social-media-on-auto-pilot

Blogging platforms

blogger.com

wordpress.com

wordpress.org

tumblr.com

typepad.com

Blogging tips and advice

Lots of useful blog related advice: hernewleaf.com/primp-my-blog

10 great blog headlines: visual.ly/10-blog-titles-drive-massive-traffic

Many great craft blog tips: ukcraftblog.com/2011/09/blogging-tips-and-tutorials-craft-blog.html

How to get more followers: poppyloves.co.uk/2013/02/top-tips-how-do-i-get-more-blog.html

Common blogging mistakes to avoid: jeffbullas.com/2011/04/13/are-you-making-these-20-mistakes-on-your-blog

Ways to make money blogging: problogger.net/moneymap

Blog readers

feedly.com

bloglovin.com

feeddemon.com

reederapp.com/ios (for Macs)

newsblur.com

netvibes.com

SELLING

ONLINE

THE ONLINE MARKETPLACE

Selling online is a good way to start a new business. It saves you the expensive overheads of a shop, removes any limit of a single geographical area, and you can fit the hours around the rest of your life. However, you do need a willingness to learn and a good USP to make you stand out from the many other online businesses. Selling online is not as simple as just setting up a website or shop and sitting back to wait for the orders to come in.

Before selling online, it helps to have or build a knowledge of search engine optimisation (SEO) and online marketing. The ability to set up a simple site yourself will help keep costs down, and an understanding of web analytics will help you to grow your business. Photography skills and branding knowledge (see pages 68–103 for more information) will help your shop or site stand out.

Learning the ropes

When I started The Sewing Directory I knew nothing about online marketing, SEO or analytics, but was prepared to put in the time to learn. These areas are constantly evolving and it really helps to keep on top of trends.

My aim for this part of the book is to explain the basics, but I suggest following some of the websites and blogs in the useful links section (see pages 210–211) to keep up to date with any changes. This will help you to stay one step ahead of your competitors and make sure that you are using your time as efficiently as you can.

Keeping up to date

It does not take a huge amount of time to keep up to date on SEO, analytics and online marketing. Putting aside an hour or so a week to read up on any changes will ensure that you can keep your site ranking well in the search engines and that you are not wasting time on something that will not return any benefits. I would much rather spend an hour a week than pay someone else to do it on my behalf. Check my Twitter account, twitter.com/craftabiz, and this book's accompanying website, craftacreativebusiness.co.uk, for posts and updates on selling online.

Legal requirements for selling online

There is some legislation you need to be aware of when considering what to include on your site. Below is a brief summary of the UK legislation and rules you need to consider. Use the links on pages 66–67 to find the relevant requirements for other countries.

Distance selling regulations and e-commerce regulations

You must provide your customers with the following information:

- Your identity.

- Description and price of the goods being offered.

- Details of delivery and payment options.

- Full address. If you are trading from home you are obliged to give your home address.

- When they can expect to receive the goods.

- Information about your customer's cancellation rights.

- Your e-mail address and VAT number, if registered.

- A way to store or download your terms and conditions.

Sale of Goods Act

Under the UK Sale of Goods Act 1979, your products must:

- Match their description. Anything you say about the product (in advertising, on your site/shop) must be factually correct and not misleading.

- Be of satisfactory quality: free from any defects, safe to use and in good working order.

- Be fit for purpose.

Customers who have purchased online/by phone/by mail order can cancel up to seven days after they have received their goods, even if the product is not faulty. However, this does not apply to personalised or tailormade items. It is worth looking through the full details of this act to find out more about your customer's refund rights.

Privacy and Electronic Communications Regulations

These regulations cover a couple of different areas of which online sellers need to be aware.

Cookie law Site visitors must be notified if you use cookies (see page 172) on your site, be told what they are for and must give consent to their use. Many sites do this through the use of pop-ups, or by a clearly indicated cookies notice on their site.

Marketing rules You can only electronically market people who have consented to receive promotional communications from you. For example by signing up to your newsletter or ticking a box to consent to future marketing when buying your products.

Data Protection Act 1998

When handling your customers' data, you must ensure that you take measures to keep their information safe so that it cannot be used unlawfully. You must get consent to store customers' details and tell them how they will be used.

Companies Act 1985

If you have your own website and are a registered company, you must make sure that the company's registered address and the company number are included somewhere on your website.

Nominet

Nominet governs the registration of .uk domain names. It can suspend or cancel the domains of anyone who does not comply with their rules.

The main rule to be aware of is that companies or individuals using their websites to trade cannot opt out from having their names and addresses published on the WHOIS database, but private individuals can. Find out more by visiting nominet.org.uk.

Latest rules

For more detailed or up to date information on any legal requirements for selling online in the UK, visit the Office of Fair Trading website (oft.gov.uk).

Online marketplaces

If you just want to get going, or are not sure if you want a website yet, you can try an online marketplace first, then build your own website at a later date. Online marketplaces are a good place to start when just starting out as you do not have big set-up costs or the time or hassle of designing your own website.

First steps

Popular sites like Etsy and Folksy have a lot of advice and guides on how to use their sites. You can also find many 'off-site' guides to those selling platforms too. However, whichever one you choose, there will inevitably be a lot of competition from other users, so you need to be ready to compete against hundreds if not thousands of other craftspeople and creatives.

Smaller sites may have a lot less traffic but also have a lot less competition. Ideally it is worth listing your products with two or three different platforms (if allowed by their terms and conditions) and compare sales over a set number of months to see which works out best for you.

Etsy advice

There are literally thousands of places you can get advice on selling on Etsy. I have listed a few on page 210.

Where to sell

There are many smaller sites you can use to sell your handmade products, but the main online marketplaces for handmade businesses are listed below. The statistics noted are taken from their respective websites or press releases.

Etsy Etsy (etsy.com) is the biggest of these platforms and probably the best known too. It has hundreds of thousands of sellers all around the world, many of whom who run full-time businesses purely on Etsy. There is no denying Etsy gets a lot of traffic and makes a large amount of sales: its November 2013 sales figues indicated it sold over seven million items that month, equating to $147.5 million of goods being sold! There were also over two billion page views. Unfortunately, Etsy's popularity means there will be a lot of competition for you. You need to put a lot of time into your SEO, your marketing and your product research to make sure you stand out amongst the other shops.

Folksy Folksy (folksy.com) is a UK-based equivalent to Etsy. Only UK residents are allowed to sell on Folksy, and as a result it is the most popular UK site for selling handmade gifts and supplies. As its tag line says, they are focused on 'Modern British Craft'. As of October 2013, there were 13,300 active shops on the site, around 170,000 items for sale and three and a half million page views per month. Folksy is significantly smaller than Etsy which means less competition but equally less traffic too.

Not On The High Street A more exclusive marketplace, Not On The High Street (notonthehighstreet.com) is not open to all sellers. Instead, it chooses what it considers to be the best creative small businesses to sell on its platform. It may approach you or you can submit an application to them. If accepted, you agree not to sell on any similar online marketplaces.

Not On The High Street gets two million unique online visitors per month and promotes the site on television as well as online and in print. The site itself is very visually appealing and has very good quality images. It charges a one-off joining fee rather than listing fees per product. Like Folksy, the site is currently limited to UK sellers, although at the time of writing it plans to expand to international sellers.

Misi Misi (misi.co.uk) is a UK marketplace that had a change of ownership in 2013. The new owners have added more features, streamlined processes and improved the ease of use. The site gets around 150,000 visitors per month and has around six thousand sellers.

DaWanda DaWanda (dawanda.com) is a German platform which covers many European countries. The word means 'something extraordinary, unlike any other'. It is a large site with over 200,000 shops and around three million products. The website gets on average thirteen million visits per month.

Artfire Artfire (artfire.com) is a US-based site which charges a monthly fee for selling products. As of December 2013 it had over a million items for sale on its site, the majority in the handmade section.

Changing costs

Selling costs for the sites shown here are subject to change. They all have their selling costs on their websites so just pop over to their sites and check out their 'sellers' sections or FAQs.

How to sell using an online marketplace

Once you have settled on which online marketplace(s) you want to use, how can you make sure that your shop and listings have a good chance of being found and how will your products stand out amongst the others?

Photography As discussed in the chapter on presentation (see pages 68–103), good photography will really make your products stand out. Use clear, bright photographs that show your products from several different angles, show the products in use and giving an indicator of size. Make the most of being able to upload several photographs per listing and do not just stick to the one shot. Remember that you can use editing software to enhance your photographs too.

Shop front Personalise your shop front. Use a banner with your branding, make sure you fill in your profile with your back story (use this as you would the 'about us' section on a website). Complete the welcome message with details of what you offer, any special offers or new products. If you have a blog, website or social media accounts, include details of these in your profile too so prospective customers can find out more about you. Use your shop title as a tag line, a chance to tell people about your business in a few words.

Product description Make the most of the description to tell people exactly what they are buying. List the dimensions of the product, what it is made from, what inspired you, how it can be used, which of your other products complement it and so on. Let people know if you are happy to customise the item, or make it in different colours/sizes. You can also use your product description for SEO benefits too (see page 180 for more information).

Product title You are often limited to certain number of characters in your descriptions. So you need them to be concise, descriptive and contain your product keywords. Get into the mind of the buyer and think what they would type into the search box to find your product.

Reviews Encourage customers to leave feedback. Having several positive reviews will allow people to see that you have sold many items and have lots of happy customers – always an encouraging thing to see when you are deciding from whom to buy.

Great customer service If people are very happy with your service not only are they likely to become repeat customers or leave a positive review, but they are more likely to spread the word and tell others about your shop.

first words

Only the first few words of your product title will show in search results, so make sure the most important words are at the start of your product title.

Get your pricing right On many marketplaces you are competing with hundreds, if not thousands, of other similar products. Trying to compete on price is a big mistake. People are often sceptical of cheap items and you will find there is always someone willing to undercut you. Read the pricing tips on pages 28–33 for more information.

Get the right category There can be a lot of different categories to choose from, and on some platforms you are limited to just one. Again, getting into the mind of your buyer will help. Where would they look for your products? Try searching for similar products to yours and see where those sellers are listing their products.

SEO Search engine optimisation will help your products come up in more searches on the marketplace itself and also help search engines pick it up. This allows people off the online marketplace you are using to also find your products. Some more help on keywords can be found on page 182.

Social media Rather than depending on search engines or the online marketplace itself to send you customers, build up a following on social media and send people to your shop. Showcase your products, tell them more about you and build up brand recognition and loyalty. Use social media to promote your offers and new products. See the chapter on social media (pages 104–159) for more detailed information.

Marketing Other ways to get your shop found include online marketing and advertising (see pages 200–202 for more information), handing out business cards with your shop link on at events, getting press coverage and cross-promoting with other businesses. Anything you can do to get your business name, and ideally shop link, out there will help send customers to your shop.

Be unique A good way to compete against all the other shops is to offer something a little different. If you are the only person offering a particular item, you do not have to worry about the sale going to someone else, but if hundreds of shops offer an identical item, the buyer will often simply choose whoever is first in the search results. If your product is not completely unique, think of reasons why people should buy your product as opposed to one of the others, and include them in your product description. See the information on USPs on page 22–25 for further details.

Keep learning Follow the blogs of the selling platforms you are using to keep up to date with any policy changes or tips for selling. If they have a discussion forum, you can often find useful advice there. Use the links sections on pages 210–211 to keep learning about SEO, marketing, photography and social media. As your skills grow so will the reach of your shop, leading to more sales.

> **Play to your strengths**
>
> One advantage you have over mass producers is that you are selling handmade products, so make sure the word 'handmade' appears several times in your shop.

Setting up a website

Having a website – even if it is just a simple three- or four-page information site – makes you look more professional. Indeed, some businesses trade only on online marketplaces, or on Facebook, without having their own websites.

A website offers you control. If all the information about you and your business is on an external platform, you are at risk: that platform can decide to delete it, or can simply close down.

Domain names can be purchased cheaply, and free software can be used to design your site, so why leave yourself at the mercy of others when you could have a site you control yourself?

Choosing your domain name

The first step of setting up your website is choosing and registering your domain name. Do this as soon as possible when setting up your business in order to make sure no one gets there before you. You do not need to use it straight away, once the domain is registered, you can sort out the hosting and web design at a later date when you are ready.

Your domain name should match your business name, if possible. This helps ensure there is no confusion when people look for you online. For instance I was able to register thesewingdirectory.co.uk for my business site and craftacreativebusiness.co.uk for the site that supports this book. However it is not always that simple. The availability of a domain name may form an important part of your choice of business name – if your first choice has been registered, you might want to adapt or use a different form of your business name in order to ensure that both match.

When searching online, most people will try the business name and add the most common extensions to it (.com, .co.uk, .au or similar regional variant), but you can try more unusual domain extensions if those are already registered. Consider an extension like .net, .biz, .co, or .org.

You could try a descriptive name if your business name is not available. A business called Lisa's Bakery which specialises in cupcakes might try homemadecupcakes.co.uk or lisascupcakes.co.uk.

Some businesses hyphenate their name – sewing-directory.co.uk, for example. However, people often forget to add the hyphen, so if you take this approach, make sure your web domain is very clear on your marketing materials so people come to remember it has a hyphen in it.

Investor's opinions

Theo Paphitis (of television's Dragon's Den fame) addressed a conference I was attending by saying that, when choosing winners of his Small Business Sunday awards, he tends to rule out companies that do not have websites. He feels that those who do not take the time to set up a website are not serious enough about their business.

Preventing confusion

If a competitor runs a website with a name similar to yours, there is a chance your customers may think it is you and order from them by mistake – or someone may intentionally register a similar name to benefit from your hard work.

There are a few ways to help prevent confusion for your customers and help protect your investment.

- If you take the option of a more unusual extension, check who owns the more common extension.

- If you choose a hyphenated name, check who has the name without the hyphen.

- Where possible, register any domains similar to your main domain so that no one else can. For instance I own: thesewingdirectory.co.uk, sewingdirectory.co.uk, thesewingdirectory.com, and thesewingdirectory.net.

ADAPTING THE NAME

You could shorten the name of your business for your domain name – I could have registered sewingdirectory.co.uk or even sewdirectory.co.uk if I had not been able to get my preferred choice.

Alternatively you can add to the name. My mum's business was called Make Do and Mend. Unfortunately, both makedoandmend.com and makedoandmend.co.uk were taken, so she added the word 'online' after the name.

If you have a physical shop, you could add the location to your domain, for instance makedoandmendcornwall.co.uk.

Hosting and creating your site

If you are skilled at coding, the best option is to design and build the website yourself. If this is not the case, there are a number of avenues available to you.

Free sites

Hosts such as Wix, Moonfruit and Weebly will provide you with a free website and hosting, usually in exchange for allowing them to place adverts on your site. They have a selection of templates for you to choose from, so you do not need any coding or web design skills. This means you can easily set up a simple site in an afternoon that includes a little bit of information about you and what you do, along with contact details and details of how to buy your products or retain your services.

Some free blogging software, like WordPress and Blogger, can also be used to design your business website. Again, these offer many templates, most of which are designed to look like blogs but there are some that look like websites.

There are a couple of downsides to this approach. Firstly, you may have adverts appear on your site, the content of which you have no control over. Secondly, the hosts tend to offer only a limited selection of templates which either cannot be edited or can have only limited changes made to them. As a result, your site will probably look similar to many others. However, if you have no budget, free sites are better than no website. There is nothing to stop you upgrading your website in the future as your budget grows.

Self-designed paid-for website

Services like Create.net, Mr Site and WordPress allow you to design a website yourself using either templates or easy-to-use software. These have a monthly or annual cost, and are a good compromise between free sites and paying a web designer to make a site for you. These sites are ideal if you do not have a large budget, or prefer to have total control over your website. Websites made with this method cost around £5.00–£10.00 ($8.50–$17.00) a month plus the cost of registering the domain, which is usually around the same amount per year.

These sites give you much more freedom than free sites when it comes to design and personalisation. Several offer free trials so you can play around with the software before committing any money. If you want to get technical, you can write or edit the HTML and CSS, but you can also use the more limited but more user-friendly design software many of these sites provide if you are not familiar with coding. If you do not have a knowledge of HTML you may find yourself limited in how much you can do with the site, so as with free hosting, your site could look very similar to others when using the supplied templates.

Most of these services are supported by users help forums, YouTube video guides and blogs dedicated to designing sites using their software. As a result, it is easy to work out how to get your website to do things like linking to your online shop on certain selling platforms, showcasing your products with scrolling galleries, or showing a stream of your social media updates.

---

craftacreativebusiness.co.uk

I used Create.net for the website that accompanies this book: it was recommended by several people I know and easy to use. Wordpress also came highly recommended because of the amount of plugins and themes designed for that platform.

Instructing web designers

The third option is to pay a web designer to make your site for you. This is the approach I used for The Sewing Directory. I needed a fairly complex website and although I could easily make a template-based simple website I had no idea how to create databases (for the directory part of the site), how to create user accounts, or how to integrate payment systems. I got quotes from a few local web designers and met with my favourites to discuss what I wanted from the site, before deciding on which company to use.

If you will be having a site that will require regular updating, I would recommend asking for a site with a content management system (CMS) which allows you to update the content yourself. This means you do not have to pay the web designers for every little change you want to make, only for bigger structural changes. This usually costs a little more initially but saves you money in the long run if you plan to make regular changes. If you do not plan to make many changes in the future then you can normally get a basic site of three to five webpages (without a shop) made for you for around £100.00–£200.00 ($170.00–$340.00).

Using a web designer means you do not need to spend time creating the site yourself, and they should produce a high quality site. They will normally do the design for you too, if you have no idea how you want it to look. The downsides are the cost – mine cost several thousand pounds – and the fact that you need to refer back to them for big changes. Often this can mean waiting several days for changes to be made and having to pay quite a lot for the changes to be made instead of being able to do it yourself for free.

If you do not have the time to set up your own site, or you need a very complex site, using web designers is the route to take.

Go local

Using a web design company local to you will allow you to visit and talk face-to-face if there are any problems or you want to make changes to the site in the future. It is easy for someone to ignore your e-mails or telephone calls, not so much so when you are on their doorstep!

Complete cost

When comparing web designers make sure you ask not only the initial cost of the site itself but the cost of hosting (if they will be hosting it). In addition, clarify the cost of updating and how long you should expect to wait for any changes to be made if you should need them in the future.

Activity: Plan your site

Think about, and write down, what you plan to have on your site. Will it be just text and some photos, or a full e-commerce shop with user accounts and databases?

Once you have made your decision, read about the website building sites (see the links section on pages 210–211) and look up some local web design companies and decide which option will be best for your website.

What should be on your site?

Once you have decided how you are going to go about building your site you need to figure out what will actually be on your site. This will then help when it comes to thinking about the layout of the site. There are a few essential sections that should be included on your site:

About us People love to find out more about who they are buying from. Including a back story and a photograph in this section of your site helps people to relate to you.

Contact details Not only do you legally have to have your contact details on your website but people are much more trusting of a site that has full contact details (including address and phone number) than one that just has an e-mail address. It assures them that if there is a problem with their order they have several ways of getting hold of you.

Terms & conditions/privacy policy/cookie policy
This is covered in more detail on page 163 under the legal requirements for selling online section, but your customers need to be aware of their rights. They want to know when to expect delivery of orders, how to complain if they have a problem, whether you are tracking them with cookies, and what you intend to do with their data amongst other details. You can either buy standard versions of these terms and conditions that you then customise to your own business, instruct a solicitor to write them for you, or you could write your own. If writing your own look at those on other similar sites to get an idea of what to include.

Newsletter/social media/blog Including highly visible links on your website to these different platforms will encourage people to follow you so that you can engage with them, tell them about your latest products and build a following for your brand.

Shop/how to book Your site should highlight how to buy your products or book your service. Even if you do not host your shop on your website, or your booking system, you still want a clear tab on your site which can route them to the site where they can place their order.

Gallery or product details People like to see and read about your products or services. Small or unclear photographs along with poor, short descriptions could lead to a loss of sales, or a lot of enquiries from people wanting more information. If you can include testimonials or customer ratings, that can help people make a decision. Customer photographs are also a good idea, showing potential new customers how previous buyers have used your products or services.

Prices/postage Be up front about prices and postage. Visiting a website that does not show the price or cost of postage will put off a lot of buyers. You may not be able to confirm the price of one-off commissions, or bespoke services without the full details, but providing a guide price gives people an idea of whether they can afford it. It is annoying to fill out a whole quote form, and then wait for a reply when that product/service was always above what you could afford anyway; and even more annoying when the postage turns out to be prohibitively high after the customer has spent time browsing, setting up an account and placing their order. This breeds bad will.

Spam reduction

Putting your e-mail address as an image rather than text can help reduce spam. Spambots use text recognition software to harvest email addresses to which to send spam mail. However, they cannot read addresses which are contained in images; while people can still read them easily. I wish I had known this a few years ago!

Blog/news section/other content An area where you can regularly add fresh content is very good for SEO (see pages 180–181) and can also bring customers back to your site on a regular basis. Some suggestions include: how-to guides, reference guides, technique guides, interviews, and details of forthcoming events, book or product reviews.

FAQs This stands for 'frequently asked questions'. You can save both yourself and your site visitors a lot of time if you put the answers to commonly-asked questions on your site. It will reduce the number of queries you get and allow the visitors to find out what they want to know quickly. Examples of FAQs you may want to include are: Do you post overseas? Do you offer personalisation? Can I get one of your products made in a different colour? Do you make to order? Do you sell wholesale or give discounts on bulk orders? What is your refunds policy?

Activity: Organising your site

Make a note of the sections you need to include on your website – both main sections and subcategories. This will help you build the skeleton of your site. For example:

Main category:
- Necklaces

Subcategories:
- Silver
- Aluminum
- Bead
- Semi-precious stones

WEB DESIGN TIPS

This advice is from Rebecca Kimber, managing director and CEO of Create.net.

Plan ahead! You would not open your high street shop without careful consideration around how you will be displaying your products, and a customer's journey. The same goes for when you are building your own online store.

Start by mapping the pages you will want to include on your website and how you want them to be linked. If you are not sure about what the pages will be, think about the content you want to display, then work on grouping similar information to be placed together on the website. This process will help you to form your pages and the links between them.

Designing your site

Following the activity on page 167, you should have a list of all the sections and subsections you want on your site. This list can be combined with the branding you want to use for your site (see chapter 3) and some high quality images to bring this together into your final site. The main thing your site design should consider is the end user. Your company's website should:

- Make it immediately obvious what it is that you do or sell and how to order.

- Be easy for the end user to navigate and get straight to the bits they want. Most people expect to find the navigation options across the top or down the side of the page. If you put them in different places you risk confusing people who may just leave the site. The main categories from your list should be in the menu on the homepage.

- Present all the information a customer needs about your business, products and services. This should be easily visible on the homepage, able to be found within a few seconds. People do not like to click through several pages to get to what they want, so bear this in mind when designing your layout.

- Be full of good quality images to make your site visually appealing and break up the text.

- Be compatible with mobile phones. Many people now browse and buy on their telephone or other mobile gadgets, so it is essential to make sure your website works just as well in a mobile browser as on a computer.

- Make it obvious what you want your customers to do once on your site. Your 'calls to action' (see page 187) need to stand out. If you want people to visit your shop, make sure the shop button is highly visible can be found in a couple of places. If your aim is to get readers to sign up to your newsletter, or follow you on social media, make sure you have a 'come and join us on Facebook/Twitter/Pinterest' message and that the social media icons stand out. Remind people what you want them to do. Do not give them too many options or they can get confused. Do not distract them with flashing gadgets, lots of moving pictures, or bright adverts which send them off your site.

- Be easy to share with their friends. Throughout your site you want to have social media share buttons, and 'pin it' buttons to encourage people to share your products and promote your site for you.

Presenting information

Drop-down menus work well for presenting information. Rather than having to click from one section to another, a customer can hover the mouse over the area they want and choose from the drop-down.

First impressions

Bear in mind that the top half of the page — referred to as 'above the fold' — is what people see without having to scroll down. There needs to be enough above the fold to tempt them to look at the rest of the page, or a call to action in the top part of the page.

Usability and site flow

Ensure your site loads quickly. This is useful from both a SEO point of view and to keep your visitors happy. If a page does not load within a couple of seconds most readers will tend to go elsewhere. Google Analytics can measure the speed of your site and make suggestions on how to speed it up.

Ensure your branding remains consistent throughout the site and make sure your logo is prominent on the home page, and ideally throughout the site. Aim to keep the site visually uncluttered: avoid having huge blocks of text, images and gadgets all over the place. It can be tempting to put as much information on a page as possible – especially your home page – but this can be overwhelming, leaving readers unsure where to click or what to do.

The Google homepage is the perfect example of good design. Almost the entire page is blank other than its logo and the search box in the middle. This tells people exactly what Google wants them to focus upon, using the search box.

A good design will direct people through certain pages of your site, so make sure those pages link together and send people to your desired destination. This 'site flow' is best explained through an example, see below.

Google Analytics

See pages 192–197 for more about optimising your website using Google Analytics.

SITE FLOW EXAMPLE

Assume you have a popular article on buying watercolour paintings on your site. This article gets a lot of Google traffic and social media referrals. You want readers of the article page to come and look at your paintings, so you need something to attract them to your gallery or shop. A big button saying 'browse my artwork here', or a revolving gallery of your paintings on the side of the page with the article on it will draw the eye and encourage a click through, while a simple link at the bottom of the page saying 'shop here' is much less likely to attract attention.

Once the reader is on the gallery or shop page, you want them to either order an existing painting, or to commission a new painting, so present just two clear options for them – buy or commission.

Once they have ordered you may want to encourage them to sign up to your newsletter, or follow you on social media, so have these options highlighted on your sales confirmation page. This will then give you the chance to sell them something else further down the line.

MAKING YOUR PRODUCTS STAND OUT

Tips from Harriet French, PR Executive at Not On The High Street (notonthehighstreet.com).

Photography The way you present your products is key to catching the customer's eye and encouraging them to make a purchase. Product images are hugely advantageous for improving your sales levels. Include as many images per product page as you can, and research simple but effective ways to brush up on your photography skills.

Product titles It is important to think about how you are positioning your products to customers. Product titles are vital in tempting the shopper to click through and see more – they are often the first things your customer will see. Keep product titles clear and concise but make sure they include vital or enticing words such as 'handmade' or 'personalised'. It is always safer to state the obvious than to choose a fancy product title.

Be savvy In order to stand out small businesses need to be very savvy to the ways of online marketing. At Not On The High Street we ask our businesses to make and source brilliant products that we know our customers want; the rest can be left up to us. If business owners also want to have a say in their own marketing, they should have a clear understanding of SEO, social media and the importance of photography and written copy.

Know your customer The customer may not always be right but they are at the heart of your entire business. In order for your business to succeed you need to know your customers well and to be on as good terms with them as you possibly can. The customer should be at the forefront of everything you do for your business – each and every decision should be made based on them. We have had a great experience with our customers; many seem almost as excited as we are to have discovered Not On The High Street. To this day, one of our favourite pastimes is sharing lovely customer comments around the office.

Use of photographs

Your images will do the most to sell your products, so it is incredibly important to use great photographs of your goods in your design. Use a consistent background in your photographs as this will look good when images are displayed together on your site.

The photographs you take can also be used to convey more about your brand, so think carefully about how they should look and do not be afraid to try out different styles until you find what is right for your products.

Include photographs of your items from different angles too, and have these visible in a gallery or lightbox on your product pages. Give your customers the opportunity to see product detailing, close-ups and different angles, this will help them with their purchasing decision.

Space and colour

Sometimes less is more. Do not be afraid of a bit of space. By ensuring that your site is uncluttered and not too busy, you will ensure your photographs draw the eye to reflect the quality and uniqueness of your products. 'White space' is the term for empty space on your page – it does not literally have to be white, but can be your background colour or any other colour. Good use of white space makes your page more inviting and the information easier to read and digest.

Once you have decided on your brand's colour scheme, use it consistently throughout the site. Ask yourself how you want your customers to feel: calm and relaxed or alert and excited? Feed this through to the types of colours you use in your site design. Soft pastels will relax whereas bright colours will excite, for example. See page 72 for more on the use of colour in your brand.

Your shop

If you are selling online, your shop will be a very important part of your website. It has to be very easy to navigate, so people can find what they want in the minimum amount of time. The use of clear categories and subsections will help, as will a text search box so people can type in what they are looking for.

- Consider categorising your products to help people browse the products that interest them most. Many online fabric shops, for example, allow you to search their range by colour, by fabric type, by designer/manufacturer and by collection. Write a full keyword-rich product description for each item so that people can not only find your product through search engines but also when using the search box on your site.

- To encourage people to order more items, add a 'related products' section under your product image and description – if they are looking at a knitted hat, show them the matching scarf and gloves too. Amazon is the perfect example of a company that does this well with its 'customers who bought this also bought' section under the product details. I know I have certainly ended up ordering a few extra items when I look at them. An alternative or complementary option to this is the option of 'add-ons' at the cart stage.

- Make sure you have a good selection of high quality images of your products, as explained in chapter 3. Allow your customers to see the whole item and perhaps a lifestyle shot showing it in use too. Just remember for website use you do not want to be uploading high-resolution images as it will slow your page loading time. Make sure you compress them first.

- Consider your checkout process. Asking people to fill out several pages of information will probably lead to a high drop-off rate as customers grow impatient or annoyed. Keep it to the essentials: name, contact details, delivery address and payment details. Do not have any distractions which may make them click away from the cart and not complete the payment process.

- Make sure your postage cost is clearly visible before the checkout process, not just at the end. Be clear about where you will post to – I wanted to order from an Irish company a while back but nowhere on its site did it tell me if it shipped to the UK, so after reading through several pages of the site I gave up and went elsewhere. You could have a postage tab at the bottom of the site with these details, along with expected delivery times.

Payment options

Related to the shop is payment, and there are many different ways of processing payment, the most popular of which are explained in the payment gateways box below. As with postage costs, it is useful to indicate before the end of the checkout what payment options you accept. You can do this by showing the logos of the cards or payment systems you accept or communicating these details at the very start of the payment process, not the end.

> ### Add-ons
>
> My friend Dionne runs a piñata website and when people checkout it asks them if they want to add on a filling for the piñata, or the stick with which to hit the piñata. Could you do something similar with your products?

PAYMENT GATEWAYS

Using a well-known brand will help to create a sense of trust in your customers; this is important because many people are wary of internet fraud. I have put a few other payment processing options in the useful links section, but here are the most common.

- Paypal is one of the most recognised and trusted payment services. Easy to integrate into your site, Paypal allows people to pay using a special Paypal account, or using their credit or debit card.

- World Pay are another well known payment merchant, plus many of the banks have their own payments systems you can integrate into your site.

- For regular payments/direct debits Go Cardless is a good alternative to Paypal.

- Braintree is excellent if you are handling multiple currencies. It will allow you to accept over one hundred and thirty different currencies with no extra processing charges. It also has a recurring payment option and handles a lot of mobile transactions.

When weighing up the different payment gateways, consider the following:

- Fees: both monthly and/or per transaction.

- Ease of integration into your site.

- How well the gateway meets your needs. Can they process different currencies, or subscription payments, for example?

- Is there an option to use discount codes or reduce prices across the site when you want to run a promotion?

- If you want to take payments at shows and events, over the phone, or in a physical shop, check the gateway has mobile processing options.

- Support. Can you call someone if you need help? Are there help forums, useful FAQ sections? How quickly will they reply to an e-mail? Are they available out of hours?

If you are unsure of what to go for, ask around and see which payment options other people recommend, and if they have had problems with any of them. You could use market research questions (see pages 18–19) to ask your target market which payment methods they prefer to use; or try looking on craft forums or small business forums for advice.

Be creative!

Once you have figured out what will be on your site, how it will look, and what payment system you will be using, it is time to put it all together into your website design.

Given that you run a creative business, be creative with your website too. Add quirky touches, buy illustrated social media buttons or design your own, avoid the standard commercial look website and make yours unique. The little touches are what will make your website stand out from all the others.

Beautiful buttons

You can buy artist-made graphics, or buttons to add to your website on sites like Etsy or Creative Market.

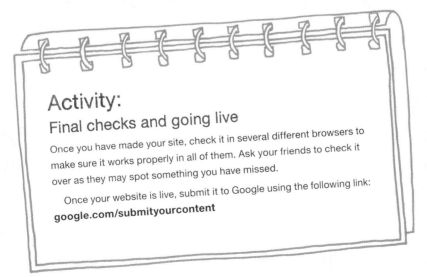

Activity:
Final checks and going live

Once you have made your site, check it in several different browsers to make sure it works properly in all of them. Ask your friends to check it over as they may spot something you have missed.

Once your website is live, submit it to Google using the following link:

google.com/submityourcontent

Search engine optimisation

Search engine optimisation, or SEO, is the practice of trying to get your site to rank well in search engines so that people can find and visit it.

SEO can seem very daunting when you first start looking into it, and can get really complex if you want. However, it is essentially based on common-sense principles, so you do not need to be technologically gifted to make sense of it.

Bear in mind that the search engines' goal is to make sure that people get the most relevant search results to their query. You will find that most of the factors they consider relate to that goal.

GOOGLE

Google Search, commonly known simply as Google, is the most-used search engine in the world, with more than three billion searches a day. There are millions of websites on most subjects so in order to ensure the most relevant sites appear at the top of people's searches, Google has a system known as the 'Google algorithm'. Google does not reveal exactly how its algorithm calculates how it ranks pages, so the majority of what we know comes from hints and guidelines given by Google and from people finding out what works and what does not work.

Google is constantly adapting its algorithm to attempt to combat spammers, so quick fixes that fool the search engine now may not work in a year's time. The best advice that I can give is to concentrate on delivering what your customers want and not to focus on tricking Google to optimise your results in the short-term. Google measures various factors which tell them how much people like your website, so the more customer focused you are the more Google will see that people like your site and will rank it higher. Some of the main factors that Google and other search engines consider when ranking a page are summarised on the opposite page.

Search engine strategy

SEO is not just one technique. Focusing on just one aspect will not reap the full benefits of SEO, and you risk losing everything if the search engines alter their method of measuring rankings. If you have a strategy that combines all four of the main points below, you should be relatively unaffected by any future changes to Google's algorithm.

Quality content Optimising content for search engines does not mean ramming it with keywords, as this can compromise the information's usefulness and readability – its quality. Make your content unique and do not use content from elsewhere on the web. The more people like your content the more likely they are to link back to it, or to share it on social media. The content does not have to be written by you. Invite people to guest post on your site or pay people to write for you if writing is not your strength. Base content around your keywords so you attract the right kind of traffic with your content (see the Keywords activity on page 183 and content ideas on page 186 for more on this).

Backlinks If your site is linked to from other well-ranking sites, Google considers your site to be important too. You can check your backlinks in Google Webmaster Tools (see pages 198–199). Offer to guest post or give people a reason to write about you: set competitions and offers or write interesting news and great content that people will want to share. Your backlinks should develop as organically (naturally) as possible, and also to build over time. Google can track when you have had a sudden unnatural increase in backlinks, so concentrate on building over time and not just putting your link everywhere you can find or paying for backlinks.

Social share Google places importance on the amount your content is shared socially. They see this as a sign that your site has quality content. Make it easy for people to share your content by adding share buttons to your site, using good quality images for people to pin to Pinterest and having your own social media accounts so followers can share your updates directly from your social media pages. Having good quality content or something of interest is more likely to lead to social shares, so this also links back to the quality content point above.

Regularity If your site is regularly updated, it shows search engines that the site is still active, kept up to date and worth them directing people to. Having a news section or blog on your site is an easy way to do this, but any section that you can regularly add new content into will help. This might be a projects section, articles section, special offer section, trends section, or a combination of these. Remember to go over your existing content from time to time and update that too. Re-promote older content as well as adding new content to drive a steady stream of traffic to both, indicating to Google that it is still relevant.

Anchor text

Anchor text is the visible part of a clickable link to a site. It usually appears blue so you know it is a link. Google used to place importance on those words which contained the link, – if you had lots of sites linking back to you with the link embedded into the words 'quality glass beads', Google would assume that keyword is relevant to your site. Of course, before long people started manipulating this and paying for sites to link to them using specific anchor text. Since realising this, Google has changed its algorithm; when it sees a site with lots of identical anchor text on its inbound links, it now disregards them.

Keywords

Keywords are the words or phrases that people are most likely to type into search engines when looking for your website, or the products you sell. Keywords are very important when it comes to SEO. They tell the search engines what your website is about and allow them to match your site to specific search queries. Focus on using the right keywords in your online marketplace and on social media too – in fact, anywhere that search engines can scan and index content.

People tend to use different words when looking for the same thing. People looking for sewing classes might type 'sewing workshops', 'sewing lessons', 'sewing tuition', 'sewing school', 'sewing teachers', 'sewing tutors', or 'sewing courses'. If you only use the keyword 'sewing classes' on your site you could miss people who are searching using the other terms.

The more specific your keywords, the less competition there will be on the search engines' results. For instance, if you type in 'sewing classes' to Google you get almost twenty-four million results! The more specific 'sewing classes Cardiff' has under 300,000 results so including the keyword 'Cardiff' in your site already improves the odds of your site being seen. The more specific you are, the fewer results: for 'beginner's dressmaking classes Cardiff' you are down to 24,000 results, 'beginner dressmaking classes Roath' (Roath is a district of Cardiff) gives you just over a thousand results. Geographical location is just one way of breaking down your keywords. Consider the materials you use, the style of your products or how your products are used to get more specific keywords.

Learn from the competition

Why not put some of your competitor's websites into the keyword tool to see if it gives any useful keywords for your own?

Further reading

To learn more about keywords I recommend reading the following link: seomoz.org/blog/how-to-rank

HELP ON KEYWORDS

If you want more help on coming up with keywords for you site, take a look at the Google Keywords tool (see page 211) or one of the many other alternatives. These tools allow you to generate similar keywords to one you suggest, or you can put in a website and it will generate keywords based upon the content of that site. Not only will it suggest keywords for you but it will tell you how many searches per month those keywords tend to get.

Activity: Identifying your keywords

Grab a notebook and write down the words that you think are important and relevant to your site and the products you sell or service you offer. These words will be your starting point. For example, if you run a sewing school in Cardiff called Stitched Up, write down words and phrases like: sewing, sewing school, learn to sew, sewing classes, Cardiff, Stitched Up and so on.

Refine your list

Go back to your list and think of alternative ways of saying each of the keywords. Write those alternate keywords below the initial keywords. Get other people to suggest refinements, as we all tend to use slightly different language.

Be more specific

Break your list down into more specific keywords. You should now have a long list with lots of keywords phrased in different ways, and broken right down to the specific terms you think your target customers will be using in search engines.

Incorporating keywords into your site

Once you have a list, incorporate these keywords into your site or shop. Your options include:

In the text Fit different keywords into your content, but make sure it sounds natural. Write for people, not search engines.

Page titles Give your page a relevant title, but try to keep it to the point so people can see at a glance what they will get.

Product titles or descriptions Again, use different keywords for each of these. If the product title is 'Bespoke red leather bag', use 'A unique handmade handbag made from leather, lined with Liberty fabric and closes with a magnetic clasp' for the description to avoid duplication.

Meta descriptions The meta description is a summary of your page that shows in search results and when people share on Facebook. Use these to encourage people to click through. Do not just leave them blank! Try to keep meta descriptions under one hundred and sixty characters, otherwise search engines will cut them down.

Headings and subheadings These are great for breaking up your text and making it more readable but also allow you to emphasise your keywords.

Image titles Never give your images generic names like 'image 1'. Give them relevant titles using your keywords so people find them when doing an image search. If you are using several images on a page, give each a slightly different title: it is the perfect chance to get alternate versions of your keywords in.

Image description Use different keywords or phrasing for the description and title of an image in order to get more alternate keywords in.

Link descriptions When you add a link into your text or to an image, you have to chance to describe that link. This is another chance to squeeze in more relevant keywords.

Using keywords effectively

Meta tags are a way of adding keywords to your site. When adding new content or pages to your site, many sites will generate a keywords box. Keywords typed into that box show as meta tags on your site. You can also add keywords directly in your html. Due to people using adding large numbers of often unrelated keywords which they thought would help them rank well, Google declared in 2009 that meta tags would no longer make any difference to their ranking. As a result, do not waste time planning the perfect list of meta tags for your page. Instead, concentrate on having an enticing meta description which will encourage people to click through to your page when they spot you in search results.

On blogs this is slightly different; you have the option to add keywords to your blog post which can allow you to divide your posts into categories. This can be useful for helping people navigate your blog content when you have a lot of posts so I would continue to use these for that purpose even if it has no SEO benefit.

Focus on a few related keywords at a time and plan your content around them. Work through existing pages on your site to see if you can fit the keywords in anywhere (see page 183). With that done, track how well you are ranking for the keywords using Google's Webmaster Tools (see pages 198–199). After a few months, pick another few keywords and repeat. This focused approach is much less overwhelming than trying to work with all your keywords at once. Remember: SEO is a long-term strategy. You do not have to do everything at in one go.

Lists

Keep your list of keywords by your computer so you can refer to it when adding products to your shop, or content to your site. With the list in easy reach, you will likely be able to sneak a few keywords in to any addition to your site.

SOME INTERESTING SEO FACTS

A 2011 study by content promotion agency Slingshot SEO (slingshotseo.com) found that:

- 1st place in Google gets you 18.2 per cent of all click-through traffic.
- 2nd place gets you 10.1 per cent.
- 3rd Place gets you 7.2 per cent.
- 4th Place gets you 4.8 per cent.
- 5th place or lower gets you under 2 per cent.

The Search Engine Journal (searchenginejournal.com) found that:

- 75 per cent of users never go past the first page of search results.
- 70–80 per cent of users focus on the organic results, and ignore paid results completely.
- 65–70 per cent of internet searches are done through Google.
- Search engines are the number one source of traffic to content sites, sending more traffic than social media.

SEO FOR BEGINNERS

This advice is by Ruth Burr, inbound marketing lead at Moz consultancy (moz.com), a leading authority on SEO.

Whenever possible, build your website with SEO in mind. Often, businesses will design, build, and launch a website and only then call in someone to 'do SEO' to it. This usually means there is more SEO work to do and that changes will be harder and more expensive than if SEO was a consideration in the first place. Part of building your website to be SEO-friendly from the beginning is making sure you choose a content management system (CMS) or platform that allows you to make back-end changes to the website; it also means having someone on staff or under contract to make continuing changes to your site. Too many companies hire a 'one-and-done' developer to build their sites and end up stuck with a website that they cannot improve.

Think of the processes of getting inbound links to your site and getting social shares and likes of your content as one giant strategy. To that end, make sure it is easy to share your content on social networks, and start building your social followings so that when you have something really cool to share, you have people with which to share it. It is tempting to buy links or to resort to get-links-quick strategies like submitting to many online directories, but the best links are ones that will drive potential customers to your site, not merely links for links' sake. If you are outsourcing link building be wary of companies who promise a set number of links per month; instead, look for vendors that focus on stellar content creation, promotion and relationship building to get the right links.

If there is one area to invest in, it is content. Do not fall into the trap of thinking 'I work in a boring industry.' You have a lot to say. Investing in a long-term content strategy will ensure you have plenty of unique content that earns links (something search engines love) and gives you an opportunity to engage with your customers (something people love). It is the foundation of a good SEO campaign and helps you build your brand online.

Content and SEO strategy

The main focus of your SEO strategy should be relevant content; if you have good content, people will find, share and link to it. If you use social media, guest posts, work with other sites or blogs to get the word out there, your content will be discovered more often and more quickly.

Content is the core of a long-term strategy. It takes time to build up and to be picked up by search engines and other people, but it does pay off. Once search engines recognise that you have good content on your site, any new content you add jumps up the rankings a lot more quickly.

Types of key content

The following types of content should help you attract plenty of visitors to your site or blog.

Evergreen posts These are posts that will always be popular and get lots of traffic. They are normally problem-solving posts or questions: How can I do x? Where can I find y? How can I use z? Evergreen posts can also be the kind that save people time. If you sell cloth and create a post with links to fifty great projects using linen, followers can go to your site and choose the project that sounds most like what they were searching for rather than trawling through hundreds of blogs or search engine results.

Evergreen posts are the sort most likely to be bookmarked or shared on social media. They save visitors time and make things easier for them, and you benefit by including keywords relevant to your business in those posts. Identify relevant subjects that people search for time and time again (use keyword tools to help with this). Do not think only in terms of current trends; what will people still be searching for in three, five or ten years' time?

Linkable assets Similar to evergreen posts, linkable assets are content that people want to link to. They will generate you a lot of natural back links over time. Unlike evergreen posts, they are not limited to being articles; they could be a video, a free download, a software program, or a free tool or e-course.

On-trend content This kind of content may not have long-term benefits but can be give short-term results. It can be related to a season or date: Christmas, or St. Valentine's day for example. While there is only a limited amount of time that these will be relevant, they can attract a lot of traffic in that time. Updating and re-promoting such posts the following year will pay dividends.

On-trend content can also be based upon current events, industry shows, a hot new product, or even a new television series.

Benefiting from your content

There is no point driving lots of traffic to your site and not informing or reminding visitors people what you actually do, sell or offer. It is important to link from your content to your end goal – to your shop if you are selling products, or to your workshop timetable if you teach. Add a sentence at the end saying 'if you liked this, try this product' or 'if you want to learn more about this, book onto one of our classes'. You may be able to squeeze this link into the article itself, or add a box or banner on the side or top of the page.

When writing content or creating something for your site, it may not be immediately apparent that it will become an evergreen post or linkable asset. Keep an eye on your analytics to see if anything is attracting a large amount of traffic, then make sure you keep it updated and promoted.

The key to event-led content is speed. Be ahead of everyone else. Get as much information as you can and post as soon as possible after the event. This gives you something to promote that people to look at immediately, but which can be clarified and updated when you have more time.

Be fast when writing about trends. If you know someone is bringing out an innovative product in your area, find out as much as possible and get a post live before it hits the shops. When people hear about the product and start searching for details, your post will be ready for them to find, and at that early stage it is likely to be one of the few posts from which to choose. A few months later you will probably find that others have written about the subject and you will have more competition for the front page of Google and other search engines, but you will have already benefitted from your prompt action.

When writing about trends, remember that you do not need to know everything. Even some basic details and some (properly flagged) speculation can form a good post. Let people know there is only limited information available but that you will update the post when more emerges. Follow manufacturers, wholesalers and distributors to keep on top of upcoming products and trends. Industry trade shows are also very good for this.

Immediate results

When **The Great British Sewing Bee** was on television, I wrote posts featuring the supplies used and put them live immediately after each episode. Those posts trebled my site traffic that month! Even once the initial rush was over I gained an extra 15–20,000 regular monthly visitors as a result of those posts, which took only an hour each.

Activity: Generate ideas

Brainstorm and note down content ideas for your site. What customer queries could you resolve? What news could you tell everyone about? What ideas can you share? If you are at a loss for ideas, ask your customers what they want on your site.

Taking it further

Draw up an editorial calendar of content for the next year. Where possible, tie it in with seasonal or industry events.

Other factors to consider in your content

Site speed People like things to be fast when browsing the internet. When they click on a page they expect it to load quickly, so site speed is one of the factors Google take into account when ranking. In Webmaster Tools they will tell you how your site speed is doing and what you can do to speed it up. Images and gadgets can slow a site, so make sure you compress your images and that you do not overload your site with widgets/gadgets. If possible check your site loading speed before adding them, and again afterwards to see if it adversely affects your speed. Some types of adverts slow or crash sites so be careful with what you add to your site.

Bounce rate People can bounce – that is, leave your site after a few seconds without clicking to any other pages – for a variety of reasons. One can be because the content was not what they were looking for. If this is the case you may want to check you are using relevant keywords. Google can take a high bounce rate from traffic they have sent to you as an indicator that your site is not resolving the search query and push you down the rankings for those particular keywords. Google Webmaster Tools will show you how you rank for various keywords, so make sure they are relevant.

People may also bounce because they cannot make sense of your content or find it to be low quality. They can be put off by poor web design or slow loading speed. Check your bounce rate in Google Analytics and if it is high, assess your site with a critical eye. If you cannot work out why the rate is high, ask a few friends or other business people to take a look over it for you.

Internal linking Having lots of links between the various sections of your site helps search engines to index your content to ensure they discover all the content on there and not just some of it. A good way to do this is to include references and links to other articles on your site in the article you are currently writing; or, at the end of the post have something directing people to another part of your site, such as 'if you liked this why not look at our projects section' or 'find our latest new and offers here'. This also helps your site visitors to discover other parts of your site too.

The copywriting site Copyblogger is a great example of good internal linking. If you read any of its articles, you will find embedded links to many of their other articles, products or services. It is hard to just read one page of the Copyblogger site as you find yourself clicking through to many others.

Be relevant

When I started my site, I was confused to find I was getting lots of traffic for the word 'logo'. Eventually, I discovered the cause – when uploading company logos to my directory I had named the images with the company name followed by the word 'logo'. Having mentioned that word over one hundred times, Google presumed my site had a lot of information about logos!

GUEST POSTING

Matt Cutts, head of Google web spam, confirmed in January 2014 that guest blogging as a strategy to get more backlinks and help improve your rankings will not work (source: mattcutts.com/blog/guest-blogging). Once again, it is an area that has been abused by spammers to the point that Google is now having to stop using it in its ranking algorithm.

However, that is not to say that you should not guest post. Guest posting is a great marketing strategy because it can help introduce you and your brand to a whole new range of potential customers or followers. So keep it in your marketing plan but do not expect any SEO benefits from it.

Concentrate on making your content as good as you can. As Matt Cutts put it: 'Try and make a site so that is so fantastic that you become an authority in your niche'.

A CALL TO ACTION

A call to action is a prompt towards the action you want your site visitors or social media followers to take. It is a way of reminding people what you want them to do – whether that is placing an order, attending an event, or joining your newsletter.

The example below shows a call to action on my website – the grey button with a link to sign up to my newsletter (highlighted).

Analysing your site

This section explains how to use Google Analytics and Webmaster Tools to help measure the performance of your site, your online advertising, social media campaigns and SEO efforts. It is important to keep track of whether these efforts are paying off – if not you need to re-think your strategy or focus elsewhere.

Google provides free and very useful tools that help measure traffic to your site and how you are doing in terms of SEO. There are of course other analytics providers (see the links section for more) but the two I cover here are widely used and free, which is always good for a small business. Just to warn you, checking your site's stats can be addictive!

You need a free Google account to register Analytics and Webmaster Tools, but both are fairly simple to set up. Both tools generate a line of code which you need to insert into your website to prove you own the site. Once inserted, the program will start to track traffic to your site. You can register multiple websites at no charge. You can also add other team members or your web company to the account so they can also view your stats.

The fastest way to learn how to use these programs is to click through the different links and see what information it brings up. Do not be afraid to explore the different options and experiment – you will find useful new information all the time.

updates

Keep an eye on this book's accompanying website craftacreativebusiness. co.uk for further information on these tools as they are updated.

OTHER ANALYTICS

Sites like Facebook and Pinterest have their own analytics that give more precise stats for interactions with your accounts. To access the Pinterest analytics you need a business account. You can convert a personal account into a business account in the account settings.

USEFUL TERMS

Bounce rate The number of people that visit just one page of your site, then leave.

Conversion rate The number of people that complete a goal you specify, such as purchasing from your site, viewing certain pages or signing up to your newsletter.

CTR This stands for 'click through ratio', which is the percentage of people seeing your site in search results (or viewing your adverts) that go on to visit your site.

Direct traffic Visitors who typed your web address (URL) into their browser taskbar and went straight to your website – i.e. people who already knew your web address.

Impressions Impressions are the number of times something (such as a webpage or advert) is seen by viewers. For example, an advert may have one hundred impressions and eighteen click-throughs; which means that only eighteen of the one hundred people that saw it clicked on it (an eighteen per cent CTR).

Landing page The first page people see when they visit your site – the page they 'land' on. Note that this is not always your homepage.

Referral traffic Traffic sent to you from other websites. This could be due to online adverts, guest posting or someone writing about you on their site or blog.

Organic search The number of people finding your site through search engines such as Google or Bing.

Social referrals People who come to your site from social media platforms like Facebook, Twitter and Pinterest. These visitors include those referred from your own social media accounts along with those referred by others who have posted links to your site on these platforms.

Traffic sources Where the visitors to your site are coming from.

Unique visitors or page views Some people will visit your website more than once, or view a page more than once on your site. The 'unique' figure counts visitors to the site only once, not once per visit or view.

Google Analytics

To set up Google Analytics, visit google.co.uk/analytics and follow the instructions to set up your account. This service can tell you many useful things, including the following:

- Exactly how many hits you have had per day.

- Where the hits came from, including how many from search engines and how many from referring sites.

- What content is most and least popular on your site.

- Which search engines people used to find your site, along with what keywords those people used.

- What browsers your visitors are using so you can ensure your site is compatible with those browsers.

- Your bounce rate: how many visitors look at only one page of your site, then leave.

- What percentage of visitors convert, i.e. complete an action you specify, such as purchasing a product.

Keeping a close eye on Google Analytics' statistics for your site will make you aware of any potential problems as soon as they start, and help you measure any successes accurately. If you do something that leads to a huge surge in traffic, you want to know as soon as possible so you can quantify and replicate that success. Equally, if you do something that causes your traffic to plummet, the sooner you know, the sooner you can resolve it to get your traffic back to normal levels.

Google Analytics is a powerful tool that can help you with many aspects of your business, including helping you identify and track which areas of your business are best for you to invest your time and money. If you are spending hundreds of pounds in advertising, for example, you want to be able to track the response you are getting in order to check it is a worthwhile investment. If you are spending large blocks of time writing content for your site, the statistics can show you the traffic the content is attracting, and the results of the visits. If you are considering investing in a mobile site, it will allow you check that your site visitors do actually view it on mobile devices.

Save and export

You can save and export any of the reports in Google Analytics by using either the e-mail or export options.

My experience

I use Google Analytics to make sure I am advertising in the right places online, and getting my money's worth. I also use it to make sure my social media, SEO and content marketing strategies are paying off. From looking at the statistics for my site I can see what is and what is not working, and where to concentrate my efforts to increase my levels of traffic.

Site traffic

When you visit the Google Analytics homepage for your site, the first thing you are presented with is the site traffic for the last month in the form of a graph with a summary of some basic statistics written underneath. At a glance you can see which days you have had a lot of traffic and which days have been quiet. You can see how many visitors visited your site in the last month, how many pages they visited on average and how long they spent on your site on average.

If you want to change the date period – to view the whole last year for instance, or to check out today's traffic – click on the box with the dates in the top right corner and adjust them. Remember to press the 'apply' button after you have selected the dates you want.

Under the date box there is a tick box to compare the dates with another date period. You can use this to see how your traffic is improving over time. Keeping an eye on the amount of traffic you get to your site can be useful to help see the following:

- Whether your SEO efforts are improving your traffic.

- Whether adverts you have are generating traffic.

- What social media activity increases your traffic.

- Which content you have added is bringing new visitors.

- Peaks and troughs in your traffic.

Annotations

Clicking the grey downward-pointing arrow just under the dates on the bottom of the graph will show a 'create new annotation' option. You can use this to make notes about any events which led to an increase or decrease in traffic for you. When you look back on your stats in the future it will help you remember why your traffic was so different that day.

Activity: Looking for patterns

Look at your website stats for the last year (or the last few weeks if you have not had Analytics running for long) and look for any pattern in your peaks and troughs. Write down the day of the week that tends gets the most traffic, and the day of the week that gets the least traffic in your notebook.

Try to identify any reasons that these days are busy or quiet. If the reasons are something within your control – for instance, if Monday is always busy because you add new products that day, or weekends are always quiet because you do not do any social media updates at weekends – plan to try to increase your traffic on the lower-traffic days. Some examples for achieving this are below:

- If you do not update at weekends because you are not working, consider prescheduling your weekend updates.
- Space out adding new content over a few days, rather than in one big update.
- Run a special offer on the quieter days to increase traffic.

It is important to realise that some things are out of our control. If your traffic drops at weekends because people are not at their computers, there is not much you can do about that. Rather than trying to increase your traffic on those days, save your content for the weekdays when more people will spot it.

Acquisition

The 'acquisition' tab on the Google Analytics menu (on the left of the site) contains information on how people found your site. The 'overview' option in the submenu will bring up a summary and tell you about visitors' behaviour and conversion rate. This is split by traffic source, so you can find how long visitors from a particular source stayed on the site, how many pages they looked at, and the bounce rate.

This lets you see if certain sources attract better quality traffic than others. Site visitors who spend time or purchase something from your site are good quality traffic; those that just read one page and then leave are not. This information can help you prioritise. For example, If you spot that visitors who come via your newsletter tend to place double the number of orders than visitors from other sources, focus your efforts on getting more newsletter sign-ups. If visitors from Pinterest have a very high bounce rate and low order rate, you need to either re-think your Pinterest strategy or spend less time on there.

Selecting 'search engine optimisation' and then 'queries' under the acquisition submenu will reveal a list of the top ten keywords used in searches to find your site. Click on the arrows in the bottom right corner to see other keywords that people used to find you, then compare the results to your keyword list that you generated earlier (see page 183) to see which keywords are proving effective.

Next to the keywords you can see the following headers:

- **Impressions** How many times your site appeared in search results viewed by a user.

- **Clicks** How many people using that keyword in a search clicked through to your website.

- **Average position** Where you ranked in Google for that particular keyword.

- **CTR** This is the click through rate – the number of people who saw your site link in their search results and clicked through to visit.

Selecting any of these headers allows you to sort the results based upon that metric. Clicking on 'average position' will allow you to see your rank in Google for those keywords, for example.

Clicking on 'all referrals' in the menu on the left-hand side of the site will list the sites sending traffic through to you. This information can help you assess the effectiveness of your social media campaigns, any online adverts you have run and any guest posts you have written for other sites. It can also help you see when someone has written about you. Click on the name of the website to see the exact page from which they linked to you. Click the double square symbol (with an arrow on the top square) to the right of the website name to load the webpage the traffic came from. The 'social' tab in the sub menu on the left will give you a more detailed breakdown of traffic from social media and blogs.

> ## Protected keywords
>
> The phrase 'keyword not provided' is common. Search keywords are protected while logged into a Google account, so data from people using one is not provided in the stats.

194

Each of the referral sections (social, search engine optimisation, etc.) has a landing pages tab on which you can click. This shows you which specific page of your site visitors first visited (landed on). This lets you see if any particular products on your site are ranking well in search engines, or being linked to by a lot of other sites, or shared a lot on social media.

Behaviour

The 'behaviour' tab shows you how people act once they are on your site. Click on the overview tab to get the summary of this information including page views, average time spent per page and bounce rate. You also get a list of the top ten most popular pages on your site in that period. You will normally find one that just says '/'. This signifies your home page.

On the bottom right of the page you can click 'view full report' to see the full list of content viewed on your site in order of popularity. Clicking any of the content page names will show you a breakdown of how many clicks it got per day. You can also find out which sources sent traffic to that page. If you want to see how many people have looked at a particular page of your site, use the search box to the top right of the list to type in the page name to bring it up.

Just under the graph to the left, there is an option that says 'secondary dimension'. This allows you to break the data down further. Selecting 'acquisition' and then 'source' in that menu will show you where the traffic to that particular page originated. There are plenty of other options there to play round with too to get even more detailed data. Getting as much information as possible about your site visitors will help you attract more.

Take a look at the 'in-page analytics' option under the behaviour tab too. Select the 'load in full view' option to load your home page and show you exactly where people are clicking on that page, and what percentage of that page's traffic click on each individual link. You can then click through to other pages on your site to see where people click on those pages. Studying this is fascinating, as site visitors often click where you least expect them to – I could spend hours looking at this!

Site speed

The 'behaviour' tab also gives information about site speed and help to identify ways to improve your site speed.

Audience

The 'audience' tab tells you more about your visitors – which countries they are from, what age and gender they are, what browsers they are using, and more. A few things worth looking at under this tab are:

Browsers Seeing which are the audience's most popular browsers will allow you to make sure your website works as it should in them. You can find this under the 'technology' subheading.

Mobile If many of your visitors use smartphones or tablets to view your site, be sure that your site works well on these devices.

Demographics This details the age and gender of your visitors. Aim your content appropriately and appeal to your target audience.

Geo Use this to see where your visitors are based geographically. Click on a country to break it down further by region or city.

The information in this tab can help you ensure you are reaching the correct audience with your marketing and SEO efforts. It is worth cross-referencing this with the notes you made on your ideal customer (see page 16) to see if your customer base is what you expected it to be. The results may surprise you.

Conversions

The 'conversions' tab helps you set goals. Using the goal setting function in Google Analytics allows you to check if visitors to your site are doing what you want them to do, which shows you whether your site is fulfilling its purpose.

For instance if you want to track how many people spend money on your site you can create a goal to measure that. If you want your visitors to sign up to your newsletter, or visit a particular page of your website you can set goals to record how many people do so.

Geo

The Geo information is particularly useful if you have just done an event or advertising in a particular location and want to see if people are looking you up there as a result.

USING YOUR EVERGREENS

Most websites have a few 'evergreen' pages – those that, like evergreen content (see page 186), continually attracts steady amounts of traffic. When you identify your evergreen posts, make sure you update them every now and then. Keep building on them and putting more information in them and they will keep attracting good amounts of traffic.

Make sure your call to action (see page 189) is included on each of these reliable pages to remind people what you want them to do while on your site. You do not want them to simply read one post and then leave your site again.

The four types of goals you can set are as follows:

Destination goals Getting people to visit a particular part of your site, such as the 'transaction complete' screen which would show they have placed an order.

Duration goals Measuring visits which last for or exceed a particular period of time. Visitors staying on your site for more than five minutes, for example.

Pages/screen goals Tracking how many visitors look at a particular number of pages or screens. For example, if a visitor views eight pages (or the number you choose) on your site, this type of goal is recorded as completed.

Event goals This is completed when a visitor performs a specific action such as clicking on an advert or a social share button.

Bear in mind that you do not have to have a shop on your site to set goals. Even if you do not sell any products on your site, you can track particular content on the site that you want people to view.

Using this tab, you can specify the web address (URL) that you want to track and you can see not only how many people visited that page, but what their route through the site was, which pages fed traffic into your goal page, and where the visitors went after that. You can use this information to try to refine your site flow, as described on page 175.

Using Google Analytics

The best place to get information on how to set goals and track e-commerce is in the Google Analytics help section (support.google.com/analytics), which walks you through the practical side step by step, so I will not repeat it here.

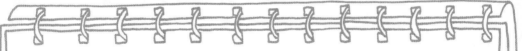

Activity: Increasing traffic

Scroll to the end of your popular content list in Google Analytics and find your site's least popular pages. Ignoring pages which concern a particular event in the past (it is obvious why these are no longer popular!), write down a list of the ten least popular pages in your notebook, along with the number of hits they had last month. Identify why these pages do not get much traffic. Are they old articles you have not re-promoted since writing? Are they for products you no longer sell? Are they not properly linked into the rest of your site?

Next to each of those pages, make notes about ways you can increase the traffic to those pages. Can you post a link on Facebook or Twitter? Could you pin some of the images from those pages onto Pinterest? Could you update them so they are more relevant, then re-promote them? Could you link to those pages from other pages on your site?

Over the next few weeks, work your way through the ten pages and do what you can to increase traffic to each. Repeat this activity on a regular cycle to help drive traffic to the less popular parts of your site.

Google Webmaster Tools

Google Webmaster Tools helps you understand how Google views your site. To set up Webmaster Tools, visit google.com/webmasters. These tools can tell you:

- The number of clicks you are getting for certain search queries.

- Your page speed and how to speed up your site.

- If you are violating Google's policies on spam.

- If there are broken links on your site or pages that do not load.

- The number of impressions and what your average position is in Google for those keywords.

- Incoming site links – i.e. who is linking to your site.

- You can also use the Webmaster Academy, which gives lots of useful SEO information.

In contrast to the data from Google Analytics, which are focused on who is coming to your website, how they found it and what they are looking at, Webmaster Tools is more focused on how your site is perceived by Google, from the point of view of a search engine.

A lot of the data from Webmaster Tools can also be found in Analytics but personally I still prefer to keep both running as there is a lot of useful information you get from them separately. Do not be scared to take a good look through these free resources and learn where to find the information you need to help improve your website.

Main tabs

In Google Webmaster Tools, the navigation bar is on the left-hand side. The main menu tabs give you the following information:

Site messages This is where Google will notify you of any problems with your site such as it being down when they tried to crawl it, your site suffering a spam penalty or being hacked. Keep an eye on these messages!

FETCH AS GOOGLE

'Fetch as Google' is a very useful tool in the Google index section of Webmaster Tools. The tool allows you to give Google a link and ask it to crawl that page. Once it has successfully done that, it will ask if you want to submit it to Google's index, which makes it far more likely to appear in search results.

This is a huge bonus for time-sensitive content, which you want Google to find as soon as possible. This tool will get it indexed straight away so people can find it. It can also be very useful when you first launch your new website and want to make sure it starts appearing in Google straight away.

Timely posts

I used fetch as Google for all of my 'Supplies from The Sewing Bee' posts that I put live straight after the show (see page 187). It is the kind of thing people would be searching immediately and not so much a few weeks or months down the line.

Search appearance How your site appears in the search engine. This section includes alerts about things like duplicated meta tags or titles, or content that cannot be indexed.

Google index This shows the total number of pages indexed from your site. This number should correspond with the number of pages on your site. If it does not, it may mean you have not linked your content into the rest of the site so Google can find it, or you may have recently added pages which have not yet been indexed. If you want them to be indexed quicker use the 'Fetch as Google' tool (see the box on page 198).

Search traffic This tab has useful statistics including 'search queries', which shows where you rank for various keywords, how many impressions you get in search engines for those terms, and what CTR you get. This section also shows you all the links to your site, where they come from and who links to you the most, as well as your most linked-to content. The 'manual actions' tab in this section is where Google will let you know of any spam actions taken against your site, why they were taken and what you can do about it.

Crawl The crawl section will let you know if Google is having any problems crawling your site, if there are any pages which are no longer found or pages that cannot be accessed. This can be useful to see if you have accidentally taken a page offline or password protected something unintentionally.

Interconnecting your site

Associated articles and pages strengthen the authority of an already-popular page as Google identifies your site as having more than one page using those keywords. As a result, your site as a whole will be considered more of an authority on the subject — in this case, birthstones.

Activity: Increasing your popular content

Identify and analyse your most popular pages using Google's tools. Do you spot a trend? Are projects very popular? Is it a particular type of product? Once you know what is popular you can produce more related content elsewhere on your site to increase good quality traffic. You can also make sure you use those pages to link through to the areas where you want to direct more traffic.

If the popular content is a product, consider:

- Producing variations on that product.
- Writing an informational guide about that product.

Assume you sell jewellery, and you identify that birthstone necklaces are very popular on your site. You could add a guide to birthstones; telling people which stones are for which months, explaining the history of the tradition of birthstones in jewellery, and detailing how different counties use different birthstones for different months. When writing the article, include the word 'birthstones' and associated keywords where possible without making the text seem unnatural.

If you also sell birthstone rings then make sure you include a mention and link to them on that popular page to help direct traffic through to other parts of your site which will hopefully lead to sales.

Online advertising

Social media, which we have looked at in more detail in chapter four, is an important way of promoting yourself online, but there are many other ways. Some are paid for – such as Google Adwords or Facebook adverts – and others are free, such as getting press coverage on a website for local or industry news.

However, it is important to track the results of any advertising and promotion that you do, whether you are paying or not. If you are giving out free products in exchange for a mention on a website, for instance, you want to be able to see you are getting results from it, otherwise you are giving something away for nothing. Even if all your are investing is time, you still want to know that it is worthwhile.

You may want to sell advertising space on your site to generate some extra income. There is information on this in this section as well.

ADVERTISING AND PROMOTION

Advertising and promotion both have the same goal, increasing the awareness of your business and ultimately bringing you more sales. However, they are different concepts, and an understanding of this is necessary to get the most from both.

Advertising

Advertising usually takes the form of a set format which will appear in a specified place for a fixed period. You tend to pay a fixed price up front and know that your advert will run for a certain period of time. Advertising includes press adverts, television/radio adverts, online adverts on blogs and websites, and advertorials in magazines.

Promotion

Promotion is a more fluid concept; it is a variety of methods for making people aware of your business. Promotion includes articles in magazines or newspapers, online blog or news posts about your business, giveaways, listings with online directories, social media business pages/accounts, flyers, product demonstrations and samples. It encompasses any way you can think of that gets your business name out there.

Where to advertise?

Advertising – of any kind – can be expensive, so you want to make sure you are putting your money where it will give you the best results. Unfortunately there is no set list of places that guarantee you will get brilliant results; this depends upon the nature of your business, where your customers spend time and the actual adverts you use.

Google Adwords

Google Adwords is a paid-for service that places advertising copy above or to the side of the organic search results. Many online shops do well with Google Adwords, as they can target the precise names of the products they stock, so that when people are looking for those terms they will see their shop.

However there can be a lot of competition for popular terms and it can be expensive, so using this service tends to work best if you have something unusual or hard to find, such as a fabric by a designer not many retailers stock, or a product that not many people make. In addition, bear in mind that seventy to eighty per cent of users ignore paid-for results in search results.

Blogs and networks

If your target customers spend a lot of time browsing blogs for inspiration, then you need to find out which blogs and look into whether you can advertise with them. Not all bloggers accept adverts, so if you cannot advertise, ask if you could work with them in another way, providing supplies for their tutorials, or supplying products for them to give away.

You may identify particular networks where your target customers spend a lot of time. Most social networks now sell advertising so it could be worth experimenting with them. Facebook not only has sidebar adverts but also lets you pay to promote a particular post from your Facebook page, either to just your current fans or to friends of fans too. Facebook adverts can be targeted to a very set demographic and to people with particular niche hobbies. Twitter, Instagram and Pinterest are all going down the sponsored post route now too so take a look on their sites to find out how they work.

Some bloggers use advertising networks like Passionfruit where you can bid to place adverts on certain blogs. These are usually done at a daily or monthly rate. You can also search their database for relevant blogs on which to advertise.

Magazine websites

Many magazines have websites as well as their print publication. It may be cheaper or more measurable to advertise on the site rather than in the magazine itself. You may be able to negotiate a discount if you do both.

Google's vouchers

I have found that if you sign up for a Google Adwords account but do not purchase any Adwords they send you a free voucher after a few weeks. If you do not use that voucher they then send a larger voucher a month or so later to tempt you to try their service. #
I cannot guarantee they will continue to do this forever, but it is worth trying.

Finding out

A customer survey is an excellent way to find out which blogs your customers follow.

Budgeting for advertising

Using the funds allocated to marketing at the business planning stage (see page 44), draw up a monthly budget for advertising and each month look at the different places you could advertise. Try a different place every few months and by the end of the first year you will have a much better idea of where to advertise and where not to. Remember to stick to your budget!

Activity: Advertising your business

Make a list of ten popular websites, magazines and blogs in your industry which you think have a similar target audience to you. Make a point of engaging with them on social media or through their sites/blogs over the next month. Once you have established a connection, look into their advertising costs, and whether they accept guest posts or competition prizes. If they do, approach one at a time with an offer.

Space out the approaches so you are not suddenly appearing in several places at once. People get bored of reading a similar thing over and over, and after that sudden rush the response will die down. It is better to space them out and have one feature per month driving a steady stream of traffic – and customers – to you. This will help to spread the cost, too.

KEY ADVERTISING LESSONS

Advertising your business on other sites

The key to advertising your own business online is identifying where your target customers are and then advertise to them there. There is no point advertising to people who are never likely to purchase from you.

Use your website stats to measure the effectiveness of your adverts and make sure you are still getting value for money. Consider changing your adverts around every few months so that they reach people in different places. This is a good option if you cannot afford to advertise in several different places at once.

Advertising other businesses on your site

People do not want to be one of many, so limit the adverts you sell on your sites. The more advertisers you have the less response they will each see. As your traffic goes up you can add more advertisers, but do not just take as many as possible because you will probably find they will drop of the site after a few months when they do not get much traffic.

Think about how much traffic you would expect to get for the price you charge and ensure your advertisers get the same. If they start to drop under that level, this is a sign you have too many advertisers. If they go well above that, there is space for a new advertiser.

Selling adverts on your site

Of course, rather than buying advertising, you may have a business model that revolves around make money by selling adverts on your own site or blog. If you have a popular site and want to start making money from it, this is a great place to start. To do this you need to have:

- The facility to add adverts to your site or blog (preferably ones you can track).

- Provable statistics for your website. Google Analytics is the best thing for this, as it allows you to extract reports that show how many visitors you get per month. If you run a blog, the number of followers you have is also something advertisers like to know. Find out your page rank too, as some people will ask for that. This helps you to show them how important Google thinks your website is.

- A target list of businesses with which you want to work. Promote products and companies you believe in. If you seem to be promoting anything and everything just for the money, your followers will lose faith in you. In addition, you will not be happy if you feel obliged to promote something you do not really like, and that will show.

- Details of any extras you will offer advertisers. Will they get a mention in your content? An annual feature in the newsletter? The option to run giveaways through your site or blog?

- An idea of how much you want to charge. This part is difficult. It is best to look at other similar sites and blogs to see what they charge to help you decide on the right price for you. Where possible, fix people in for three to six months or longer to reduce the amount of administration you have to do. Offering discounts for longer terms helps to sell a few months at a time.

Once you have your statistics to hand, an idea of what you can offer advertisers and your pricing, contact the businesses on your list and offer them an advert on your site. Explain that you have handpicked them and only want to work with businesses you love. Tell them how it will benefit their business to be working with you and if you have time design a press pack and send it over to them. See the links section on page 211 for more on this.

My incentives

I give my advertisers priority when it comes to editorial content or giveaways. This is a simple but effective incentive that encourages them to advertise with me.

Networks or not

You can sign up to networks like Passionfruit or Google ads but you will have less control over the adverts. I prefer to work directly with my advertisers to make sure I am advertising companies I like and with which I want to work.

The personal relationships you develop with these direct links can also help lead to you working with them in other ways.

Online promotion

Getting your business featured on blogs or websites is another way to get coverage online. There are a few ways to go about this:

Press releases If you have something newsworthy that you think certain website would like to write about, send them a press release and a couple of web size images. Press releases should be reserved for important news: do not send them all the time for every little thing you do with your business. Target only relevant sites who accept press releases – do not annoy people by sending them to anyone and everyone! One of those people you annoy may be someone you want to work with in the future.

Giveaways Most websites and blogs love the offer of a prize for them to give away. It is usually win–win for both parties: the website owner or blogger gets more traffic to their site and gives something back to their readers, while you get promotion and traffic. Where possible, ask them to make the competition question something about your website, so that they direct traffic to you.

Guest posts Many website owners are always on the lookout for good quality content to share with their followers. If you can offer that to them it saves them having to write it themselves. Remember that by guest posting you are asking to use someone else's platform that they have spent time, energy and effort building, so you need to convince them to allow you to use that platform by providing good quality material.

Target your offer appropriately and show how it is relevant to them. The website owner will want to know it is something you are specifically offering to them and not anyone who will reply to your group e-mail. Most website owners that accept your guest post will credit and link back to the writer, and if people like your content they will visit your site to look for more.

Give freebies If you offer a review product or supplies for people to use in their projects that will normally lead to exposure on their site or blog and sometimes social media too. Track the response to the promotion and make sure that is is worth the cost of what you are giving away.

Promote someone else Whether you feature their products, interview them, or ask for their tips on something, if you promote someone else on your site they will often promote you back. If nothing else they will usually share with their followers and send them to the post on your site. Sometimes they will offer to return the favour and feature you on their site or blog.

> ### Finding the right blogs
>
> A great place to find craft blogs split by subject matter is the directory on Craft Blog UK (craftbloguk.blogspot.co.uk).

Building relationships

Wherever possible, try and build a relationship with people before approaching them for promotion. If you have commented on their blog a few times, had a chat with them on Twitter or met them at a show they are more likely to remember you and want to work with you. Make sure you emphasise the benefits for them. They have no obligation to promote you and need to get something out of it too.

Always take the time to find out the name of the person you are approaching and tailor the e-mail to them, not just a 'Dear blogger' type e-mail which will go straight into their trash folder. When an offer of content looks like a form e-mail, most recipients will simply delete it. Taking time to address an e-mail personally and tailor it to the recipient is much more likely to get a response.

If the business you approach does refuse the offer, take it in your professional stride, but do persevere. You could respond by asking if they have any suggestions of how you could work together, or let them know that they can contact you in the future if they need anything. The company might have turned down your offer of a prize because they have their next few months' worth of competitions booked. If they know the offer of your giveaway is still open, they may contact you when planning their next block of contests.

Bad guests

I get endless 'I can write you any content you want so long as you will promote me' types of e-mails. These get ignored: I want to know exactly what you would write for me and how it will benefit my readers.

IS IT WORKING?

The good thing about online advertising and promotion is that it is very easy to measure the results. Using Google Analytics's goal tracking you can see exactly how many site visitors you have received as a result of a particular campaign, how many signed up to your newsletter and even how many of them purchased from you.

Newsletters

Creating a newsletter allows you to build a customer database, which can be more valuable than simply accruing social media followers. Social media is out of your control: if Facebook or Twitter closed down for some reason, or your account got hacked, you could lose all your followers and have no way to contact them. Having a newsletter mailing list means you always have the details of people who are interested enough in what you offer that they have given you their e-mail addresses.

Back up

Make sure you download your mailing list a couple of times a year to keep it backed up.

If you sell anything through your site, add a 'join our newsletter' tick box at the end of the checkout process to encourage customers to join. Take a newsletter sign-up sheet to shows and events that you attend, and have a newsletter sign-up option highly visible on your homepage.

Attracting subscribers

The important things with newsletters is that customers have to 'opt in'. You cannot just add people's details to a database and e-mail them whenever you feel like it – this is spam and will not get good returns. Encourage people to sign up by offering something of interest to them, whether that is a regular delivery of great content, a free download, a discount code, a competition entry or something else. Once signed up, let them know what to expect from you, and when. Will you be e-mailing daily, weekly or monthly? Will the e-mail have special offers, freebies, great content, useful tips or just sales messages? If subscribers do not get what they expect they will unsubscribe or even worse mark your e-mail as junk. Be realistic and up front from the outset as to what people can expect from your newsletter.

The goal of a newsletter

Use newsletters in conjunction with your site and social media to give value to your customers/potential customers. 'Value' means something that viewers will find useful and which will keep them coming back to you. Many newsletters contain free advice or content such as downloadable patterns, technique guides, or free webinars, podcasts and projects. The aim of this is to lead them to your website and to buy from you.

Use your newsletter to support your business. Let people know about any news, things that have recently been added to your website, customer or sponsor's news and any events you are holding. People do expect that there will be a certain amount of promotion in your newsletter but often when it is all promotion it tends to switch people off. People do not like being marketed at but when you mix it with something attractive to them they mind it less.

The benefits of a newsletter

Apart from being in direct contact with people interested in your business, a mailing list will tend to generate a better response than social media when asking for something like a feedback survey to be completed.

You also tend to reach a higher percentage of people through your newsletter than you do through social media.

NEWSLETTERS AND YOUR BUSINESS

Your newsletter should support the goal of your company. For example, the core concept of The Sewing Directory is bringing sewing suppliers, teachers and groups into one place. My website is built around pages with details of current fabric sales, sewing events and places to buy particular themes of fabric (Christmas, Halloween, floral and so forth) so that people do not have to visit lots of sites searching for that information but instead can find them all on my site.

My newsletters – and social media – build on the same goal as my website. I continue to expand on this concept in my newsletter by picking a theme each month and providing details of and links to useful projects and articles relating to that subject. For instance in September I send out a newsletter with a 'back to school' theme; which includes links to bag projects, pencil cases and similar material.

Other themes I have used for my newsletters in the past include working with different fabrics or projects and tips for people learning to sew. In this way, the newsletter becomes an extension of my site, with the subscribers benefitting from getting the content before it goes onto the main site.

Activity: Planning your newsletter

How can you continue the ethos of your company into a newsletter? What can you offer readers to make sure they open your newsletter and stay subscribed? Make a note of some ideas.

You might consider using your newsletter to send exclusive discount codes, access to new products or sales before non-subscribers; or send subscribers useful tips and advice.

Think about some of the newsletters to which you subscribe, and work out why you signed up, why you want to receive them, and what makes you want to read them when they arrive. This might suggest valuable leads on generating your own ideas.

Newsletter providers

You can create your own newsletter using whatever e-mail program you prefer, by you do not have to. There are a number of services, like MailChimp or AWeber, that make creating and sending newsletters easy. Most have design templates for you to use, simple subscriber option processes and detailed statistics. The statistics tell you who has opened your newsletter, what links they clicked within the newsletter, if any newsletters failed to deliver and if so why.

How often to send a newsletter?

Many people are unsure of how often they should be send out a newsletter. Ultimately, the answer comes down to what works best for you and your subscribers. If you have new things to promote every week, along with other useful content or benefits to share that frequently, a weekly newsletter is suitable. Unless you are giving something really valuable that people will take the time to read every day, a daily newsletter is likely to be unwelcome.

   As with social media, consistency is important, do not over-promise and then fail to keep up with what you said you would deliver. If your newsletter is in-depth and takes several hours to draft, a monthly rate is more sensible to ensure you can keep up a regular schedule.

Tempt them in

I promote the sign-up link for my newsletter on social media a few hours before I send it out. I give people a hint about what will be in the newsletter to tempt them to sign up before it is sent.

BUILDING AND RETAINING YOUR READERSHIP

Make sure your newsletter sign-up link is obvious and easy to find on your website to help build your subscriber list. I had mine moved from my menu bar to a box at the top right of the site and my subscription rate tripled! It was so easy to find and one of the first things people saw, so I got a huge number of sign-ups.

   Do not panic if you notice you get people unsubscribing after you send an e-mail. It is normal for a few people to unsubscribe each time. Sometimes they find the content is not what they expected, or they forgot they had signed up, or they may be no longer interested in your business. If you are getting over a five per cent unsubscribe rate then look into the causes. Are you not delivering something interesting? Are you e-mailing too frequently or not frequently enough? Is the newsletter too focused on sales? Once you identify the problem, you can start to fix it.

TOP TIPS FOR NEWSLETTERS

- Think about the timing. When will your target customers be free to read the newsletter? If it is going to work e-mail addresses, then during working hours is best; while sending to personal e-mail addresses will likely get more readers out of hours. First thing on Monday and last thing on Friday are normally not good times. People tend to come into lots of e-mails on the Monday so will skip non-urgent ones, and by late on Friday most people are thinking of the weekend. Of course, if your product or service is more relevant to the weekend that could be an ideal time for you.

- The subject line is important. It needs to tempt the recipients to open it and to be able to see what it is straight away, but it also needs to pass through people's spam filters. Most people are wary of opening e-mails if they are not sure what they are or who they are from.

- Ensure your company branding is on the newsletter so people can see it is a genuine newsletter from you. Also do not forget to include your social media links as this may lead to an increase in your follower numbers.

- Use images! Text-only e-mails are boring. They do not tempt people to click to your site and after the first few, most readers will probably stop even opening them. Make sure the images you use are clickable too.

- Double check all your links. You do not want to have to re-send an e-mail and risk annoying people because your links did not work. If they do not work most people will just give up and not bother trying to figure out what the link is or find it another way. Send yourself a test e-mail and check that the links work before you send it to your mailing list.

While they wait

Consider setting up an auto responder, which automatically sends an e-mail to new newsletter subscribers a set time after they join. You can use this to direct them to the most popular content or products on your site, or to offer them an exclusive discount whilst they wait to receive your newsletter.

USEFUL LINKS AND FURTHER READING

General online selling advice

Tips for choosing a domain name:
agreatplacetobe.co.uk/get-started/whats-in-a-name

Checking domain availability or ownership:
whois.com

Free websites:
wix.com; moonfruit.com; weebly.com; yola.com; wordpress.com; blogger.com; tumblr.com

Paid-for websites:
create.net; mrsite.com; wordpress.org; streamline.net; 123-reg.co.uk/make-a-website

Legislation for selling online: See links on pages 66–67.

Useful articles for your web design

Call to action buttons:
copyblogger.com/call-to-action-buttons

Using white space:
bigbrandsystem.com/use-white-space

Checkout page optimisation:
moz.com/blog/checkout-page-optimization-just-follow-the-facts

Web design tips: create.net/blog

The Paypal blog: paypal.co.uk/blog

Things to get right on your website:
enterprisenation.com/blog/make-sure-you-get-these-5-things-right-on-your-website

Ten critical home page elements:
marketingtechblog.com/critical-homepage-elements

Payment systems

Paypal: paypal.com

World Pay: sme.worldpay.com

Streamline: streamline.com

Go Cardless: gocardless.com

Braintree: braintreepayments.com

Paypoint: paypoint.net

Stripe: stripe.com

Card save: cardsave.net

Graphics to add to your site

etsy.com or creativemarket.com

Online marketplaces

Information about selling on Etsy:
handmadeology.com/10-real-tips-for-successfully-selling-on-etsy;
everythingetsy.com; etsy.com/blog/en/category/seller-handbook;
youtube.com (search 'selling on Etsy'); dummies.com/how-to/content/starting-an-etsy-business-for-dummies-cheat-sheet.html;
blog.hobbycraft.co.uk/selling-craft-makes-etsy

Information and advice about selling on other online marketplaces:

Folksy:
folksy.uservoice.com/knowledgebase;
blog.folksy.com/category/seller-tips;
sayitsays.blogspot.co.uk/2013/08/top-tips-for-selling-on-folksy.html

Not On The High Street:
notonthehighstreet.com/email/10goldenguidelines/guideline-1.html

MISI: misiuk.blogspot.co.uk/

DaWanda:
en.dawanda.com/cms/c/en/Seller-Portal

Comparison of several platforms:
thecraftynetwork.wordpress.com/where-to-sell/where-to-sell-your-crafts

Differences between Artfire and Etsy:
theartfireblog.com/2010/11/03/if-you-started-on-etsy

Selling on Artfire: theonlineseller.com/2012/09/17/marketplace-focus-artfire/

Where to sell art online:
artcove.co.uk/blog/internet-markets-for-artists-the-ebay-copycats.html

Selling handmade products online: smallbiztrends.com/2011/10/29-places-sell-handmade-creations.html

SEO

Google Keyword Tool: adwords.google.com/keywordtool (You will need an Adwords account to access this, but it is free to sign up and you do not have to run any ads.)

Google trends: google.co.uk/trends

Keyword generator: ubersuggest.org

Moz's whiteboard videos can be very useful and their free beginner's guide to SEO is worth downloading: moz.com/blog

Information on linkable assets: moz.com/blog/9-tangible-linkable-asset-ideas-and-how-to-build-links-to-them

Information on meta tags: descriptions: moz.com/learn/seo/meta-description

For an alternative view on SEO (sign up to the newsletter for bonus content): viperchill.com

Content marketing advice: copyblogger.com

Useful tips for blogging, content creation and a little SEO relevant to the craft industry: ukcraftblog.com

Useful advice on all aspects of building a business including SEO: buildalittlebiz.com

Information about evergreen posts: ukcraftblog.com/2011/09/evergreen-blog-posts.html

Advice on using Google Analytics, including setting up goals and conversion tracking: support.google.com/analytics

Beginners guide to Google Webmaster Tools: blog.kissmetrics.com/beginners-guide-to-google-webmaster-tools

Google Adverts: google.co.uk/ads

Google Adwords: adwords.google.co.uk

Passionfruit, a blog advert network: app.passionfruitads.com

How to make a media kit for your site: theblogmaven.com/make-a-media-kit-that-rocks

Page rank checker: prchecker.info

Newsletters

Mail Chimp: mailchimp.com

AWeber: aweber.com

Advice on e-mail marketing: moz.com/blog/category/email-marketing

YOUR LINKS AND NOTES

You can use this space to keep a list of links to websites and services you find helpful.

SELLING

THE OFFLINE MARKETPLACE

In addition to – or instead of – selling online you may want to also sell your products 'offline' at craft shows, in galleries or at retail outlets. This chapter will explain how you go about getting other people to stock your products, and looking into the best way to set up your own shop or stall.

It is also worth complementing any online marketing you do with offline marketing such as features in the press. This section of the book will help you get started with both selling and promoting your business offline.

Why sell offline?

It makes good business sense to have several streams of income rather than being solely dependent on one source. That way if something goes wrong with one of your sources of income you still have money coming in from other areas. Offline selling can be the perfect complement to selling online, and it gives you the chance to get out and meet your customers or the people selling your products in person rather than just dealing with them by e-mail.

Offline selling also ties in to online sales. Including your web address on your product packaging, and business cards or flyers handed out at events, may lead to future business being driven to your online shop or service.

If offline selling is not for you, it is still worth looking through this section for information and tips on promoting your business offline through advertising, and through the press and broadcast media, all of which will help you to direct people to your website or online shop. It also includes guidance and suggestions for networking at events to make contacts, build your brand and strengthen your business.

Selling at craft fairs

You can do craft fairs for publicity, to get feedback from potential customers, or simply to make money by selling your products. Whatever your focus, you need to decide in advance what you want to get from the event, and how much you are prepared to spend.

The first practical step of selling at craft fairs is to conduct research. Find out what events are going on around you, and you can then decide which are worth the investment of a stand and, if appropriate, which products to sell on that stand.

It is easy to be tempted by fairs with cheap stall prices, but although you may not be spending a lot of money you are still spending time, so you want to make sure you are getting something back for that time – whether this is cash, publicity or customer interaction. Remember to check back on whether you achieved your goals after the event.

Choosing an event

When looking for events at which you could sell, good places to start are your local newspapers or magazines; websites like ukcraftfairs.com or stallfinder.com; local 'what's on' websites; discussion forums such as the UK Handmade forum (ukhandmade.ning.com) or Crafts Forum (craftsforum.co.uk); or you could ask other crafters which events they recommend in your part of the world.

As part of your research, once you have identified a few potential events, attend them as a visitor before investing any money. Look at how many people are attending, who else is exhibiting, what kind of prices they are charging and whether they are successfully selling their products at that price. Take a look at both the layout and the visitor flow – you want to be situated somewhere where you get a good number of visitors and not hidden in a corner. Take a look at the vendors' stall displays for inspiration: which ones are attracting the most visitors, and why?

See how well the event was advertised, and whether it attracted a large number of visitors. Will those visitors be interested in your products at the price you need to sell, or are they just looking for bargains?

If you do not have chance to attend the show beforehand, you can still contact the event organiser to ask for information about the advertising, expected visitor numbers, other sellers and similar information. If you look on the event organiser's social media accounts, you may find photographs of the event and feedback from both visitors and exhibitors.

Preparing for the show

Once you have chosen which events at which you want to exhibit and have booked your stand, the next stage is planning. Think about what stock to take – and how much. Think also about how you will transport it to the show, lay it out, and what to charge.

Tips to help with planning

- A tablecloth on your table allows you to store things out of sight. Take one that reaches the ground, and keep it fairly plain so that it does not draw attention from your products.

- Do not clutter your stand. Giving people too much choice can lead to them buying nothing at all.

- Making sure everything is clearly priced will leave you free to serve your customers rather than having to answer constant price queries. In addition, some people may be afraid to ask and may just leave if they cannot see a price.

- Pricing in round figures (to the nearest pound for instance) means you do not have to have lots of different change on you.

- A supply of easily-accessible leaflets or business cards allows people to look you up later. If they do not have time to stop, they can grab a card on their way past. Take lots – it is better to have too many than not enough.

- Bring food and drinks with you so you do not need to leave your stand unattended.

- A money apron will allow you to keep your cash safe and to hand.

- If it is a long or busy event, bring a friend with you to allow you to take breaks and to help serve when it gets busy.

- Take something to sit on if you have space; your feet will thank you by the end of the day!

- Keep pen, paper and calculator to hand. You never know when they will come in useful.

- Talk to the other stall holders when you get the chance. You can use down-time for networking or getting useful advice.

When to stop networking

Stop when you have a customer at your stand: some will be reluctant to interrupt and you could lose a sale.

- If another seller seems to be very popular and getting lots of sales, try to identify why and think about whether there is anything you can learn from them.

- Make sure your products can be seen from a distance, and that your signage tells people what you do. This allows customers to see if your products are of interest to them.

- Do not be afraid to use props, but make sure they enhance rather than overshadow your products.

- Do not be too pushy and sales-focused. Smile and greet people, and then let them browse. Engage them if they want to chat to you.

- Craft in the quiet times if you can; this could lead to people taking an interest in what you are doing which could then generate a sale. It also demonstrates that the products are handmade by you.

- It is good to have things at a range of prices to suit all budgets.

- Put a card or flyer in with everything you sell, in case the buyer wants to buy more in the future.

- Look happy, no matter how bored or exhausted you are. If you look like you do not want to be there, it will put off potential customers.

After the show

The first thing to do after a show is to reflect on how the show went. Did you sell what you expected? Was there anything you could have done differently? Did you get any useful feedback from the customers? Did any of your products prove unexpectedly popular or surprisingly disappointing in terms of sales? Note down in your notebook anything you learnt and want to do differently at the next event.

A report on the show makes a good blog post or social media post. Let people know how it went and what you thought of the event. If nothing else, it may help send you some search engine traffic from people looking for information about the event. If you took photographs, include these. As discussed earlier, images help generate interaction. Make sure that some of the photographs are of your stall and products, as that is another way for you to showcase them online too.

If you had the chance for any networking (see pages 230–232), leave it couple of days after the show for people to catch up and then send them an e-mail or get in touch on social media. It will start building a relationship that could in time turn into a good business relationship or a friendship.

Ongoing effects

Remember that you may not see all the effects of the craft fair while at the fair itself. If you have handed out lots of business cards, for example, you may find you get orders in after the show too. One way to track this is to hand out a unique discount code at the show.

Craft fair displays

When exhibiting at a craft fair, find good ways of displaying your items so that people can see them properly, can touch them and can look through your selection at a glance. Your products should face outwards, towards your customers, not up at the ceiling.

You can use boxes or shelving to raise your display and place some products at eye level. Do not limit yourself just to the table itself: you could have things attached to the walls of your stand, hanging from the top of it or standing beside the table if you have space.

There is no need to display all of your stock at once. If appropriate, put a few samples out with a sign to explain that different colours and sizes are available on request. You can rotate your stock throughout the day to get an idea of what sells best at that particular event.

Think about the layout of your products, you may want to keep more valuable products towards the back of the table so they do not get taken. Remember that children may be able to reach the items you put at the front of the table, or they could get knocked off as people brush past. You will want bestsellers within easy reach of both the customers and you for quick restocking as they sell.

Your stall and you

Ideally you want your stall to stand out from the others, to catch potential customers' attention and draw them in. If you have electricity, use it to your advantage. Light up your products so that they stand out. You can use spotlights to highlight your bestsellers or major pieces. If not, you can still use signage to tell people why they should buy your products: explain what is unique about them, how they are made, what materials or techniques you use, and suggest how they could be used.

If possible, have a banner or poster with your branding on to help build brand recognition, and to help people remember your business name, which will make it easier for them to search for you after the show.

Finally, remember that you will also form part of your display. Think about what you are going to wear and whether it fits in with the image you are portraying with the rest of your stall.

Pinspiration

I would highly recommend looking at Pinterest for craft fair display ideas. You will find a huge amount of inspiration there.

Be organised

Having to rummage through your products like they are at a second-hand sale may lead to customers expecting to pay second-hand prices.

WHAT TO DO AT CRAFT FAIRS

These tips are from Wendy Massey from Handmade Harbour (handmadeharbour.co.uk).

Before the fair

Do your research! Attend fairs as a customer, speak to stallholders and organisers and read what people are saying online. Look for more than just dedicated craft fairs: carnivals, car shows, county shows, green events, winter markets, wedding fairs and even local school events might be good choices.

Make sure you have a web presence in place: a blog or Facebook page gives people something to look at and a way to contact you – a phone number is not enough to generate repeat sales. Being able to see your products online makes it easier for people to spread the word as well as return and buy from you themselves. Tell your online followers about the fair – they may want to attend and see you in person.

During the fair

Be friendly but not pushy. Hand out business cards like they are sweets. Do not take it personally if people stroll by without a glance – you cannot appeal to everyone. Chat to customers, listen to feedback and write down any comments so that you do not forget them. If you offer a bespoke service, you may find that customers come up with ideas that could become bestselling items. Have an order book or print out your own order sheets to use with a clipboard and carbon paper (give the customer the top copy).

After the fair

Analyse what went well and what you could do better next time. Look at the comments you noted down – is there anything useful you could use? A slight change to a product might increase sales, someone might like to sell for you (have you considered wholesale or drop shipping?) or you may have a new product idea. If you sell online, alter your PayPal settings to automatically ask where people found you – this is a great way to discover if fairs are working to promote online sales.

Remember that fairs are much more than just a selling platform. They work really well for face-to-face market research, promoting your online presence and showing off your range to independent shop owners who may want to stock your products. Other stallholders may also become friends – you can learn a lot from each other, too, so try not to be shy!

Selling through art galleries

Selling your art through galleries gets them in front of the relevant audience without you having to sell directly. It can free you up to spend more time creating your art rather than selling it.

Approaching galleries

The first step towards getting your artwork stocked in art galleries is to research the galleries, as they all have their own niche. Make sure your work fits their style before approaching them.

The next step is to check out their website, as many art galleries now handle applications online rather than in person. Make sure you submit good quality images of your work, both for the best results, and for future licensing.

Payment

A few galleries will buy your work outright and pay you within thirty days. Most will take it on a sale or return deal: you only get paid if the artwork sells, and if it does not sell it will be returned to you at the end of the agreed period. Sale or return is less risky for the gallery, so it tends to be the most common option.

Some galleries may try to make you pay to exhibit with them, or to pay for the opening event. You should not have to do this. If a gallery likes your work and is confident that it can be sold, they will not need to charge you upfront. Be sceptical if the gallery asks you to pay to exhibit.

It is important to build up a good relationship with the galleries with which you work so that they will continue to stock your work in the long term. If your art is in the same gallery a lot you will start to build a customer base in that area. It is better to do that than to distribute your work all over the place and not have the time to form proper relationships with the galleries.

Nel Whatmore

Artist Nel Whatmore (nelwhatmore.com) is a friend of mine. She has been making a successful living from her art for over twenty years, and was a valuable contributor to this part of the book.

Search more widely

Do not limit yourself to local galleries. You may find your work sells better in other parts of the country.

OTHER WAYS OF SELLING

In addition to selling through galleries, Nel Whatmore (see box, above right) also sells her artwork directly, through her website and at local shows and events. This has allowed her to build a mailing list so she is not solely dependent on galleries to sell her work. It has also allowed her to build a personal relationship with her customers.

However, she does find it cuts into her painting time: you need to be happy to be on stalls all day, chatting to the public. It is not suited to everyone: if you would rather be in the studio painting all day, then galleries are probably the better option for you.

TIPS ON SELLING YOUR ARTWORK

These tips come from award-winning artist Kerry Darlington (kerrydarlington.co.uk).

Before approaching a gallery with your work, it is important that you have at least the beginning of a strong definite style. You can have a mixture of subject matter but if the same style of painting runs through them all, the galleries will have a strong image to promote and your work will stick in people's minds more. As a result, you will be remembered and requested, and you will be commissioned to paint more as the first ones sell.

Artists that have not formed their own style often look to popular current work and are tempted to bend their work to try and 'fit in'. This is all very well if you can give a current trend a complete twist, but being heavily inspired by someone else means it may be hard to be taken seriously and it could affect your reputation long term. It is always better to create a trend than to buck a trend.

Before approaching a gallery, do a bit of research first. There are several streams of galleries, from independent highly priced art shops representing a handful of artists, to small framing shops using a wall or two to sell very affordable art to their customers. See what type your art would fit into first. All are open to new artists, they too are looking for the next big thing, so never be frightened of approaching them.

Some artists use publishers or agents to get their work into galleries. This can be great for some artists but terrible for others. Publishers usually take over all of the framing and distribution, which means more promotion but much less of the retail price. It is a good idea to contact other artists who are currently with an agent or publisher you are looking at, and also artists who used to be with that same agent/publishers to see how it worked for them.

Most importantly, create work of which you are proud and are happy to represent. I believe that the viewer can often feel the passion that has gone into creating something, and that alone can sell the work.

Getting your craft products into stores

Getting your products stocked in stores can give you more time making and less time selling directly at events and shows. If your products sell well, being stocked in stores means you are likely to have a steady stream of orders which can help with your cash flow.

Independent stores

As with selling anywhere else your first step should to be research. Make sure that your product fits with the range in the store before approaching them, and check that they do not already have something too similar to your product.

Contact the store to make an appointment, and using your research, tell them why your product is perfect for their store. Explain why and how it is better than, or different from, items they already sell; and lay out the benefits to them of stocking your product. Let them know what your USP is. Make sure you have the answers ready to all the questions they may ask. Be ready to let them know:

- What variations (size/colour, etc.) you can offer on your products.

- How many you can produce for them and by what date.

- How your product will be packaged or presented.

- What your wholesale price is.

- What your payment terms are.

- Whether you are happy for them to take them on a sale or return basis.

- What the postage costs are.

- What your returns policy is.

- Whether you are prepared to offer any discounts.

Prepare samples of your products ready to show buyers, as well as samples of packaging and any display or promotional materials you may have. Also, remember to take your order form in case they want to place an order.

Big retailers

The ultimate dream of most makers is to get stocked in one of the big retailers; to bag the kind of order that will keep your company afloat for the next year, regardless of whether you get any other orders or not.

Benefits

There are of course many benefits to getting a large retailer to stock your products. As well as increasing sales numbers, the presence of your products in a big store will help build your brand recognition by getting your products in front of thousands of people who would never otherwise have seen them. It also gives your business kudos. One big company paying you attention and wanting to work with you could lead to others.

Getting noticed

The advice opposite for selling to smaller independent stores applies equally to larger retailers and chains, but the following additional steps can help to get large retailers to notice your products and want to stock them:

Be unique Make sure your product is different from the retailer's current range.

Research Take the time to look into who you should contact and personalise your approach to them. Address them personally and by name, not just 'dear head buyer'.

Minimise risk The retailer is more likely to take a chance with your products if you can minimise risk to them. Examples of this include offering sale or return, or smaller pack sizes.

Have a clear aim Be clear who your product is aimed at and communicate that to the retailer.

Send samples It is much more convenient for buyers to see the quality of your products through samples than descriptions and photographs.

Events Some big brands run events where they invite people to pitch products to them. Keep an eye on likely sites or social media for details.

Attend trade shows Ask around and find out which trade shows are worth exhibiting at, and which shows are attended by the buyers from the shops in which you want to be stocked. You can always contact the buyers before the show and ask them to visit your stand or arrange a meeting.

Be prepared Make sure you have wholesale pricing and details ready to send to anyone who inquires.

Potential problems

Before you think about approaching big retailers you need to make sure you have the capacity to make large quantities of your products in a short time scale. There is no point taking on a large order if it is going to badly affect your business. If you will not be able to deliver in the time scale promised it will affect your chances of ever working with a big retailer in the future.

You will need to ensure you have the systems in place to cope with large orders before you start to seek them. If you will have to close your online stores for a month while you work on the order, your other customers may end up going elsewhere. If you do not have anyone who can help you and you fall ill, you may end up unable to complete the order. If you do not have enough packaging available the retailer will not accept your product.

Larger companies can have complicated accounting systems which may result in you having to wait for months before you get paid. Clarify when you can expect to receive payment; and make sure you have sufficient cash flow to survive at least another two months without that payment in case of problems.

Getting featured offline

In the previous chapter we covered getting featured online to help increase your brand awareness and drive traffic to your site – and custom to your business. Although it seems like most people are online nowadays, a good business does not neglect offline promotion too. Look for coverage in local newspapers, trade magazines, industry relevant magazines, and on radio and television.

Press releases

A press release is a communication that you send to the media to tell them about your business, which you hope they will use. News about new premises or product ranges, or about events you are attending are good examples. The press are often looking for stories, and if you can send them something that is ready to use it saves them time and effort. Do not wait for them to approach you. Be proactive and send out targeted press releases – that is, to the right people at the right publication. Do your research to see how your business can fit into the publication, what angle is best to take in your press release, and to whom you should send it.

Contacts come in very useful. If you build a good relationship with staff at magazines and newspapers they are much more likely to feature you, and to let you know if they have anything coming up which they could include you in. If you get the chance to meet journalists at local events or industry shows, introduce yourself and establish that contact. Build on the relationship by thanking them when they feature you, and let them know that if they have some space to fill, they can get in touch with you.

Unfortunately some publications will only feature you if you advertise with them. If that is the case with the publication you are approaching, you need to weigh the cost of advertising against the benefits of the promotion, especially if there are others that will feature you for free.

Writing a press release

Editorial space is often at a premium, so keep your press releases succinct. You can include further information at the bottom for the journalist to use, but the core of the piece should be concise. Try to include a few quotes with your press release so that the publication can make it sound as if you have been interviewed you if they choose to do so.

MY FREELANCING

In my experience of freelance writing for craft magazines, the biggest problem I faced was submissions not having images of a high enough quality, or simply not having the correct images available. Do make sure you keep high quality images of all of your products, even if you only need web quality ones to go onto your website.

Another common problem I encountered was people replying after the deadline. Even if it is going to take you a few days to get together everything the journalist is asking for, do reply and let them know that you do want to be included and will send them what they need by the deadline. Journalists have to submit an article on time or risk it not being printed. If we do not hear anything at all, we will look for someone else as we need to ensure we can finish our article.

Because the piece may need expanding upon, always include details of whomever they can contact from your business for more information. You should always send over relevant, high-resolution images (see page 82 for more details on supplying images) to go with your news story. It helps if you can send a selection so that they have a choice of which to use. Do not forget to include your web address along with your business name and premises address (if you have a bricks and mortar shop).

The more effort the publication has to make to use your press release, the less likely it is to use it. Send all the images, the text ready to be cut and pasted plus full contact details, so they should not need to get back to you for anything. When writing your press release, you can make the journalists' life easier by writing it in the third person, as the story would appear in a magazine. Do not say 'me' and 'I' but rather 'the business' or 'they'. This means it will not have to be entirely reworded, and press releases that require little editing are more likely to be accepted.

Activity

Create a contacts database of the people to whom you could send press releases, both online and offline. Create a spreadsheet with the person's name, their job, the publication for which they work, their website, their e-mail and then have a notes column at the end to make notes about the kind of thing they feature in their publication. This will save you a lot of time when you have something ready to share.

Television and radio features

As with print media, having contacts in the industry will help with television and radio features. If media journalists know you and have your contact details, they may think of you when they need someone. Visiblity and good SEO will also increase your chances of being approached. I have had a few television offers from researchers who found me via Google – it seems some television researchers will simply use a search engine to find experts in the subject they want to talk about, so it really does pay to get your SEO right.

If you are looking to be on television, identify the productions companies that make television programmes that cover your area of business, along with any local television companies. Keep an eye on their websites and follow them on social media. You will then see any announcements when they are looking for people to get involved in what they are filming. You will normally see the production company in the credits, or you can use a search engine to find their details.

Other ways of getting featured offline

Sending out press releases when you have something newsworthy is one way to get featured offline. However, you may not always have something big to publicise but still want to have a presence in the media. How can you do this?

Editorial content Magazines and newspapers are often looking for content to fill the editorial side of their publication. If you can offer them something that fits their usual style, the chances are that they will be very happy to use it. If you can write a project or technique guide for a publication, it creates exposure for your brand. Ensure that the publication credits it to you and includes your business name and a link to your website. This ensures the feature will also be promoting your business.

Writing for publications helps to establish you as an expert in your niche, and raises your profile. Some publications will also pay you for the content, offer you an advert in exchange or give you a feature elsewhere in the magazine for helping them. It also helps with building relevant contacts which could come in useful when you have something you want promoted.

Competitions Competitions are always popular, and if you are willing to give away prizes, most publications will be happy to work with you. Competitions are also a good way of making people aware of your products, which helps to build brand recognition. Remember that your products have a cost to your business, so weigh up the cost of what you provide against the exposure and potential business you will get in return. Ensure your competitions are targeted at people who might potentially buy from you in the future.

Shopping features Many publications do seasonal shopping features such as gifts for St. Valentine's day, Easter-themed products, Christmas decorations and so forth. If you have products that would fit, you could contact them with details, explaining why they would be ideal for their feature. Most publications work a number of months in advance, so contact them in plenty of time, not a few weeks before.

Many magazines run 'new products' features. When you have a new range to promote, try sending details and images to those magazines to see if they will run it.

Awards Winning awards can help to publicise your business. Some awards require you to apply yourself, while others require a third party to nominate you. Local awards often get coverage in local newspapers, trade awards tend to be mentioned in trade publications, and online awards can lead to an increase in traffic, online coverage or support from other winners.

Glittering prizes

Don't be afraid to put yourself out there. Sometime an award will come with a prize that can be very useful. I won the Theo Pathitis Small Business Sunday (#SBS) award in 2011; and won promotion on the dedicated SBS website. I also gained access to a Facebook group where winners swap advice and help each other, and annual networking events too.

MARKETING TIPS

Freelance PR consultant Francesca Weeks (franfreelance.co.uk) provided these useful tips on marketing.

Network Put yourself out there to get work; and attend as many local or national events and meet-ups as you can. As the old saying goes, 'people buy from people' so attending events can be a great way to bring your brand to life.

Target your PR Be targeted with your PR efforts. If you are sending out a press release, for example, spend time researching the journalists and publications you want to send it to and ask yourself why it might be of interest to them or their readers. Try to address each journalist personally and avoid being too generic and blind copying everyone into one blanket email.

Keep your eye on the media Always be aware of the national news agenda and trends. If something is getting a lot of media attention or gaining momentum on social media, have a think about whether it is relevant to your business in any way. If it is, act quickly and make the most of the media hype and buzz!

Watch awareness campaigns Similarly, tapping into national awareness days and weeks is a great way to generate extra publicity. There are a great many awareness campaigns out there, from National Knitting Week to National Cupcake Week, so do some research into the awareness campaigns that might fit with your business and plan your marketing activities ahead of time.

Combining offline and online marketing Combine marketing offline with your online efforts. Make the most of social media! It is such a fantastic free tool and can really help grow your fan base. Make sure you use it to listen and have real conversations with people, not just for broadcasting your own news. Getting social media right is time-consuming but in the end it is worth it. If you are not sure where to start or which platforms are right for you try taking a course.

Follow journalists Make sure you follow key journalists to stay up to date with what they are writing about. You can also search the #JournoRequest hashtag on Twitter. You never know when a journalist might be looking to write about something you make!

Promoting yourself offline

It may be easier to promote your business online, but not everyone spends their time on the internet. Combining offline and online promotion will help your business reach as many people as possible.

Local promotion

Local advertising can work really well if you sell only in one geographic area. Most of your customers will be local people so advertising nationally is not really going to benefit you as much as promoting yourself in your area. You could look at advertising in the local papers, or local magazines. On a smaller scale, the area or parish magazine and local free ads are good choices.

Look for local publications within your niche in which you could advertise, such as a local quilting group's newsletter if you sell fabric. If your products are for babies or children, will the local toddler group let you put up a poster or display your products?

Well-placed posters or locally delivered flyers could also lead to more business. Many local shops and post offices let you put up an advert for a nominal cost, or some even do it for free. If you do not want to deliver flyers yourself, is there someone you could pay to do it for you?

INDIRECT PROMOTION

If your customers are happy with the products or services you deliver the chances are they will tell others about it. Word of mouth is a great method of promotion for your business, but you can only influence it indirectly. Focus on delivering great customer service alongside quality products.

You can try to encourage word of mouth referrals by offering 'refer a friend' incentives, or even by simply prompting people to spread the word: when you package an order, include a business card or flyer with the note 'if you have a friend who may be interested in what we offer, please pass this onto them.' Sometimes people just need a gentle nudge.

Activity: Publicity research

Set a day aside to research ways in which you can promote your business offline. Draw up a plan of action for the next six months.

- Which publications are you going to contact and how do you want to be featured in them?
- Are there any awards you can apply for?
- What are the deadlines for entering the awards?

Schedule in at least one thing per month to try to generate some offline publicity for your business.

Product demonstrations

Product demonstrations at industry shows or local events can be a good way of getting people to discover your products. It shows people what you sell and gives them ideas of how to use the products. Your aim when demonstrating is to make them think that what you sell is something they cannot live without. Contact local shopping centres, event organisers and your product stockists to see if they would like you to do any product demonstrations.

Measuring the effects of advertising

Advertising can be expensive, especially on a national scale. It is therefore important to avoid wasting money by making sure your adverts target the correct audience. You also need to measure the effectiveness of your adverts to make sure that your money is being well spent.

As with online advertising, one way of tracking an advert's reach and effectiveness is to use a unique discount code. This allows you to track any orders that come from the advert. Similarly, you could put a voucher in the publication which people can cut out and bring with them. This will help to attract people into your premises, looking at whatever it is you have to offer.

Tracking the effectiveness of your offline advertising can be easier if you have an online presence. Look at your website's analytics to see if you can see a spike or other change in traffic and/or sales around the time your advert comes out. If it is a regional advert or local you can go further into your visitor demographics for your website and see if there is an increase of visitors in that particular geographical area.

If you have sales premises, keep a notebook to hand by the till and ask new customers how they found you, while serving them. Make a note of their answer and you can see whether advertising is driving new customers to the store. If they say they saw an advert for your business, ask if they remember where they saw the advert.

Another way to track leads generated from certain advertising is to use a different phone number. You could put your land line number in one advert, and your mobile in another.

Ring the changes

Changing the artwork for your advert regularly can help attract more people.

Activity: Monitoring advertising

Make a list of your current adverts, how much they cost and whether you see any noticeable increase in business as a result.

If the results are inconclusive, stop all but one advert for a couple of months, and then change it to a different advert for the next two months. This will allow you to measure the effectiveness of each advert in isolation, rather than paying for lots of adverts when only one or two may actually be working for you.

Networking at events

Events like trade shows, craft shows, networking events and even local craft fairs can be great places for networking. Ideal for meeting like-minded crafters with whom you can share business tips for finding new suppliers, finding new buyers or meeting people who can help promote your business.

Time is limited at these events as there are a lot of people to talk to so it is best that you go prepared with a plan of action, ready to make as many useful contacts as you can.

Before you go

Make sure you have plenty of business cards ready to take with you, take a lot more than you think you will need. It is amazing how fast they go!

Notes Take a notebook and pen so you can take down details of people you meet or write down notes.

Know your way around Print a floor plan if possible. They are often available to download on the organiser's website. Organisers sometimes send floorplans by e-mail, so it could be worth signing up to their newsletter.

For big shows you can also normally find an exhibitors list on the organiser's website. Work through the list or floor plan and write down the people you want to see in order of importance and their stall number. It can also help to make notes as to what you want to see them about to remind you on the day.

Research Read up about the exhibitors you want to target before you go. Have a look at their websites and check out their social media, so that you can approach them with knowledge about their businesses and have some concrete ideas about how you can work with them.

Dress appropriately First impressions count, so dress smartly to give the best impression of your business.

Network with other attendees

Look on social media and see if anyone you would like to speak to is attending rather than exhibiting. If so, you could contact them in advance and arrange to meet them at the show.

At the show

Once at the show, work your way through the list of people you wanted to visit, in order of importance. At big shows it can be best to contact people in advance and ask for a meeting so they can schedule you in. If you can see someone is busy, come back later: you will not get chance for a proper conversation if you try to speak to them while there are other people vying for their attention. If you go back to them a few times and they are still busy, ask when the best time to come back would be, or offer to take them for a coffee when they get a break.

Be sociable and strike up conversation where you can – you never know who you will end up meeting. Hand your business cards out and take cards whenever you get the chance. When taking cards, add a note to the back about what that person does, what you talked about or what you would like to speak to them about after the show. If you have space note down where you met them, this will help serve as a little reminder when you get in touch. It is useful to carry an envelope to put all the cards in so you do not lose them.

If they do not have a business card, write their name and business name down in your notebook along with the reason you want to get in touch. You can go online when you get home and find their contact details. If they are exhibiting at an event usually their details will be on the organiser's website.

If you have time left after seeing everyone you wanted to see, take a wander around the show and look at the stalls you have not yet visited. You may find someone you missed off your list, or someone who booked at the last minute, and so was not on the floor plan or exhibitor's list.

Picking the right time

Shows are often quieter towards the end of the day, so you may find people are more able to talk then.

NETWORKING AT SHOWS

Many of the tips for selling at craft fairs (see pages 216–217) also apply to attending shows in order to network. In particular, take refreshments; and while you should look smart, comfortable shoes are a godsend for tired feet. In addition, you may want to take some cash. Some shows have no cash machines once you are inside, and there may be exhibitors who are not able to process card payments on their stand.

Paying attention to all of these details can help you stay alert, approachable and making the most of your networking opportunities.

Following up

You will often meet a large number of people at an event or show that you would like to speak to or work with in the future. Attending the show itself is only the first stage of networking; you need to follow up after the event. This ensures people have your contact details, reminds them of anything you discussed and makes it easier for them to get back to you.

Make the subject of your e-mail the name of the event at which you met. Start off with a polite 'nice to meet you at…' sentence, where you can insert a reminder as to where exactly you met them. If it was a big show over multiple days, they probably met many people in different parts of the show. If you remind them that you met them in the queue for the coffee shop on Saturday afternoon, or at a particular social media seminar, it will help them recall exactly which person you are.

Next, explain why you are getting in touch, how you think you can help that person, and how you could work together. Give specific examples and include links to the relevant parts of your site. Anything that saves them time and effort is worthwhile. Make sure you include a telephone number as well as an e-mail address that they can use to contact you.

While contacting people within a few days of meeting them is a good idea because it ensures your meeting is fresh in their mind, the day immediately after a big event may not be the best. They will likely be coming back to an e-mail backlog and you do not want yours to get lost in the midst.

If you do not receive a reply to your initial e-mail after a couple of weeks, follow it up by calling by telephone, or by sending a polite follow-up e-mail asking if they received your previous one – be sure to attach the original e-mail for them.

If you sell products and the contact is a potential stockist, it could be worth posting them a sample and including a letter with your post-show follow-up rather than an e-mail. It will make you stand out from all the other people they met at the show and will remind them of the products you create. This also works for magazine editors too, who are often swamped with hundreds of e-mails after big events.

If you do not have a specific reason for getting in touch with someone, you can still follow them on social media and send a quick message or tweet to say 'nice to meet you at the show'. There may be a way for you to work with them in the future so it is worth establishing an online relationship.

USEFUL LINKS AND FURTHER READING

Craft fairs

How to find craft fairs: ukcraftfairs.com; stallfinder. com; craftsforum.co.uk; ukhandmade.ning. com/events; gogomargo.com

Craft fair display ideas: pinterest.com/ lifethriftylane/craft-show-display-ideas/

Craft fair tips: pinterest.com/kirameku412/for-craft-shows

Lots of useful posts on selling at craft fairs: blog.folksy.com

Lots of links to craft fair tip posts: ukcraftblog. com/2011/08/craft-fair-display-tips-and-ideas. html

How to prepare for a craft show: thedesigntrust.co.uk/how-to-best-prepare-for-a- craft-show-or-design-trade-fair

Useful series of posts on craft fairs: handmadelives.wordpress.com/2014/01/24/craft- show-preparations

Getting your craft products into stores

General information: missmalaprop.com/2009/07/ how-to-sell-your-product-in-stores; prime.org.uk/ how-to-sell-to-department-stores

Ten reasons gift stores reject handmade products: squidoo.com/gift-stores-reject-handmade-items

Lots of useful links and information about selling to retailers: squidoo.com/selling-to-retailers

Offline promotion and advertising

How to get featured in magazines: handmadeharbour.blogspot.co.uk/2012/07/how- to-get-your-products-in-magazine.html

Ideas for getting magazine features: info.thatsgreatnews.com/blog/bid/256175/18- Ways-to-Get-Featured-in-a-Magazine

How to get press features: blog.folksy. com/2010/11/09/get-featured-in-the-press

Getting value from your magazine advertising: abcmag.co.uk/ad_info/advertsguide.asp

Tips for magazine advertising: ephealy. com/2012/01/24/7-magazine-advertising-tips

Networking tips from The Design Trust: thedesigntrust.co.uk/networking-if-you-dont-like- or-cant-network-the-usual-way

Useful networking tips: passivepanda.com/networking-tips

How to run a successful competition: success.com/article/how-to-run-a-promo-contest

Word of mouth promotion strategies: blog.livehelpnow.net/7-strategies-word-of-mouth- customers

How to encourage word of mouth promotion: bit.ly/1ime2bc

YOUR LINKS AND NOTES

You can use this space to keep a list of links to websites and services you find helpful.

ENDNOTES

Your business

Now that your business is up and running, you can look at ways of streamlining your processes so you can do things more quickly, and be more efficient. Over the years I have learnt ways to save time, cut costs and generally make running a business easier. On the following pages I have listed ten free tools which I use to make my life easier. Hopefully you will find them useful too.

The biggest thing I have learnt is not to give in to what other people think. There is no 'one size fits all' for your business. We all have different needs and what matters is what you want from your business, not what someone else tells you that you should want from it.

Remember, the business is yours. Keep striving towards making it the perfect business for you; whether this is working as much as possible and earning as much as possible, or something that fits around the rest of your life and earns enough to cover the bills or for some extra pocket money. There is a lot of pressure to keep your business growing and building all the time, to employing people and managing staff, but this may not be for you.

Personally, I just want to pursue the craft I love without any extra pressure. For me, my focus is streamlining my business so that I keep the same level of income but gradually reduce the hours I put in; by improving my productivity and gradually cutting out the work that earns me less.

Your goals may be different to mine, but it is crucial that you make sure you know what your goals are and that you do not let other people distract you from them. It is your business, so make it work for you.

THE TEMPTATIONS OF OVERWORK

When you run your own business it is easy to put all your time and energy into it, and hard to take time away from your business to recuperate. You can easily find yourself working seven days a week, and before you know it, you burn out. This leads to you being too exhausted and ill to work for weeks or even months, which sets you back a lot more than if you had just taken a day or two off when you first started to feel tired or ill.

Understandably, you want everything to be perfect with your business, and this can lead to setting yourself impossibly high standards. Even after many years of running my business, I must confess I still struggle with the temptation to overwork, but I have finally come to realise that close to perfect is just as acceptable and much less stressful!

My top tips

This is my own list of ten of my favourite free services that I use in my own business. They will all help you save time, money and effort when running yours.

1 Dropbox (dropbox.com)

A free online cloud storage for your documents, photos and other files. You can earn free space by inviting friends to also use Dropbox, or you can upgrade to a paid account if you need more space. It is very useful for backing up your computer as well as sending large files that will not fit into an e-mail.

2 Google calendar (google.com/calendar)

Most of us have Google accounts nowadays. One is essential if you want to use Google Analytics on your site, or Google Plus, so why not take advantage of its other free programs? Google have a free calendar app which you can use to synchronise appointments and reminders between your computer, tablet and mobile phone. It works with Apple devices as well as Android.

3 Image resizer (imageresizer.codeplex.com)

Image resizer is a free download which allows you to select single or multiple images on your computer and resize them. This is ideal for when you need images for your website and social media, or if your camera takes very high quality, large sized images.

   You can either use one of their standard sizes or specify your own, and you can set it to keep both the original file and a smaller version. This allows you to keep a high-resolution image for print and have a smaller web-sized version too. Using this service only takes a few seconds to resize big batches of images – so much easier than opening each image individually and re-sizing it!

4 and 5 Google Analytics and Google Webmaster Tools (google.co.uk/analytics and google.com/webmasters)

As you will see in the SEO section of this book, Googles give you huge amounts of useful information about your website, and all for free! You would be a fool not to make the most of them. Information on how to use these programs is on pages 192–199.

6 Hootsuite (hootsuite.com)

Ideal for prescheduling your social media updates, and for streaming your Twitter lists, Hootsuite allows you to view several of your social media platforms at once and manage multiple accounts. Just remember that it does not work so well for Facebook, as your posts will have less reach. See page 122 for more information.

7 Evernote (evernote.com)

A popular multiple device app that allows you to store to-do lists, research and similar notes. It allows you to snip things from the internet and separate your notes into different projects.

8 Google Keep (drive.google.com/keep)

I use this in a similar way to Evernote, but find it easier to use. It is essentially a collection of digital post-it notes into which you can add images and schedule alarms in order to remind you when to do the things on the note. It works well for to-do lists and storing ideas for future use. I also use it for saving links that I want to look at properly when I have more time.

9 PicMonkey (picmonkey.com)

Free image-editing software that will allow you to create adverts; images to use on social media or your website (such as banners and sharable images) and also to enhance images. If for any reason you do not get on with PicMonkey try Pixlr (pixlr.com) which offers a similar service.

10 Bitly (bitly.com)

Bitly shortens unsightly long web address (URL) links so they look neat and tidy. It also stores statistics for those links so that you can see how many people clicked on them, when they clicked and where those people are geographically.

A few final tips for going forward with your business

- Set aside some time each week to read business sites, SEO sites and marketing sites to keep up to date with changes that could affect your business, and to learn new things. If you keep learning, you can keep ahead of new trends and continue to work efficiently, without wasting time on things that no longer work, or are not very effective any more.

- Thinking of a second business? If you have another business idea make sure it will not adversely affect the first (or your health from doing too much) and plan carefully. It will be easier the second time around in many ways because you will have learnt a lot of lessons from the first business. However, a second business will add new pressures. Do not stretch yourself too far and end up doing neither business properly. The problem with being an entrepreneur is that we have too many ideas and not enough time!

- Take the time to build relationships with other entrepreneurs, with magazines, with blogs and enjoy the social side of business. Working for yourself can be very isolating, especially when working alone, or from home. Make plans to go to events regularly, or meet with other people in a similar situation to you so you do not feel lonely or depressed. Social media is great, but it does not compare to leaving the house and meeting up with people in real life.

- Have a clear goal. Knowing what you are working for will help you through hard times, while having a clear goal in mind keeps you focused. Make sure the goal is of your choosing, and that you do not let other people distract you from it or allow them to dictate your aims.

- Repeat custom is the easiest way to grow your business. It is easier – and cheaper – than attracting new customers, so do your best to make sure your customers are very happy with the service and products they receive.

- Have fun! Most of all, have fun and enjoy what you are doing. There is so much freedom that comes with self-employment so make the most of it. If it is a lovely sunny afternoon and you want to go to the beach, then go. If you are having an 'off day' and do not feel like working, take some time off. So long as you are sensible and still get your work done, it is up to you when you do it.

  As a self-employed businessman or woman, you no longer have a boss dictating that you must work on set tasks at set times. Instead, you get to spend your time doing something that you love. Make sure you enjoy it.

Good luck on your new creative adventure.

INDEX